D1213074

INTRODUCTION

During the past four decades a great deal of experience has been gained in using various forms of interviewing, and there has been a steadily increasing interest in the systematic investigation of the methods employed. But despite the knowledge and sophistication that have developed, there are numerous questions that still lack empirically based answers and numerous assumptions that have not been subjected to careful analysis and testing. In what circumstances can information be collected more effectively by intervewing rather than by observation or the use of documents? In what respects are the various forms of interviewing similar, and how do they differ? On what assumptions is each form based? What criteria can help an investigator select the form of interview best suited to his particular purpose? In each of the main forms of interview, how do the interviewer's behavior and the formulation of the questions affect the quality and quantity of the response and the level of respondent participation?

Each of the several schools of interviewing has sought *the* correct approach. Rather than advocate any one of these, we have examined the various approaches to determine the assumptions underlying their use; we have described the specific methods requisite to each form and the circumstances and conditions under which each method may be most appropriate.

It was fortunate that, at about the same time we began our systematic examination of interviewing, tape recording had been developed so that interviews could be recorded easily and economically. This enabled us to examine in detail verbal specimens of actual interviews. These examinations proved to be important for two reasons. First, we frequently found that an interviewer's account of how he had conducted an interview bore little resemblance to the actual recorded interview. This raised some question as to the validity of the generalizations suggested in the literature by experienced interviewers that were based only on recollections of their performance. Second, recorded interview specimens enabled us to develop a systematic and detailed way of describing the verbal behavior that they contained. We found this to be important because nearly all accounts of interviewing, although suggestive of techniques of questioning, lacked definition and specificity. Terms were used somewhat differently by various authors.

A prerequisite for any interview is that the respondent be willing to be interviewed. We examined the experience interviewers have reported in gaining and maintaining the cooperation of the people they study. From the numerous reports, we have developed a set of general considerations or queries that need to be taken into account in planning and executing any interview study. Then we have shown how these may be used.

In line with our thesis that there is no one correct way to interview, we believe there is no one optimal set of interviewer characteristics. Rather, the skills required of the interviewer, his role, and his personal characteristics may vary widely, depending on the form of interview selected, its purpose, the subject matter, and the characteristics of the respondents. For some forms of interviewing the interviewer may require formal training and considerable experience in one of the social sciences. He may need to thoroughly understand the over-all objectives for which the interviews are being used and—if in research—the conceptual approach to the problem, the design, and the analysis of the study. He may well be the principal investigator. On the other hand, for the "survey" interview in which all questions are prepared in advance and read from a schedule, the interviewer may need no professional training and little knowledge of research. After having explored the various skills required in the various forms of interviewing, we consider, in the last section of the book, the question of the personal characteristics needed for various forms of interviewing.

Because we deal with the collection of information, we have emphasized the collection of data in connection with the research use of interviewing. It is beyond the scope of this work to treat systematically the subjects of research design, sampling, analysis of data, or the logic of science; we have introduced these subjects only insofar as they relate to the central issue of data gathering.

The reader will find that the character of the book varies considerably. In some sections we make specific recommendations and suggest tactics and techniques. In others we raise issues and questions for consideration and investigation. The difference in levels reflects our judgment on the quality and amount of knowledge that exists for study and application of the many aspects of interviewing.

PART I

The Interview as
a Research Instrument

I

THE INTERVIEW
AND OTHER METHODS OF
DATA COLLECTION

Regardless of its specific purpose, form, or context, the interview is essentially a method of collecting information. The purpose for which the information is sought varies with both the seeker and the respondent:[1] the physician seeks from his patient information on which to base a diagnosis; the personnel officer seeks from job applicants information about their qualifications; the lawyer seeks from his clients and witnesses information that may serve as legal evidence; the journalist seeks information to retail to his readers or to lead him to further sources; the market researcher seeks from consumers information that will help to design or market a product; the social scientist seeks from a wide variety of respondents information by means of which he can explore a problem or test a

[1] The terms used to describe the person being interviewed connote something about his function. In survey research, the commonly used term "respondent" implies an expectation of brief responses to questions posed by the interviewer. In anthropological and other forms of nonschedule interviews, the usual term "informant" implies the provision of information on such general and complex topics as organizational structure or life histories. For the sake of simplicity and consistency, we shall use "respondent" as the term for all persons interviewed, including informants.

hypothesis; and everyone, in the course of daily life, seeks information as a basis for short- and long-range actions—or even for its own sake.

The nature of the information sought varies even more widely. It may consist of a description of events—a narrative account of "what happened" in a situation in which the respondent was a participant or a witness; it may involve behavior—past, present, or intended; attitudes—conscious and unconscious; moral values—overt and covert; habits—of recreation, purchasing, or ethical choice; modes of perception; or feelings—habitual or stemming from a specific event.

The information may be given freely, or with the greatest reluctance; it may be given accurately, or with conscious or unconscious distortion. It may take the form of a single word, a number, or a response to one of a series of alternatives; or it may have to be sifted out from a flood of response material given by a respondent who either is doing his best to cooperate with the interviewer and to understand his questions, or is doing his best to mislead. The information may be elicited in a casual, extemporaneous, two-minute conversation; in the course of an hour of intimate discussion; or in a series of interviews extending over many months.

Despite the almost infinite variety of the interview, however, its basic purpose is to collect information. Although the interview is the only feasible method for acquiring certain kinds of information, and although it is often the most effective method for gathering information that could also be acquired by other methods, it is only one of three commonly used methods. Its use must be based, therefore, not only on the investigator's subjective preference for it or his familiarity with it but also on an objective assessment of its advantages and limitations in terms of the information to be gathered; the available sources of information; and the personal characteristics, resources, and skills of the investigator. The use of the interview must be based, as well, on an objective assessment of the other methods that might be used. Such an assessment requires some familiarity with the two other general methods of information-gathering: observation and the use of documents.

Interviewing, Observation, and the Use of Documents

The following discussion of the three basic methods of gathering information is obviously not exhaustive and is not intended to provide a basis for the exclusive selection of one method in preference to another. Its purpose, rather, is to indicate certain advantages and limitations that are peculiar to each method and to suggest the possibilities of combining methods for maximum effectiveness. All three methods are often used in the same study, either concurrently or in sequence, to verify or to supplement the information gathered by any one of them or for the peculiar advantages of each at various stages. An investigator intending to use the interview as a primary method, for example, may have to rely heavily on documents in the selection of his respondents. Similarly, an experimenter who relies primarily upon observation of his subjects' responses in a laboratory may lose much valuable information if he neglects to interview them for introspective data on their behavior in the experimental situation.

OBSERVATION

Observation—that is, the purposeful and selective watching, counting, listening to, or even smelling of objects or of phenomena as they take place—is basic to the physical and natural sciences, but its uses in social research are probably equally various. In some situations, it is the only feasible method, in others it is an essential precursor to interviewing, and in still others it serves as a check on the accuracy of interview responses.

Observation is essential when documents do not exist and accurate and full information cannot be obtained by the questioning of respondents. There are several reasons why people may be unable to give information to an interviewer. A person who is participating in an event may be so thoroughly involved in his own participation that he cannot be aware of dimensions of the event that would be apparent to a detached observer. Thus, the perceptions of a speaker at a meeting, or those of a participant in a race riot, are likely to be focused on specific details different from those that an investigator may need.

A second kind of information that usually cannot be elicited by questioning pertains to behavior that is so habitual to the individual as to be outside his awareness. Most individuals have personal idiosyncrasies of which they are not aware and which, therefore, they are unable to report to an interviewer, even if they wish to co-operate with him as fully as possible. Such behavior—whether it involves modes of personal interaction, habits of dress, or aspects of physical behavior such as tenseness or skill in a motor task—is usually more easily and accurately discovered by observation than by interview. Similarly, cultural differences in behavior are more likely to be noted by an outside observer than to be reported by a respondent who, as a member of the culture, is likely to believe his customs are universal and, hence, neither novel nor interesting to the investigator. A Briton who has had no contact with Americans, for example, is unlikely to volunteer the information that he holds his fork with his left hand while eating, because he may well assume that this practice is universal. The investigator, in his turn, is unlikely to question him about it unless the practice has come to his attention through observation.[2]

Observation is useful, too, when the information sought is likely to be repressed, as in the following account of an interview with a mother concerning her child-rearing practices (E. & N. Maccoby, 1954, p. 484):

During the interview she held her small son on her lap. The child began to play with his genitals. The mother, without looking directly at the child, moved his hand away and held it securely for a while . . . later in the interview the mother was asked what she ordinarily did when the child played with himself. She replied that he never did this— he was a very "good" boy. She was evidently entirely unconscious of what had transpired in the very presence of the interviewer.

[2] Even the outside observer can become so habituated to certain facets of behavior or custom peculiar to the culture he is studying as to lose his awareness of them. For this reason, anthropologists and others entering a culture different from their own find it valuable to record their initial observations carefully in order to preserve the aspects that appear unusual to them before they become familiar with the culture.

Although this single observation may not be reliable, the discrepancy between it and the mother's statement raises questions about the validity of the mother's reporting.

Thus far, we have noted the uses of observation in situations in which persons may be *unable* to provide information in response to questioning. It is also useful, however, when a person is *unwilling* to be interviewed. In some situations, the group being studied may regard an interviewer as a less familiar or more threatening figure than an observer. Hence, if the investigator can initially assume the role of an observer, he may be able to gain the confidence of the group that he intends subsequently to interview. For example, in a study of the social organization of a laundry, Bain (1960) spent a preliminary period observing the machinery layout and work flow of the plant, making his observations in full view of the workers whom he intended subsequently to interview. Although the primary purpose of Bain's observation was to make him a familiar and nonthreatening figure to his potential respondents, an initial period of observation can, as we shall note later, enrich the study by permitting the investigator to familiarize himself with aspects of environment and interaction that make subsequent interview responses more meaningful.

Information on certain kinds of criminal, illicit, taboo, or deviant activities is often difficult to obtain by interview because of the understandable reluctance of participants to serve as respondents. In such situations, observation may provide information. When William Whyte (1955, p. 303), for example, was studying gambling activities, he found himself unable to get information either from one of the prominent gambling operators or from any of numerous neighborhood residents who obviously knew what was going on. One resident advised him, however, ". . . just hang around, and you'll learn the answers in the long run without even having to ask the questions." The advice proved entirely sound. In such situations, observation in advance of interviewing may provide the investigator with enough information to put him "in the know"—that is, to enable him to identify potentially useful respondents and to display to them sufficient knowledge and sophistication about the activity to encourage them to reveal further information.

Even when respondents are not unwilling to reveal information, they may be powerfully motivated to distort it. The frequency of church attendance, for example, may be exaggerated by some respondents. Officers of clubs, unions, or fraternal organizations may exaggerate the number of members who participate regularly in meetings. Here observation—of the Sunday church service or of a lodge meeting—may be useful, either as a more accurate method than interviewing or as a check on the accuracy of response material.

In addition to being more effective than the interview for collecting certain kinds of information, observation is useful in conjunction with a study that will depend primarily on interviewing. Often, at the outset of a study, an investigator will be clearly aware of his general goals but unable to specify the foci of information he seeks or the kind of interview that would elicit them effectively. In these circumstances, a period of observation can help him identify and sort out the most useful variables and can help him identify those individuals who are most likely to have relevant information. During this period, too, he can learn about the various factors that will enhance or inhibit the responsiveness of those he intends to interview (see Chapter 4).

Introspection—which is essentially the observation and consideration of one's own behavior, reactions, and feelings—is also useful before and during an interview. One sociologist (Roy, 1953), for example, while working at an unskilled job in a factory, discovered through introspection that he was using the piecework incentive system as a kind of game to help the time pass more quickly. Baldamus (1951), through the same kind of participation and introspection, discovered that the sequence of physical activities and the rhythm of work movements were important elements in job satisfaction. Both these insights eventually became foci of interviews with other factory workers.

In the course of the interview, observation can be used in several ways: First, observation of the respondent's style of life—the furnishings of his home, for example, or his interaction with his children or neighbors, or any number of other clues—can help the interviewer assess his behavior, socioeconomic status, and various other characteristics more fully than on the basis of his responses to questions alone. Secondly, careful observation of a respondent's nonverbal responses—his tone of voice, the hesitancy or positiveness of his response, his general attitude toward the interviewer—can produce information which will help the interviewer to appraise the accuracy and other characteristics of the respondent's verbal responses. Thirdly, as we have already noted, observation can be used to check on whether the respondent in fact behaves in the ways he has described to the interviewer.

Warner (1941) suggests an especially effective combination of interviewing and observation: the interviewing of respondents before a specific event, the observation of the event by the investigator, and the interviewing of the same respondents after the event. The value of comparing the information thus collected through different eyes and at different times is clear enough.

Counterbalancing its numerous advantages, however, observation has several severe limitations. Its primary liability is, of course, its cost in time and manpower. Both the interview response and certain kinds of documents can compress long periods of time and span vast geographic distances. A single interview response can encompass many years of behavior, and a file of documents can provide information from sources that are geographically dispersed. Observation, by contrast, is confined to "real" time and place. It can proceed no more rapidly than the event itself. And it cannot be used for the study of past or future events. It is limited entirely to the "now" as well as the "here." Moreover, in many situations, observation requires the services of a highly skilled individual over a long period of time. Hence, often the values attainable through observation must be sacrificed for reasons of budget, time, or manpower.

In addition to its spatial and chronological limitations, observation cannot be used directly to study feelings, beliefs, values, attitudes, or cognitive processes except insofar as these can be inferred from behavior. Often, too, the observer is barred from witnessing certain phenomena—certain kinds of sexual behavior, religious rites, etc.—on which at least some information can be elicited by interview.

Observation is, moreover, necessarily partial and selective. No observer is the equivalent of a wide-angle movie camera in being able to make a continuous and total record of an event. The selectivity of observation is clearly illustrated by the experience of Richardson who, in training observers, used a color and sound motion picture of a meeting involving five participants. The observers were asked to record as fully as possible both what happened and how the participants behaved. When their reports were carefully checked against the film, it was noted that, although each observer made some errors, the major difference between reports lay in their content—in what each observer selected out to report from the totality of stimuli. Some of the observers selected such different aspects of the characters in the film that there was little overlap between the descriptions. Moreover, when observers are deeply emotionally involved in what they are watching, what they see and how they interpret it varies widely, as any football or baseball umpire can testify (Hastorf and Cantril, 1954). Although trained observers attempt to separate observation from interpretation, their biases and feelings may well cause them to observe selectively.

Aside from idiosyncratic differences among observers, there is the additional problem that, if he is observing a culture different from his own, the observer will often not know which of its aspects to look for or, to put it in another way, will not understand the significance of what he observes. Observation, thus, may require supplementation by interview, by the use of documents, or by a lengthy period devoted to the progressive articulation, selection, and definition of the variables to be observed.

Because the data obtained by observation often seem vivid and clear, the observer may be tempted to generalize from a single observation of an event which may, in fact, be atypical. In the case cited on page 14, for example, the observation and the mother's report are discrepant, but one can no more assume that the behavior noted during the single observation is typical than one can assume, in the absence of other information, that the mother's report is valid.

Another characteristic of observation—and one that is shared by the interview—involves the effect of the investigator's presence. The observer who views behavior through a one-way screen, and whose presence is thus unknown to the persons observed, can hardly be said to influence their behavior; but, when observation requires the intimate presence of the observer, the behavior of the observed may be influenced considerably. The experimental psychologist who watches the physical response of a subject to a stimulus which he administers, the psychiatrist who is alert to observe nonverbal responses in his patient, or the anthropologist living with a family is to some extent a part of—and, hence, an influence on—what he observes. In some situations, indeed, the presence of the observer may alter, if not actually prevent, the very behavior that he is seeking to observe. On the other hand, observers may, in the course of time, become so active in the affairs of the community or organization that they are observing that they may have little time or inclination for systematic observation. J. R. Johnson (1951), in commenting, somewhat facetiously, on his experience as a participant observer in an intergroup-relations study, has remarked that he began as a nonparticipant observer and ended as a nonobserving participant.

Although the observer must be aware of his influence and attempt to assess its effect on the information he obtains, he should not magnify its importance. It is difficult for people to deviate from their customary patterns of behavior for any length of time, and the observer, if he continues to minimize his participation, may find that with the passage of time his influence on what he observes diminishes considerably.

Although the usual concern of the observer centers on minimizing his influence and determining the nature of its biasing effect, it is also possible for the observer to serve as an experimental stimulus and to observe the variations in response which the stimulus provokes. In a study of intergroup relations (Williams, 1964, p. 12), for example, the bartenders and owners of segregated bars in a New York town were interviewed about how they would respond to a Negro customer. To determine the relationship between the verbal response and their actual behavior, a Negro sociologist then entered the bar and ordered a drink. His observation and introspection about the event were supplemented by the observations of two or three independent observers who were in the bar before, during, and after the entry of the "stimulus observer."

DOCUMENTS

The documents usable by the research investigator can be considered under two broad categories: *existing* documents, which are not produced in connection with a specific study but are relevant to it, and *elicited* documents, which are produced at the instigation of the investigator by the individuals being studied.

Existing documents of many sorts—vital statistics records, personnel files, maps, weather bureau records, motor vehicle registrations, newspaper accounts, tape recordings, medical histories, and thousands of other records and reports that fill the files of every literate society—constitute rich sources of information whose usefulness is limited only by their accuracy, comparability, comprehensiveness, and relevance to an investigator's research topic.

Documents (and artifacts) are the only sources of information about past events, unless, of course, there are surviving participants or witnesses. Not only do interpretations of historical and social movements depend largely on contemporaneous documents but accounts of numerous isolated events—ill-fated polar expeditions, aircraft crashes, or shipwrecks—have been reconstructed in detail on the basis of written records left by those who perished or documents produced by various automatic recording devices.

Even when the participants in an event are available for interview, documents may provide useful complementary information. Mothers, for example, find it difficult or impossible to recall valid information about their obstetrical experiences or their children's early development; hence, medical records made contemporaneously may be valuable in helping to reconstruct such experiences and events. Unfortunately, because medical records generally are kept for clinical and service purposes rather than for research, the specific information sought by an investigator is not always uniformly available for all the cases he is studying. Documents also provide valuable corroboration of data that people are likely to distort in an interview—their level of education, their income, their history of automobile accidents, etc.—although documents may, of course, themselves contain distortions.

In some situations, documents may be less valid than personal accounts elicited by interview. If the original event aroused strong feelings, these feelings may have found their way into the contemporaneous documents. And, if subsequent evidence altered the explanation of an event, contemporaneous documents would not reflect it.[3]

The economy of using documents rather than interviews is striking—particularly if the documents have been classified or coded in a form suitable for the investigation. Certain kinds of document—the United States Bureau of the Census data, for example—provide a body of information larger than could be accumulated in several lifetimes of interviewing.

By the use of documents, an investigator can swiftly traverse not only time but also geographic distance. When access to Japan was impossible during World War II, Ruth Benedict (1946) made a study of Japanese culture by relying heavily on a content analysis of Japanese radio programs, motion pictures, and popular literature to supplement data which she had collected from individuals who had lived in Japan. More commonly, the examination of documents in a central repository—such as a state department of health or the files of a professional group or association—can provide information about persons who are widely scattered geographically.

Like observation, documents can sometimes yield information which, especially during the early stages of a study, may be withheld by respondents. In most community studies, for example, the investigators need to be able to identify, at the outset, the power

[3] *A Night to Remember*, a narrative account of the sinking of the *S. S. Titanic* constructed some thirty years after the event on the basis of survivor interviews, differed considerably from contemporaneous accounts. Similarly, the Sacco-Vanzetti trial has been given interpretations in recent years that differ sharply from those given in contemporaneous documents.

structure and the opinion leaders; yet local respondents may be reluctant to give this kind of information to an interviewer who is an outsider. The information may be obtained—with at least an adequate degree of accuracy—from a study of the files of the local newspaper, the minutes of town council meetings, or such sources as Poor's *Register of Directors* or the Rand-McNally *Banker's Register* (Lamb, 1960).

Documents have, of course, serious limitations. They are virtually useless for any information about future behavior, since even such future-oriented documents as income-tax estimates, real-estate options, and cotton futures contain an element of speculation which could be revealed only by interviewing. They are also of little value in uncovering motives, opinions, or any other information usually elicited by skillful questioning. And occasionally they can be misleading if the investigator fails to recognize that they are no more accurate than their compilers and that the compilers of such records may well have lacked the training, interest, or motivations of scientific investigators.

Perhaps a limitation more common than inaccuracy is the fact that documents often provide information that is tantalizingly tangential rather than central to the investigator's interests. The mere fact that the compiler of the documents had the same conceptual scheme as the investigator who subsequently attempts to use them does not guarantee that the data will be usable. Data may not be available for all cases, or critical data may have gone unrecorded, or the unit of measurement may be one that is useless to the investigator.

Elicited documents—questionnaires, tests of various kinds, autobiographical sketches, diaries, prior interview responses—are useful adjuncts to the interview in some situations.[4] Some of them provide a considerable measure of economy, because they can elicit information without the investigator's presence and, thus, without taking up his time. Often a questionnaire can elicit from the respondent materials that cannot be elicited as effectively *viva voce*,

---

[4] The observer's field notes and records and the interviewer's transcripts, tape recordings, or completed questionnaires may also, of course, be regarded as elicited documents.

either because it is assumed that oral questioning may cause embarrassment or because the responses require more time and thought than respondents may give to them comfortably in face-to-face situations.

For both existing and elicited documents that cannot be supplemented by data from other sources, the only test of validity is an examination of the internal consistency of the data and an appraisal of their plausibility by the investigator.

INTERVIEWING

Even so brief a discussion as the foregoing indicates some of the research situations that make the interview indispensable. Most obvious, perhaps, is the event that took place in the recent or remote past and was totally undocumented but from which there survived interviewable participants or witnesses. Such events range from the history of a preliterate tribe, through political coups or race riots, to the minor, fender-bending automobile accident. Osgood (1940), for example, reconstructed the Ingalik culture pattern on the basis of data provided by a sole surviving respondent. The Civil Aeronautics Board, by interviewing scores of witnesses, was able to reconstruct enough of the details of an aircraft's flight path on November 16, 1959, to lead to a determination of the cause of its crash (Hunt, 1960). And there is hardly a policeman of more than a few years' experience who has not interviewed participants in an automobile collision.

Although some future events may be predictable on the basis of documents and observed behavior, others are predictable only on the basis of interview data. The most conspicuous use of the interview to predict future behavior is probably the pre-election political poll or the several on-going surveys of attitudes and values relevant to political issues; but the interview is also used widely in market surveys, educational censuses, and the study of other types of future behavior.

In the study of motives, attitudes, skills, opinions, health—or of anything else that is "inside" an individual and is not directly reflected in observable behavior or appearance—the interview is often used in conjunction with observation and documents. For relatively simple information—e.g., respondents' preferences as to competing brands of gasoline or competing candidates for political office, or a patient's recital of fairly clear-cut physical symptoms— the interview alone may suffice. But, for more complex matters, the interview may be necessary but not sufficient. The employment interviewer may, before or after the interview, observe the candidate in a performance test or consult a report of his past vocational and educational performance. The psychiatrist may require a physical examination and perhaps an evaluation based on a battery of psychological tests to supplement the information he derives from the interview. The physician may read the patient's chart, laboratory reports, and other test results and observe the patient's behavior to corroborate the impressions he receives from the patient's answers to his questions.

Even in less technically complex situations, the interview and other tools are used to supplement one another. The interviewer asking about reading habits may glance around the respondent's home to see whether the absence or presence of books corroborates the verbal response. The anthropologist and sociologist may find it necessary to use interviews in order to learn the significance of what they observe. The investigator who finds that documentary evidence is superficial or otherwise inadequate may interview to discover what underlies the recorded data.

For some purposes the interview is far more versatile and flexible than either observation or the use of documents. The investigator using either without supplementing them with the interview must rely entirely on himself in interpreting the significance of what he discovers. In cases of ambiguity, he cannot ask about meaning; in cases of inconsistency, he cannot seek clarification; and, where data are inadequate, he cannot ask for amplification. Perhaps most limiting of all is the fact that the meaning that he derives from observational and documentary information is the meaning that he attributes to it rather than the meaning that it has for the persons he is studying. In the interview, by contrast, the investigator can always check his own interpretation of the data with that of his respondents—an advantage that is virtually essential if he is studying a culture different from his own.

The Criteria for Selecting a Method

As the foregoing discussion indicates, in some studies the choice of the method of data gathering is dictated by the subject matter, the group being studied, or the circumstances of the investigation. Often, however, the investigator is faced with a choice of any of the three methods or of a combination of two or more. Indeed, it is the rare investigation that proceeds from original idea to completion by use of one method alone. The investigator may develop his original hunch or hypothesis through reading (documents), through discussion with colleagues (interview), through observation of a new or familiar phenomenon, or through introspection (observation of himself). His first steps in formulating his design may likewise involve more than one method, and even in his preliminary or pilot investigation he may test two or more methods to discover the most effective one. Nevertheless, at every stage, he will find it useful to weigh one method against another in terms of four basic criteria: accessibility, economy of his resources, accuracy, and relevance.

Although the applicability of each of these criteria to the specific methods of data gathering requires some elaboration, the criteria themselves are not unfamiliar to anyone who has sought any kind of information in the course of his daily life. Each time a specific method is selected, interplay among these criteria is involved. For the determination of a person's annual income, for example, it is likely that the withholding receipts filed with his income-tax return (a document) would provide more accurate information than an interview question. But, since this document is not accessible to the investigator, and since the person is accessible for interview, accuracy must be sacrificed to accessibility. In taking the most recent United States Census, one of the census taker's questions involved the number of rooms in the respondent's house. Because of differences in definition of a room—e.g., inconsistency in the counting of bathrooms as rooms—and perhaps because of the tendency of some respondents to distort in either direction, it seems likely that observation by the census taker—that is, an actual counting of the rooms—would have produced somewhat greater accuracy than questioning the respondent. But this higher degree of accuracy was not considered sufficiently desirable to justify the enormously higher costs it would have entailed. Thus, the degree to which each method of data gathering meets each criterion needs thoughtful examination. This can be done most effectively after the investigator decides which of the criteria is most important to him in the light of the subject matter, the focus of his research, the group being studied, and the budget available to him.

ACCESSIBILITY

The accessibility of information involves two separate questions: (1) Is the information obtainable at all by one of the three methods, regardless of the willingness of its "proprietor" to make it available? (2) Will the "proprietor" of the information be willing to make it available to the investigator?

The answer to the first of these questions is, as we have already seen, often determined by the nature of the information being sought. Information on past events, for example, is obviously not accessible by observation unless it can be inferred from artifacts or technology, just as information about future intentions is not likely to be reliably obtainable from documents. But for many research subjects the question of accessibility is not so easily answered. For example, until the Cornell Automobile Crash Injury Research project developed a uniform system of accident reporting by state police, consistent and relevant details on large numbers of automobile accidents were not accessible through the study of documents. Similarly, for the study of the causes of neurological damage in children, obstetrical records were, until recently, inadequate. It was only after the laborious development of uniformity in recording—through identification of what might be information relevant to the problem, definition of terms, and training in the use of measures—that the data became accessible. Storerooms may be full of documentary records, but if these were not designed with the investigator's purpose in mind, they may be virtually useless to him.

The increasing development of archives and information repositories of films, punch cards, tape recordings, survey data, cross-cultural studies, and other documents makes a considerable amount of information accessible to the investigator who is sufficiently ingenious and persevering to locate it and adapt it to his purposes. Often, however, as we shall note shortly, the information that is thus available is not so highly relevant as the investigator would wish.

The question of whether the people who control information are willing to give the investigator access to it also requires careful consideration. Certain documents which contain highly useful information in economical form—insurance claims, tax returns, medical records, diplomatic and military reports, etc.—may be so highly confidential that they are not accessible to any investigator; some may be available only to certain especially qualified or privileged investigators. And observation may produce resistance. The residents or the authorities of many American communities may make an investigator's life extremely difficult if he attempts to observe such crisis situations as race riots or strikes. Numerous partisan organizations will not permit outsiders to observe their meetings. An investigator who wants to observe police action from the vantage point of a police car may find himself barred by insurance regulations, either actual or fabricated for the occasion.

Even if the group under study is ostensibly willing and cooperative, however, several factors may make information inaccessible. The presence of an observer may, as we have pointed out, modify or put a stop to the very behavior that he wishes to observe. Documents, even when they are made available to an investigator, may prove inaccurate or irrelevant. Forgetting or repression may make information inaccessible through interviewing. A respondent's perception of the interviewer as a person may cause him to distort information. Or he may simply not have the information that the investigator is seeking and, with the best of intentions, answer his questions with "I don't know."

Despite these obstacles, however, many investigators have gained access to information that appeared to be inaccessible. Until Kinsey

(Kinsey, Pomeroy, & Martin, 1948) completed his study, few investigators would have believed that information on sexual practices could be obtained from a large and heterogeneous population by means of the interview.

The development of small radio transmitters and receivers and tape-recording equipment has made it possible to obtain a continuous record of all verbal communication between two or more people who are isolated from the investigator—teacher and students in a classroom, for example, or a married couple in a domestic situation. Whether married couples would be willing to wear the transmitters, and, if they did, whether and in what ways the wearing of transmitters would inhibit their verbal behavior, are questions that cannot yet be answered. But the investigator's estimate of what information others will be willing or able to provide is not necessarily predictive of what he can obtain. Only the naïve investigator assumes in advance that he will have access to the information he is seeking. But it is equally naïve to assume that certain information is clearly inaccessible simply because other investigators have hitherto failed to elicit it.

ECONOMY OF RESOURCES

The cost of acquiring a body of information is difficult to estimate in advance, because it represents an aggregate of the costs of four processes: (1) locating an appropriate source, (2) eliciting information from the source, (3) editing, translating, digesting, and coding the information, and (4) carrying out the analysis so that the study provides answers to the questions originally posed by the investigator. The costs may be represented in man-hours of the investigator and his staff, in charges for the use of computing machinery, and in direct disbursements for postage, telephone calls, printing, travel, etc. Unless the total process is kept in mind, it is easy for the investigator to choose a method that appears economical in one phase of the research but proves inordinately expensive in another phase.

Observation is, as we have pointed out, expensive in terms of the observer's time, although the resulting data may be analyzed economically if the observer is able to code his observations as they occur; on the other hand, such precoded categories, although useful for standardization, will inhibit the development of insights during data collection. Interviewing costs can sometimes be reduced by the use of professional part-time interviewers in place of the investigator and by the use of interview schedules on which the answers are coded by the interviewer, but both these procedures may lower the quality and richness of response material. Nonschedule interviews often provide extremely rich response material but require skilled interviewers and may involve expensive and time-consuming coding and analysis. The use of documents, especially if they are centrally located, offers a substantial economy in travel time as well as data collection, but, unless these documents are in the form of punched cards, they may involve high costs for transcription and analysis. Nevertheless, these procedures may cost less than collecting the data by other methods.

One method commonly used for reducing the cost of interviewing is to design a single interview which can be used for two or more studies with the same respondents, thus amortizing the cost per interview. Although this "as-long-as-you're-at-it" approach can be economical, it quickly reaches a point of diminishing returns, at which response quality deteriorates and both the respondents and the interviewers become overburdened. On the other hand, economy is not inevitably related inversely to the quality of information. With sufficient forethought, planning, and ingenuity in the development and pretesting stages, an investigator can frequently cut costs with no sacrifice in quality.

Because of the costs of data collection, an investigator must review carefully the research which has already been done relating to his own interests to determine whether a usable body of data may not already be available. The responses to questionnaires used in large numbers of surveys have been collected at the Roper Public Opinion Research Center at Williams College, Williamstown, Massachusetts, on coded and punched IBM cards and are available to qualified investigators. The Human Relations Area Files, originated at Yale, provide, in classified form, the data from hundreds of anthropological studies. Copies of the files are now available at a number of major universities. The United States Bureau of the Census maintains a wealth of demographic information for the whole United States. Occasionally, too, a body of data collected for seemingly unrelated purposes in another discipline may either reduce or eliminate an investigator's need to collect new data for his study.

ACCURACY

In his efforts toward accuracy, an investigator must steer a course between two hazards: on the one hand, he must maintain a healthy skepticism about the reliability and validity of any information and a constant awareness of the possible sources of error and distortion; on the other hand, he must realize that reliability and validity are relative and that an extremely high degree of accuracy may be not only unattainable in terms of his budget but also unnecessary in terms of his study.

Error and distortion can occur in any method of data gathering. The respondent in an interview may have a faulty memory; he may distort unconsciously for a number of reasons; or he may deliberately mislead the interviewer. In subsequent chapters we shall discuss methods by which an interviewer can increase response accuracy by the formulation of his questions and by other techniques, but on some topics the interview by itself cannot eliminate all types and sources of inaccuracy.

Observation may be inaccurate for reasons originating in either the observer or the observed. The observer's biases, his preconceptions, or his expectations may cause him to see what he expects to see rather than what is there. The observed, in turn, may consciously or unconsciously modify his behavior or may draw the attention of the observer to phenomena which are irrelevant or misleading.

Documents, too, can be inaccurate. Being derived largely from observation or interviewing, they may share all the sources of bias of these methods in addition to those of recording and transcription. Moreover, inherited documents, since they were not produced directly for the investigator's purposes and since the motives, interests, and competence of their authors are often indeterminable, may contain biases which the investigator who considers using them is unable to detect.

In applying the criterion of accuracy, the investigator will try to choose the method that yields the greatest accuracy within limits of economy and accessibility, bearing in mind that other methods may be employed as cross checks. In a study of mother–child relations, for example, observation might yield the highest degree of accuracy. Not only would it be costly, however, but also certain mother–child interactions would be difficult to observe. The use of an elicited document—a diary kept by the mother—would be more economical and might eliminate error due to forgetting, but it would permit distortions which the investigator might not detect by reliance on the diary alone. The interview would not be proof against forgetting, but it would permit the investigator to question the mother about any information that he suspected to be distorted or repressed. His observation of mother–child interaction during the interview could serve as a further check on response accuracy. Similarly, the combination of a diary with the interview for the questioning of certain entries would be likely to produce higher accuracy than either method by itself.

The degree of precision of a piece of information, although not inevitably related to accuracy, does affect economy and accessibility. In general, the greater the precision required, the more costly is the acquisition of the information. Less time and effort are required, for example, to classify children as "under forty-eight inches tall" and "over forty-eight inches tall" by marching them past a forty-eight-inch-high mark than to measure them precisely—particularly since these precise measurements are likely to be grouped ultimately in a frequency distribution. Similarly, it may be possible, for research purposes, to classify respondents' occupations in terms of "skilled," "semiskilled," "unskilled," "clerical," "managerial," and so forth without eliciting from the respondents a lengthy job description, although often considerable detail is necessary if the classification is to be accurate. This establishment of a level of precision suitable for the purposes of the study seems obvious enough, but some investigators, in an effort toward maximal accuracy, choose the least economical method and produce data of unnecessary precision. It is obvious, for example, that greater precision can be obtained by consulting school records of a child's age than by asking him to tell his age to the nearest birthday; but, unless the child is intellectually incapable of answering the question or is motivated to distort his response, asking him the question or eliciting the response as part of a test or questionnaire may produce adequate over-all precision at considerably less expenditure of the investigator's time.

Within the interview, however, a high degree of precision may occasionally be necessary, not for its own sake, but in order to stimulate the respondent to a careful (and, hence, more accurate) answer. For example, the question "How many magazines do you read regularly?" may be answered without careful thought. But if the question is rephrased as "Will you please tell me the names of all the magazines you read regularly?" the answer (in terms of the number of magazines) is likely to be more accurate—even though the names may be irrelevant to the study.

RELEVANCE

An investigator's decision about the kind of information he is seeking or the relevance of any specific piece or set of data—that is, the bearing the information has on his research problem—is likely to change from time to time as the study progresses. This shift in his perception of what is relevant will not invariably consist of a progressive narrowing and sharpening of his focus. Although frequently he will begin with the examination of a broad range of data and gradually refine and narrow his conception, ultimately selecting a fraction of the original range as being most relevant, the reverse of this process is not uncommon; that is, beginning with a narrow range of data, he gradually perceives that his study requires a broader range, and, consequently, he adjusts his methods in order to collect data which at the outset seemed irrelevant. Despite the fact of change, however, an investigator has, at any given point in a study, a general idea of what is relevant, and his choice of a data-gathering method depends, in part, on whether it will yield material of maximal relevance.

The relevance of data that is obtainable by a given method has two separate aspects. First, there is the problem of separating the informational and useful "wheat" from the accompanying "chaff" that may be inherent in the method of data collection. An example may make this clear. An investigator interested in certain child-rearing practices may attempt to obtain data through a content analysis of the most popular books, pamphlets, and magazine articles dealing with child rearing (Wolfenstein, 1951). But, before he proceeds with the use of such documents as information sources, he must estimate as best he can how much reading—i.e., data collecting—he will have to do in order to obtain specific information on the practice with which he is concerned. If he must sample hundreds of volumes and periodicals in order to collect sufficient data, a different method may be more economical. He will also have to consider how to interpret the data. To what extent, for example, do they reflect ideals, norms, or actual behavior?

Superficially it might appear that by use of the interview the investigator might be able to question parents directly about the practice in which he is interested and thus obtain relevant information more economically. But, if the practice in which he is interested is generally regarded as a sensitive topic—the use of corporal punishment, for example, or the handling of sexuality in children—the relevant question may have to be embedded in an interview consisting of other questions which are not relevant but which camouflage the significant questions.[5] Ideally, these context questions are not totally irrelevant—or may be relevant for an unrelated study—but, whether or not such a subsidiary advantage is possible, the asking of these questions increases the amount of work entailed in gathering the relevant data.

Observation might also be used by an investigator, if we assume that the practices in which he is interested would not be inhibited by the presence of an observer. But, once again, the investigator must estimate in advance (1) how frequently during the course of his observation he will be likely to witness the relevant behavior and (2) how many relevant incidents he needs to observe in order

[5] Pettigrew (1959, p. 29) reported success in inquiring about intergroup attitudes in both Northern and Southern towns by embedding the relevant questions in an interview "concerned with the effects of the mass media on public opinion."

to obtain an adequate sample of behavior. It is for this reason that observation can be used neither economically nor efficiently in the study of those events that occur infrequently, for example, accidents.

From the foregoing example, it would seem that relevance is closely related to economy—that it involves essentially the amount of effort that the investigator must expend in acquiring the information he needs. But another aspect of relevance is related to the logic or the design of the study as well as to the method used in gathering data. In our earlier example of the study of child-rearing practices, the investigator must decide whether a content analysis of books, pamphlets, and magazines will provide him with information about actual current practices or whether it will provide him with ideals to which only lip service is paid. If he is studying the effects of a specific nutritional regimen on child growth, he must decide whether height, weight, both, or neither are relevant variables. If he is studying changes in the incidence of childhood accidents as a consequence of a program of safety education, he must decide whether the relevant variable is accidents per child, accidents per family, or the installation of seatbelts in the family car or fire extinguishers in the home. In a sense, each of these choices of significant variables hinges on general knowledge, insight, and logic rather than on the choice of a data-collecting method, but often the investigator does not have an adequate basis for choice. Instead, he must, by the use of documents, observation, or interview—the reading of professional literature or reports, for example, or the observation of a group similar to the one he intends to study, or the interviewing of fellow-investigators or other experts in his field—determine what is relevant for his purpose.

Even after the most careful study and review, however, the variables he selects may have only a "face" relevance. At this point, pretesting of the data-gathering method on one or more samples is essential to ensure that he can elicit the quality of information he anticipates or that the information he anticipates can in fact be analyzed so that it answers research questions. Only then can he select the best method or combination of methods for data gathering.

THE QUALIFICATIONS OF
THE INVESTIGATOR

Regardless of the logical applicability of any of the three methods, a final choice cannot be made without consideration of the personal qualities and circumstances of the investigator. The initial task of examining documents, conducting exploratory observation, and interviewing must be carried out, or closely supervised, by the senior investigator. Although in Chapter 12 we shall deal in detail with the qualifications of the interviewer, it should be apparent at the outset that some characteristics of the investigator —his age, his sex, his ethnic background, perhaps his personal values—may, in a specific study, render interviewing either impossible or inordinately difficult.

For example, it might be difficult for a young male investigator to interview women on aspects of their menopausal experiences or for a young women to interview soldiers about their off-duty recreational patterns without the risk of distorting the responses. Similarly, an investigator with a pronounced speech impediment or a foreign accent might, in studying certain groups, encounter more difficulty in interviewing than in observation.

Reality factors, such as the investigator's professional and personal commitments and responsibilities, also may preclude the use of the logically most effective method. Although it is relatively easy for the young predoctoral anthropologist to spend a period of several months as a participant observer in the field far from home, such expeditions become increasingly less feasible as he acquires a family, teaching responsibilities, writing commitments, and the other personal and professional involvements typical of an academic career. The ultimate choice of a data-gathering method depends, therefore, not on abstractly matching the method with the problem but on a careful examination of the subject matter, the group to be studied, budgetary limitations, and the characteristics of the investigator.

Thus far, however, we have referred to the interview as though it were a stereotyped process applicable in essentially the same form to a variety of uses by a variety of investigators. That this is not the case will be demonstrated in the next chapter.

2

FORMS AND PURPOSES

OF THE INTERVIEW

Although in the preceding chapter we referred to the interview as though it had fixed characteristics, interviews do, of course, vary widely, and both the task and the characteristics of the interviewer vary accordingly. In some interview studies, the interviewer knows at the outset the total number of interviews planned, and he can either describe the respondents in terms of their general characteristics or list the name and address of each respondent. In other studies, the interviewer is unable at the outset to describe or identify the respondents in advance. He may have the names of a few key respondents and know in general the kinds of respondent he is seeking, but, to a considerable extent, he will interview on a "catch-as-catch-can" basis without being sure in advance which respondents will provide the most useful data. He may, in fact, use the advice of early respondents in identifying subsequent respondents.

Studies may vary also in the degree of specificity with which the information being sought is known in advance. In some, the interviewer will be able to describe the information he is seeking only in general terms—e.g., the social effects of technological change or the behavior of individuals in mobs—or he may be able to break down the general problem into a number of component parts. More precise specification of interview content will depend on what he learns in early interviews. In other studies, once pretesting is completed, the interviewer can specify at the beginning of the formal interviewing not only the general problem and its component parts but also exactly what information he will seek and sometimes the actual questions that will be asked to elicit it.

As a consequence of these differences, the characteristics of the interviewer will also vary. Sometimes he is the senior member of a university department who has devoted years of study to the general area under investigation. Sometimes the interviewer may be a graduate student or research assistant working rather in the role of an apprentice learning his craft from an experienced senior research worker. Sometimes the interviewer will be a housewife, a school teacher, or a student working part time to conduct interviews that a professional in research has already planned in great detail.

Different kinds of interviews dictate many differences in the behavior of the interviewers as they go about their task. Some interviewers use a prepared list of questions which they read to the respondent, recording each answer on the schedule. They repeat this list with almost no variation and spend almost the same amount of time with each respondent. Other interviewers have no list of preworded questions, and they may either record responses during the interview or postpone recording until the interview is terminated. The ground covered and the length of time spent in each interview may vary considerably from one respondent to another. In some studies, the interviewer may see each respondent only once; in others, twice or several times, sometimes with a considerable interval between interviews. Other interviewers may have a series of interviews with a few respondents who seem particularly knowledgeable, articulate, and cooperative but spend only a few minutes in a single interview with others.

Finally, the style of the interviewer–respondent relationship will vary widely from one interview to another. Some interviewers take a very active role, asking one question after another and seeking relatively short answers; others, once a respondent has begun talking, largely play the role of listener, encouraging the respondent to go on talking and seeming to provide very little direction beyond asking for more information or for clarification when the response is ambiguous or vague.

The variations that we have noted in the personal characteristics, the tasks, and the behavior of interviewers tend to fall into certain interview patterns. The housewife or student hired to do part-time interviewing almost invariably interviews from a prepared list of questions, records the answers, and asks the same questions in each interview. The senior member of a university department, in all probability, does not work from a schedule of questions but seems to be exploring a problem, varying his questions from one respondent to the next and exploiting the leads, insights, and unanticipated information he receives from the respondents.

The Standardized and Nonstandardized Interview

The wide range of behavior among interviewers that we have sketched can usefully be associated with two categories of interview. The first is the *standardized* interview or, as it has sometimes been called, the *structured* interview. Although, as we shall see, it can be conducted in more than one way, this form of interview is used when the same, or predominantly the same, information is to be collected from each respondent.

Standardized interviews are used for many purposes: to determine public opinion on a wide range of issues—e.g., foreign policy or the popularity of candidates in elections; to learn about consumer preferences, human sexual behavior, leisure activities, or the epidemiology of psychiatric symptoms; and other purposes involving the quantification of data. The standardized interview may be used once on a number of respondents or may be used on a series of occasions with a panel of respondents to determine the stability of certain attitudes, values, and practices.

Because the standardized interview is designed to collect the same information from each respondent, the answers of all respondents must be comparable and classifiable—that is, they must deal with precisely the same subject matter—and differences or similarities between the responses must reflect actual differences or similarities between respondents and not differences due to the questions they were asked or to the meanings that they attributed to the questions. If, for example, some respondents are asked, "Do you drive a car regularly?" and others are asked "Do you have an automobile operator's license?" the two sets of responses will not be comparable. Similarly, if some are asked, "Are you in favor of racial integration in the United States?" and others are asked, "Are you willing to have children from minority groups transported by bus to the school that your child is attending?" the responses are not comparable.

The second broad category, the *nonstandardized* interview, includes the wide variety of interviews which do not conform to the requirements we have outlined for the standardized interview. The nonstandardized interview may be used to identify the components of a general question or problem that interests the research worker, to describe carefully the phenomena being studied, and to articulate progressively the specific information that may later be collected by means of a standardized interview. The user of the nonstandardized interview makes no attempt to obtain the same classes of information from every respondent, and the unit of analysis need not be the individual.

The nonstandardized interview may be used to explore a broad problem or research question, such as the causes of riots, the social effects of technological change, or the psychological consequences of living in a residential institution; it may be used to help explain an unexpected research finding—e.g., that people are not voting as the pre-election polls predicted—or it may be used to explore new questions that arise in the course of a study. For such purposes, little would be gained by asking each respondent for the same information because each respondent may have a very different contribution to make, depending on his position with respect to the problem under study—whether, for example, in a study of a riot, he is a policeman, a person attacked, or the leader of a participating gang.

For the standardized interview, the procedures for schedule design and data collection and analysis have been very thoroughly worked out, because the tremendous volume of research using this type of interview has aroused widespread interest among methodologists. The nonstandardized interview, on the other hand, has been used less frequently and for a far wider range of purposes; hence, its methodology is more varied, more complex, more difficult to make explicit, and more difficult to develop into a set of routine practices.[1]

Two Forms of Standardized Interview

Although there is no disagreement among investigators that, in order to obtain standardization, respondents must be asked for precisely the same information, there is a difference of opinion as to the form of interview whereby this may best be accomplished. The form most commonly used to obtain standardization is the *schedule* interview, in which the wording and sequence of questions are determined in advance and the questions on the schedule are asked of all respondents in exactly the same way. The alternative approach is the *nonschedule standardized* interview, so called because it aims at achieving standardization without the use of a prepared schedule from which the interviewer reads the questions. Instead, the interviewer is thoroughly taught exactly what information is required of each respondent and then is allowed to vary the wording and the sequence of the questions for maximal effectiveness with individual respondents. As we examine the assumptions and premises underlying these two approaches to standardization, the methods used in each will become clearer.

THE SCHEDULE STANDARDIZED INTERVIEW

To judge by current practice, most investigators believe that standardization is most effectively achieved with the schedule interview. In this form, the interviewer asks each question in its prescribed sequence and records the response on the schedule— either verbatim or in specially precoded spaces. If the respondent does not hear or understand the question, the interviewer is gener-

---

[1] Perhaps one reason for this is that, when the unit of analysis is not the individual, it is easier to obtain cross checks on the same information from several respondents and to check interview data against observation and documents. Where the unit of analysis and the source of information is a single respondent, there are no independent checks on the information obtained, and the interviewer must depend on measures of consistency within the interview.

ally instructed to repeat the question without rephrasing it. Because the interviewer's task is to read a set of questions and record the responses, his behavior from one interview to another is partly standardized. His introduction and his statement of purpose are also usually prescribed in detail in order to provide further standardization. The following excerpt is taken from a typical schedule interview (Leighton, Harding, Macklin, Macmillan, & Leighton, 1963, pp. 413–414):

86a. Has any ill health affected the amount of work you do?

1. often
2. sometimes
3. hardly ever (skip to 88)
4. never (skip to 88)

87. What age were you?
    For how long did this last?

    _____
    _____

88. Have you ever had to change your work because of poor health?

1. no (skip to 90)
2. yes

89. What age were you?
    For how long did it last?

    _____
    _____

90. Do your hands ever tremble enough to bother you?

1. often
2. sometimes
3. never

91. Are you ever troubled by your hands or feet sweating so that they feel damp and clammy?

1. often
2. sometimes
3. never (skip to 93)

92. Are you troubled by both hands and feet sweating?

1. yes, both
2. hands only
3. feet only

93. Have you ever felt that you were going to have a nervous breakdown?

1. often
2. sometimes
3. once or twice
4. never

94. Have you ever been bothered by your heart beating hard?

1. often
2. sometimes
3. never

95. Do you tend to feel tired in the morning?

1. often
2. sometimes
3. never

95a. Have you ever had spells of   1. many times
     dizziness?   2. a few times
                                      3. never

96. Do you have any trouble in get-   1. often
    ting to sleep and staying asleep? 2. sometimes
                                      3. never

97. How often are you bothered by   1. nearly all the time
    having an upset stomach?   2. pretty often
                                      3. not very much
                                      4. never

98. Are you ever bothered by night-   1. many times
    mares? (dreams which frighten   2. a few times
    or upset you?)   3. never

99. Do your arms or legs go to sleep 1. often
    rather easily?   2. sometimes
                                      3. never

99a. Have you ever been bothered by   1. often
     shortness of breath when you are 2. sometimes
     not exercising or working hard? 3. never

100. Have you ever been troubled by   1. often
     "cold sweats"?   2. a few times
                                      3. never

Actually, our description of the schedule interview is over-simplified and represents an extreme picture. In many cases, the schedule interviewer departs from the rigid restrictions of the schedule, either by instruction or on his own initiative, since it is difficult, if not impossible, for him to adhere to his script in every interview regardless of the behavior of the respondent or of environmental circumstances. Sometimes departure from the schedule is essential to maintaining the respondent's participation. Moreover, many schedule interviews are not so rigid as we have indicated. Some permit the respondent to amplify or qualify his responses; others provide alternative series of questions which the interviewer can select on the basis of prior responses. Note, in this respect, questions 45, 48, and 50 in the following example (Hughes, Tremblay, Rapoport, & Leighton, 1960, pp. 504–505):

[If R has never stayed for an extended period of time in any other place besides this community, skip to Q. 49.]

44. Why did you move (or return) here?

45. Do you ever wish that you lived back in one of the other places you've lived?

    1. yes, very much
    2. yes, some
    3. no, not at all

    [If yes]: Where is that?

       Why?

46. Were the people in _____ easy or hard to get to know when you first moved here (or last returned)?

    1. very easy
    2. medium
    3. hard to get to know
    4. other (specify)

47. How did you feel about the way people received you when you came (or returned) to _____?

    1. very good
    2. quite good
    3. didn't make much difference
    4. bothered you some
    5. bothered you a lot

48. Has moving made much difference in your life?

    1. very much
    2. some
    3. very little
    4. not at all

    [If *very much* or *some*]:
    What kind of difference has it made?

49. Have you ever wanted to move away from here very much, but didn't?

    1. no (Skip to Q. 51)
    2. yes

50. List periods of wanting to move away.

I When was it? [R's age and frequency of wish]	II Why did you want to go?
_____	_____
_____	_____
_____	_____
_____	_____

III	IV	V
Why didn't you go?	At the time, how did you feel about staying here?	How do you feel now about having stayed?

That's all about moving around; now I'd like to ask you about other kinds of changes you've seen.

Our purpose in describing the more extreme type of schedule interview, however, is to make clear the assumption that underlies its use: *to produce a response that validly differentiates one respondent from another, the stimulus must be identical.* Thus, according to this assumption, if the question is to function as an identical stimulus to every respondent, it must be *worded identically* each time it is presented. Moreover, since, at any point in an interview, every interchange that has taken place earlier in the interview is part of the stimulus context, the *sequence of the questions must be identical.* And, since the behavior of the interviewer is also part of the stimulus context, this, too, must be standardized so that, insofar as is possible, every interviewer behaves in the same way toward every respondent.

Although the schedule interview is in overwhelmingly preponderant use where standardization is required, its sheer preponderance does not constitute proof that it is the most effective form for achieving standardization. In order to evaluate the procedures used in the schedule interview to achieve standardization, we need to make explicit and to examine the assumptions on which the procedures are based.

(*1*) *In any study, the respondents have a sufficiently common vocabulary so that it is possible to formulate questions which have the same meaning for each of them.*

This assumption, in other words, is that the wording of a question constitutes an identical stimulus for each respondent. If the respondents have similar backgrounds and experiences, the assumption is, in general, sufficiently justified in that the few respondents who do not understand the same questions, or interpret them differently, will not significantly alter the over-all distribution of responses. The more heterogeneous the respondents in any study, however, the more difficult it becomes to find a sufficiently common vocabulary.

A number of methods have been employed in dealing with this problem. Where there are wide differences in the levels of education, intelligence, and language usage among respondents, "difficult" or sophisticated wording is likely to be incomprehensible to those respondents with little education. The general practice, therefore, is to phrase schedule questions in a "least common denominator" vocabulary likely to be comprehensible to the least educated. As a consequence, a question may be phrased as in the following example from an actual schedule (Cantril & Strunk, 1947, p. 842):

Everyone, rich and poor alike, pays hidden taxes as a part of the cost of the things he buys. Do you believe it would be better to tax everyone directly on whatever he or she earns, so as to lighten these indirect taxes?

Although this level of language is likely to be comprehended by the least educated, it may strike the more educated respondents as so patronizing that they may refuse to participate—or so naïve that they may feel the study undeserving of their serious thought. And if the interviewer, sensing this kind of reaction, proffers an apology or explanation for the language level, he deviates from standard presentation of the schedule.

Some investigators who favor the schedule interview, however, solve the vocabulary problem in a different way. They assume that certain topics can be usefully discussed by the better educated respondents but not by the uneducated ones. On the basis of this reasonable assumption, they do not concern themselves with formulating the question in the simplest possible terms but instead match the wording to the complexity of the subject matter. In order to avoid asking these complex questions to respondents who probably cannot comprehend them, they first use filter questions to determine the respondents' state of knowledge about or interest in the issue and then ask the crucial question only of those who, by

their answers to the filter questions, demonstrate sufficient knowledge or interest. This technique is usable if the designer of the
interview schedule recognizes in advance that some respondents
will not understand the questions and if he can design questions
to filter out such respondents.

Thus far, we have considered the possibility that, whether the
question is formulated in "hard" or "easy" language, or whether it
embodies sophisticated or simple concepts, the identically worded
question may have different meanings—or different degrees of
meaning—to respondents of high and low education. But the effect
of wording depends also on factors other than the respondents'
education. Although the development of mass media and the increase in geographic mobility have considerably reduced regional
differences in language usage, some differences persist which may
give the same question different meanings for respondents in different parts of the country. There may also be differences in the
preferred styles of questioning among respondents of different
backgrounds (see Chapter 13).

(2) *A uniform wording for all respondents can be found for
any subject matter.*

Although questions can probably be formulated uniformly for
studies dealing with subjects that are discussed widely and openly
—public issues, for example, or consumer preferences on such
nationally advertised products as automobiles or cigarettes—the
assumption becomes increasingly questionable for subjects that are
viewed from different frames of reference and are discussed in
different vocabularies by different segments or subsets of the
respondent group. For any subject that is not openly discussed in
public, there tends to develop a multiplicity of special vocabularies
known to various in-groups and subcultures. Thus, if the subject
of an interview with a heterogeneous population is sexual behavior,
toilet training, drinking, gambling, or any other sensitive topic, the
interviewer is faced with an unresolvable dilemma in phrasing his
question: If, in a study of sexual behavior, he uses the formal
medical-legal terminology, some respondents may actually fail to
understand his questions, others may understand partially but not
sufficiently to prevent some distortion in their responses, and still

others may be "put off" by the formality of the language in reference to a subject that they are accustomed to dealing with only informally. If, on the other hand, the interviewer uses the informal terminology familiar to any one subgroup, he is certain to mystify or offend other respondents.

(3) *If the meaning of each question is to be identical for each respondent, its context must be identical and, since all preceding questions constitute part of the context, the sequence of the questions must be identical.*

The assumption that an identical sequence of questions contributes to the standardization of the context is based on the further assumption that a question will have the same emotional significance for all respondents.

Generally speaking, the sequence of questions in a schedule interview is arranged according to the following principles: Questions most likely to elicit the interest of the respondent are placed early in the schedule, the rationale being that, if his interest is aroused and he becomes involved, he will be more willing to continue with questions that may be less interesting or that require considerable thought and effort. The more threatening or "sensitive" questions are placed toward the end of the schedule, the rationale being that (*a*) during the course of the interview, the respondent will increase his trust or his confidence in the interviewer and hence become more willing to respond to threatening questions, and (*b*) if the respondent balks at the threatening questions and becomes uncooperative in his responses or terminates the interview, the interviewer will at least have obtained his responses to the earlier, nonthreatening questions.

Whether the interviewer can develop a question sequence along these lines depends on the topics to be covered and the characteristics of the respondents. Inevitably, a few respondents will be highly threatened by a seemingly innocuous question—for example, a respondent recently discharged from his job may feel threatened by a question about his employment or occupation— but these idiosyncratic reactions are unlikely to have a significant effect on the over-all distribution of responses. If, however, a large-scale layoff of employees occurs in a town's major industry just prior to the interviewing, this fact could significantly affect the distribution of responses. To some extent, the writer of the schedule questions can depend on his prior experience and on pretest experiences to identify and correct errors of this kind. For some studies, however, it is difficult, if not impossible, to develop a sequence of questions that will have the same emotional meaning for most respondents.

(4) *Careful pilot investigation, development, and pretesting will provide a final schedule of questions that meets the requirements of assumptions (1), (2), and (3).*

To determine whether individual questions and their sequence have the same meaning for all respondents and are clearly understood, it is generally recommended that, after the schedule has been developed through pilot interviewing, a pretest be conducted on a random sample of the respondents. This recommendation is based on the belief that such a pretest can determine the variability in language use and reaction to the questions of all the respondents in the study. The fact that the pretest respondents answer the questions does not, however, mean that their understanding of the questions is uniform or corresponds with that of the interviewer. It is necessary not only to obtain answers but also to explore the meaning of each question by such means as asking each respondent to rephrase each question in his own words.

The extent to which this is done must depend on the nature of the questions and the characteristics of the respondents studied. The more homogeneous the respondents, and the more similar in background they are to the interviewer, the safer it may be to assume that interviewer and respondents share a common language.

To sum up, the four assumptions which underlie the use of the schedule standardized interview, although justified under certain conditions, are questionable under others. They appear to be justified where the respondents have similar personal characteristics— such as education, intelligence, and place of residence—and questionable when the respondents are heterogeneous in their backgrounds and personal characteristics, unless the subject matter is common to all.

THE NONSCHEDULE STANDARDIZED INTERVIEW

Advocates of an alternative approach to standardization, the nonschedule standardized interview, reject the idea that standardization can be achieved by the use of identically worded questions and identical sequences for all respondents; they claim, instead, that, if questions are to have the same meaning for each respondent, they must be formulated in wording that is *appropriate for each respondent*. Instead of using a schedule of questions, the nonschedule standardized interviewer works with a list of the information required from each respondent. The interviewer is thoroughly trained in the meaning of all the information required, and, when he is interviewing, he may depend on careful memorization of all the information to be sought or may refer to notes. For each respondent, the interviewer formulates questions to get at the same meaning, using his prior knowledge and training, as well as the feedback he obtains in the course of the interview, to determine the language congenial to the respondent. To put it another way, the schedule standardized interviewer asks the *same question* of each respondent and hopes this will have the same meaning, whereas the nonschedule interviewer formulates the *classes of information* he is seeking and hopes he can formulate the questions in such a way that they will have the same meaning for each respondent.

Gruenberg (1963), in describing a study of mental disorder, gives this rationale for the nonschedule standardized interview:

The questionnaire is addressed to the interviewer and it is the interviewer's job to inquire into each area of behavior until he or she is satisfied that he has the information requested. There is no standard interview method. We have discussions at different times with the interviewers to widen the range of interviewing tactics available to each interviewer. It is continuously emphasized, however, that each interviewer must use his own judgment in his approach to any particular individual or any particular question. We are now at a stage where we can, we believe, carry out this procedure on a defined population and are about to do so while simultaneously introducing reliability and validity checks.

I favor a structured questionnaire addressed to the interviewer in contrast to the commoner method of developing a structured questionnaire to be administered by the "interviewer" to the subject. Continuing refinements of the structured questionnaire with efforts to eliminate interviewer bias can lead us up a blind alley—when carried to an extreme we will conclude that the best interviewer is a tape recorder containing the questions and the best recorder of replies a second tape recorder. A questionnaire addressed to the subject of the research which becomes very highly refined and standardized in its administration so as to allay our anxieties about interviewer bias may very well throw away the most valuable characteristic of the interviewer, his humanity.

I am interested in exploring the ways in which the interviewers can be helped to contribute as much as they can to the research in a constructive and yet systematic way. I see the interviewers as interpreters, or in military parlance as intelligence agents. I want them to understand the questions *we* are asking *them*. I want them to understand the language and viewpoint of their informants. I want them to use their intelligence and ability to form relationships with other people to find out what the subject did and what certain people in the patient's environment did.

The basic assumptions underlying the nonschedule standardized interview also need to be made explicit and examined.

(*1*) *If the meaning of a question is to be standardized, the question must be formulated in words familiar to and habitually used by each respondent.*

As Kinsey and his colleagues (1948, p. 52) have pointed out, "a lower level individual . . . is never ill or injured, though he may be sick or hurt. He does not wish to do a thing, though he wants to do it. He does not perceive, though he sees. He is not acquainted with a person, though he may know him."

Thus the interviewer who is unrestricted by the fixed wording of a schedule can formulate each question in the vocabulary habitually used by people of the educational level, social class, ethnic background, and geographic location of the respondent. If the matching of vocabulary to the respondent is satisfactory, it may well have the additional benefit of improving the level of the respondent's participation because he feels that the interviewer, to a certain extent, "talks his language" and has some understanding of him.

Understanding differences in vocabulary between one respondent and another, and, hence, tailoring questions appropriately, may call for a high level of skill on the part of the interviewer. To some extent, the complexity of the task is reduced if the respondents come from two or three different but recognizable backgrounds, each with some differences in language usage. In such circumstances, three interviewers can be used, each developing skill in formulating questions for one of the subgroups.

An argument against adjusting the phrasing of the question to suit the individual respondent rests on the demonstrated fact that different question wordings sometimes produce markedly different responses. For example, when one sample of respondents was asked, "Should military training be part of the duties of those who attend CCC camps?" 70 per cent answered "Yes," whereas when a comparable sample was asked, "Do you think part of the duties of those who attend CCC camps should be training for war?" only 59 per cent answered "Yes" (Cantril, 1947, pp. 42–43). Such cases are often used to justify the rationale of the schedule—that questions must always be asked in exactly the same words if responses are to be comparable.

To see why this argument is not altogether valid, we must consider the conditions that have been found to make respondents susceptible to the influence of question wording (Cantril, 1947, pp. 48–49):

Where people have standards of judgment resulting in stable frames of reference, the same answer is likely to be obtained irrespective of the way questions are asked. On the other hand, where people lack reliable standards of judgment and consistent frames of reference, they are highly suggestible to the implication of phrases, statements, innuendos or symbols of any kind that may serve as clues to help them make up their minds.

It is difficult to reach a conclusion about the responses of people who "lack reliable standards of judgment and consistent frames of reference." Can one conclude that such responses are so unstable as to be meaningless? If they are unstable, does the wording of the question lend them stability? And how, on the basis of this reasoning, can one determine which of several alternative wordings is the "right" one? In the CCC example cited above, which of the two

sets of responses is the more valid? Nevertheless, the schedule interview must make an irreversible decision in the face of these questions.

Those who advocate nonschedule interviewing, on the other
hand, do not regard this as a satisfactory solution. They argue that,
if a respondent's views on a topic are in fact unstable, a question
with fixed wording gives the response only a spurious stability and,
hence, no validity. But, they argue further, often what appears to
be instability of response is in fact an indicator of complex or
emotionally loaded opinions, and such opinions can most effectively
be elicited by using the respondent's own language rather than the
standardized wording of a schedule. Such individual use of language can, they believe, elicit a clarification of the respondent's
values, uncover the reasons for instability of response, and, hence,
produce a response of higher validity. Thus, even the fact that responses may be influenced by the wording of questions, which
seems a strong argument for schedule rather than nonschedule
interviewing, does not necessarily dictate the choice of the former.

(2) *No fixed sequence of questions is satisfactory to all respondents; the most effective sequence for any respondent is determined
by his readiness and willingness to take up a topic as it comes up.*

There is probably no disagreement between schedule and nonschedule interviewers about the basic principle of question sequence—that is, the interview should, if possible, open with interesting and nonthreatening questions, and more difficult and more
threatening questions should be postponed until the interviewer–
respondent relationship has had an opportunity to establish itself
and the respondent's involvement has increased. But, whereas the
schedule interviewer believes that a fixed sequence is suitable for all
respondents and that standardization of this sequence contributes
to the standardization of the interview as a whole, the nonschedule
interviewer believes that no one sequence will be perceived in the
same way by all respondents. Thus, a question perceived by one
respondent as interesting may be perceived by another as threatening. If this difference in perception exists, it not only violates the
sequence principle stated above but also invalidates the claim that a
fixed sequence contributes to standardization.

Proceeding from this assumption, the nonschedule interviewer feels free to change the sequence of questions to suit the characteristics of subgroups of respondents or of individual respondents. In their interviews on sexual behavior, for example, Kinsey and his colleagues (1948, p. 48) recognized that almost any question was likely to be threatening or embarrassing to almost any respondent, but they nevertheless noted subgroup differences on specific topics.

... [T]he sequence of topics is varied in accordance with the subject's social background, his age, and his educational level. For unmarried college males the sequence is nocturnal emissions, masturbation, pre-marital petting, pre-marital intercourse with companions, intercourse with prostitutes, animal contacts, and the homosexual. For males who have never gone beyond the tenth grade in school, pre-marital intercourse can be discussed much earlier in the interview, because it is generally accepted at that social level; but masturbation needs to be approached more carefully if one is to get the truth from that group. At that level, petting is secondary to intercourse in interest and in acceptance, and it is brought into an interview only after the discussion of intercourse.

In a nonschedule standardized interview, not only can topics be ordered to suit the type of respondent being interviewed but the sequence can be readjusted whenever an individual respondent shows evidence of discomfort or resistance. The interviewer may continue with a particular topic longer than intended if the respondent is engrossed in it, or he may drop a topic temporarily if it seems to disturb the respondent. Underlying this adjustment of topic order to suit each respondent is the assumption that a respondent who is embarrassed or uncomfortable about a topic is likely to give distorted or evasive responses, if, indeed, he does not terminate the interview.

One can, of course, argue that alteration of the question sequence provides each question with a different context since this context is, in part, provided by the questions that preceded it. But, as advocates of nonschedule standardized interviewing (Dembo, Leviton, & Wright, 1956, p. 16) point out,

That we deny the necessity of maintaining a rigid formulation and order of questions does not imply that we disregard the influence of preceding events upon a given question. Rather, we assert that this kind of influence can be validly determined only when the analysis of data is made. A rigid order gives an "appearance" of the same conditions and illegitimately relieves the experimenter from investigating the effects of the actual psychological conditions upon the responses.

This statement does not, of course, constitute convincing evidence in support of the nonschedule interview, but it seriously challenges the assumption that in a schedule interview the mere maintenance of uniformity of question sequence exempts the investigator from further concern with the problem of context. Certainly the issue of sequence is not so clear-cut as to establish the superiority of one form of interview over the other.

To some interviewers, the flexibility of the nonschedule standardized interview, in terms of both the phrasing and the sequence of questions, makes it particularly useful in dealing with sensitive topics. In a series of interviews with war veterans who had suffered amputations and other visible injuries, for example, the investigators (Dembo et al., 1956, p. 16) point out that

... a rigid interview leads in many cases to a more superficial, intellectual discussion than is the case when the interviewer follows the natural course of the discussion. If a subject is developing a topic in a given direction and the interviewer goes on to the next question on the list, the interruption might be emotionally disturbing. Such interruptions promote the feeling that the interviewer is not really interested in what the subject is saying but just has to complete the task of getting answers to "twenty questions."

As this passage indicates, the case against the use of a schedule interview for sensitive topics is based upon two related points. First, the rigidity of the schedule is likely to offend the respondent. Secondly, as a consequence of its offensiveness, the schedule interview is likely to elicit responses which are evasive or superficial. The first point—that the use of the schedule standardized interview for studies of sensitive topics may offend the respondent—has occasionally been stated so strongly as to suggest that many respondents would refuse to complete schedule interviews on such topics. But this conclusion does not seem to be justified. Experienced investigators have found schedule interviewing feasible for such extremely sensitive topics as personal finances, family planning

(Cannell & Axelrod, 1956), and mental health (Gurin, Veroff, & Feld, 1960) without significant loss of respondents.

The second criticism—that respondents may give evasive or superficial answers—is, of course, much more difficult to evaluate. So far as we know, there is no unequivocal evidence either to support or to refute this contention. Thus, it remains one of the points of controversy about the differences between schedule and nonschedule standardized interviews.

(3) *Through careful study of respondents and selection and training of interviewers, the necessary skills can be achieved to tailor the questions and their sequence so that equivalence of meaning is obtained for all respondents.*

It is unlikely, especially with a heterogeneous population of respondents, that any amount of study and training can enable interviewers to obtain perfect meaning equivalence for all respondents. The real question is whether errors can be reduced to the point at which they do not alter the significance of the findings.

Nonschedule standardized interviewing seems to be used most frequently where the topic is sensitive and the population heterogeneous. In these difficult circumstances, a very high level of experience and skill is demanded of the interviewers, which will generally require extremely careful training and preparation. How the necessary levels of skill are achieved and how effectively they can be achieved are questions requiring careful study. The nonschedule interviewer has a great advantage over the designer of the schedule interview in that he does not have to formulate or order his questions in advance of each interview but can be guided, in part, by what he learns from talking with and listening to the respondent during the interview.

CONCLUSIONS ABOUT THE SCHEDULE AND NONSCHEDULE STANDARDIZED INTERVIEW

The two approaches to standardizing interviews rest on assumptions that are largely untested, and certainly there is insufficient evidence for unequivocally choosing one over the other as the best way to collect comparable information. Examination of the assumptions underlying the two approaches does suggest that the schedule interview may be appropriate either when the respondents are relatively homogeneous with respect to their background and personal characteristics or where the subject matter deals with topics that are discussed widely and openly in the mass media. Where the respondents are heterogeneous and the study deals with sensitive topics which are not discussed widely and openly, the nonschedule standardized interview appears more appropriate.

In practice, the choice between schedule and nonschedule standardized interviews is frequently influenced by manpower and budget considerations. Because schedule interviews have been used so predominantly, large numbers of people have been trained in the design and analysis of schedules, and an even larger number have experience as schedule interviewers. Numerous research organizations specialize in studies using schedule interviews, and most graduate students interested in standardized interviewing are trained to use schedule rather than nonschedule interviews. Relatively few investigators have had experience with the nonschedule standardized interview, and its methodology has not been refined and articulated to nearly the same degree as that of the schedule interview. Practice and tradition thus make it difficult to obtain trained manpower for nonschedule standardized interviews and relatively easy for schedule standardized interviewing.

The costs of the two forms of standardized interviews also differ. In the schedule interview, an extremely high level of skill is required for the development and pretesting of an effective schedule. Once the schedule is completed, however, people without previous training or formal qualifications, who do not command high rates of pay, can be taught its use fairly quickly, and, because training costs are relatively low, interviewers who do not perform adequately can be replaced without much loss. Provided a large number of respondents are involved, the high costs of development and pretesting can be amortized over the large number of relatively low-cost interviews. Because the schedule interview is designed to be precoded, the cost of transferring the responses onto punch cards suitable for electronic sorting and analytic procedures is minimized.

The development of the nonschedule standardized interview, on the other hand, demands as high a level of skill as the schedule interview. Even after development is completed, however, the discretion given to the interviewer in formulating the wording and sequence of questions requires a far higher level of experience, skill, and training than that required in schedule interviewing. Training costs are therefore higher, and so is the cost per interview, since the more highly skilled interviewers are more highly paid. The recording and coding of responses also requires far more training and skill. The degree of difficulty which may be involved in the interviewer's coding of the responses during the interview is illustrated by the perhaps extreme example of Kinsey and his colleagues (Hyman & Sheatsley, 1948, p. 187):

> The interview data were recorded in the respondent's presence by a system of field coding. The usual code ranged from six to twenty categories, and it was deemed necessary for each investigator to memorize the entire code for a maximum of 521 items which could be covered in the interview. . . . Each of the six interviewers who took the 5300 case histories was trained for a whole year, during which time he learned the code and was checked for competence by double interviewing, practice recoding of old interviews, and comparison of his results with those of an experienced interviewer. Field coding was continually checked to provide a measure of the accuracy and standardization of coding.

In brief, the availability of manpower and the lower cost of the schedule standardized interview can easily swing the decision in favor of its use. These practical considerations, however, should be recognized for what they are and should not be used as arguments in support of the validity and meaningfulness of the schedule over the nonschedule approach to standardized interviewing.

Nonstandardized Interviews

Regardless of whether it is schedule or nonschedule, the standardized interview is used when the same classes of information are to be obtained from each respondent. As we have pointed out earlier, however, a wide range of research purposes—including the exploration and development of concepts and the description of phenomena—involve interviews that do not require standardization.

Although the standardized interview has, as a prerequisite, the advance specification of all items of information sought, the non-standardized interview does not have this prerequisite and can be used at all stages in the articulation and conceptual development of a study. It can be used to uncover insights or unanticipated areas of relevance to a study, which can then be followed up and capitalized on with the same respondent in the same interview. One of the unique assets of the nonstandardized interview is that the interview content can be varied from one respondent to another on the basis of his conceptual grasp of the over-all subject matter of the study, each respondent giving the information and ideas that he is best suited to provide. Since, in these circumstances, use of a predetermined, comprehensive set of questions can be only a hindrance, the nonstandardized interview does not employ a schedule.

Whereas in the standardized interview study the investigator may select the population for study and enumerate the sample (if one is used) that is to be interviewed, studies using nonstandardized interviews generally begin with a conceptual guide to help in selecting respondents but do not begin with a fixed preselection. Often valuable respondents become identified only during the course of the study, whereas some respondents initially selected will be found to be of little or no value.

Without the restrictions of questioning procedures inherent in the schedule interview—and, to a lesser extent, in the nonschedule standardized interview—the interviewer has greater freedom both in the formulation of content and in the questioning procedures. The questioning stems from his over-all conceptual grasp of the study and considerable prior knowledge of the subject matter under investigation. For these reasons, it becomes very difficult to make a division of labor between those tasks that require high levels of skill, training, and experience and those that can be undertaken by less qualified personnel who can be trained fairly quickly. Hence, nonstandardized interviews are generally conducted by the investigator who is in charge of the study or by colleagues with whom he has fully shared his thinking.

Combining the Three Forms in a Single Interview

In the foregoing discussion, we maintained sharp distinctions among the schedule standardized, the nonschedule standardized, and the nonstandardized interview in order to clarify their differences. This does not imply that two or more forms may not be combined in a single interview.

In a standardized interview, even with a heterogeneous population of respondents, certain lines of questioning—such information, for example, as name, address, presence or absence of a telephone, age, and such background information as parental birthplace and level of education—can be scheduled. Other topics, which are more sensitive or more vulnerable to language differences, then can be pursued by means of nonschedule standardized interviewing. Conversely, even in the exploratory stages of a predominantly non-standardized study, it may be valuable to obtain standard information on each respondent—e.g., information by which to characterize each respondent and thus maintain a check on the kind and range of respondents that are being interviewed.

In a standardized interview, there may be one or two topics about which the study director does not know enough to formulate exactly the information he is seeking. In these areas, he can instruct the interviewers in general terms as to what it is he is seeking and encourage them to explore the topic at the end of the interview after the standardized section has been completed.

PART II

Respondent
Participation

3

FACTORS INFLUENCING

RESPONDENT PARTICIPATION

In view of the fact that many hundreds of research interviews are successfully completed every day, one may well ask whether gaining and maintaining the participation[1] of respondents is a problem worthy of serious attention.

Anthropologists and sociologists who have studied organizations,

[1] What we have chosen to call "participation" has frequently been called "cooperation." We prefer the term "participation" because "cooperation" is commonly confused with "rapport," even though they are far from synonymous. "Rapport" generally connotes friendliness and social and emotional intimacy. In this sense, a high degree of rapport may be not only alien to an interviewer's personal style but also quite unnecessary for, if not actually antithetical to, the collection of adequate response material. These connotations, moreover, tend to reinforce in the interviewer the existing cultural trait of wanting to be liked by everyone with whom he has dealings. As a consequence, the interviewer may spend more effort on cultivating friendship than on eliciting information and may evaluate an interview in terms of the quality of the social relationship rather than the quality of the information obtained.

"Participation," moreover, is a broader and more neutral term than "cooperation." Two persons may agree to participate as respondents in an interview. One of them responds with careful reflection, precision, and a clear willingness to provide as much time as the interviewer requires. The other provides hurried, superficial answers; is resistant if not actually misleading; and meets the minimum demands of the interview. Although both respondents participate, their degrees of participation differ greatly. One of the challenges facing an interviewer is to maintain and improve the level of participation of the respondent who initially offers minimal and grudging participation. The gaining and maintaining of adequate respondent participation also involves the various skills and techniques discussed in other sections of this book.

sects, and small communities have generally been sensitive to questions of respondent participation, or "field relations" as it is frequently called, and this concern is reflected in the literature (Adams & Preiss, 1960). Until recently (Stephan, 1964) almost no concern about respondent participation has been expressed in writings about survey interviewing. The part-time interviewer hired to conduct schedule interviews for a large-scale survey research study may embark on a series of interviews with the expectation that only a few potential respondents will refuse to be interviewed. This expectation often turns out to be correct, but the hired schedule interviewer is often unaware of the planning and pretesting that were done by the project director and field director to facilitate respondent participation. Although some studies, by a purely fortuitous combination of circumstances, obtain adequate respondent participation without advance planning, it is unwise to leave so important an issue to chance. The studies that founder or require redesign because of poor respondent participation are not published and hence do not come to general attention.

If, instead of assuming that participation will be immediately forthcoming from a preponderant percentage of respondents, the interviewer, whether a solitary investigator or the director or member of an interview team, asks why, in fact, a respondent should give freely of his time, thought, and energy, sometimes involving himself in uncomfortable self-relevation and embarrassment, the answer is not immediately apparent. In most nonresearch interviews, the respondent participates in order to gain some clearly perceived reward or to avoid some sort of punishment. In the employment interview, the respondent's "reward" is the job; in the welfare interview, it is eligibility for relief payments. In the courtroom interview, the punishment for nonparticipation may be a jail sentence for contempt of court; in the medical interview, the penalty for evasion may be neglect of a serious illness. The research interview, on the other hand, offers no tangible rewards or effective compulsion. Hence, we must seek and examine other factors that motivate the respondent to participate as freely as he apparently does.

In order to identify the factors that influence participation, one must recognize that every interview involves two *individuals* functioning in a *social context*. The behavior of each of them will be influenced by their prior experiences, their social background, and their expectations and perceptions of what constitutes an interview. And these factors will be modified further by the social context—the structure and character of the community, the characteristics of the social milieu in which the respondent lives, the impact of the study, the degree of communication among respondents, and even the physical setting of the interview. Under certain conditions, unless these factors are considered by the interviewer in advance and he attempts to modify some of them before beginning a formal program of interviewing, he may be unable to obtain the necessary participation, regardless of his skill in interviewing.

The problem of respondent participation is important to every interviewer, regardless of the type of interview he is using and regardless of whether he is a lone investigator, a study director, or a part-time schedule interviewer hired after the planning and pretesting have been completed. Even though the hired schedule interviewer on a large team does not carry out the planning of the study, an understanding of factors that influence participation will make him sensitive to the quality of participation he encounters while interviewing and will provide a valuable source of feedback to the field director during the course of the study.

Most discussions in the interview literature on field relations—or respondent participation, as we have chosen to call it—are problem oriented. These writings are sometimes so "horrific" in tone that it is hardly surprising that student interviewers who have read these accounts often exhibit acute anxiety before embarking on their first interviews outside the university or college campus. Yet, the factors that influence participation can work to the advantage of the interviewer as well as to his disadvantage.

In the following pages, we shall identify and describe a number of factors relating to respondent participation which the interviewer can profitably bear in mind during the planning and course of the study. These factors have been derived from published accounts, discussions with interviewers, personal interviewing experience, and experience gained in training interviewers.

Inherent Characteristics of the Respondent
That Facilitate Participation

Although the personal characteristics described below cannot be assumed to exist in every respondent, and although in various respondents they may be elicited in different ways, experienced interviewers have found them to be reasonably reliable as motivating forces. Indeed, in the absence of complicating factors, these characteristics are often sufficient to produce thoroughly satisfactory participation.

ALTRUISM

The desire to help one's fellow man is present, to some degree, in every human being. A respondent may direct this desire toward the interviewer as an individual, toward the sponsors of the study, or toward society as a whole, if he can be made to feel that the research in which he is participating will be of help to mankind. At one level, the respondent's altruism impels him to give information freely simply because he has it and the interviewer needs it; the interviewer is seen as an individual whom the respondent is in a position to help. At another level, the respondent may see himself as somewhat in the position of a volunteer in a medical experiment; from his participation, knowledge will emerge that may benefit society as a whole or a specific group that he can identify.

The means by which the interviewer can arouse a respondent's altruism depend on other characteristics of the respondent. Slocum, Empey, and Swanson, in discussing schedule interviews (1956, p. 222), suggest that the interviewer can focus on two elements: "(1) establish an image of social utility of the survey in terms of the value system of the society, group, and/or community under study, and (2) emphasize the special role of each respondent in making possible the attainment of the maximum social utility by the survey."

The expression of altruism does not require a full understanding of the study, nor is it limited to groups sufficiently educated to understand a technical explanation. Kinsey and his colleagues (1948, p. 36), who apparently relied heavily on altruism to obtain participation, make this point quite clear.

The appeal to professionally trained and other educated groups has involved a technical exposition of the scientific problems involved, and of the social significance of securing data which clinicians may utilize in their practice. The academic groups in psychology, biology, and sociology cooperated as soon as they saw broad, basic principles emerging from the study. Religious groups saw a need for information on the early training of children, and have shown an outstanding willingness to cooperate in any study which might contribute to an understanding of problems which affect the stability of the home and of marriage. More poorly educated and mentally dull individuals have responded to the simple and brief explanation that "The doctors need to know more about these things. They need your help, so they can help other people." The underworld requires only a gesture of honest friendship before it is ready to admit one as a friend, and to give histories "because you are my friend." For each group the mode of the appeal is different, but in each case it is based on the measure of altruism that is to be found—if one knows how to find it—in nearly all men.

EMOTIONAL SATISFACTION

For many people, the opportunity to express opinions or to talk to a good listener occurs only rarely. The reseach interview offers just this satisfaction, particularly in view of the possibility that the response material will be put to serious and productive uses. For the lonely or socially isolated respondent, a chance to talk may be a great release. For the geographically isolated respondent, the interviewer may represent a new face or an opportunity to unburden himself in ways that his everyday surroundings prohibit.

Some respondents will derive satisfaction from feeling some identification with the interviewer or with the sponsor of the study. And, although it can never be assumed in advance, the idea of cooperating with a scientist or with the university or research organization conducting the study—or of having been selected as a participant in such research—is strongly gratifying to some people. In any of these situations, indeed, emotional satisfaction may so strongly motivate a respondent that the interviewer's problem is no longer a matter of eliciting participation but rather of preventing the respondent from making revelations that he may later regret, of containing the relationship within professionally appropriate bounds, and of terminating it without hurting the respondent's feelings.

INTELLECTUAL SATISFACTIONS

Just as some interviews offer some respondents emotional satisfactions, so other interviews—by virtue of their subject matter or the personality or intellectual style of the interviewer—offer some respondents intellectual gratification. As Lerner (1956, p. 194) reported after interviewing a population of French intellectuals, their participation was elicited largely by the interviewer's skill in dialectic and argument.

The impact of the interviewer as a person was especially dramatic among Leftists, who are perhaps more richly endowed with the manipulative inclinations of the propagandist. Quite often a Leftist who began by refusing an interview sponsored by "the Americans," and berating the interviewer for using his talents under such auspices, would be drawn into heated discussions of the specific questions. After several hours of such dialogue, which furnished some extremely rich data, he might conclude by inviting the interviewer to have a drink— over which, if a relentless ideologue, he might advise the interviewer to quit this job and take more respectable employment.

Similarly, it is clear from Riesman's study (1958, p. 306) of the respondents who had previously been interviewed for *The Academic Mind* that some of these college faculty members were forced to come down to the level of their interviewers in order to communicate with them at all and that they would have responded more satisfactorily to interviewers who were more nearly their peers.

Intellectual stimulation is not necessarily limited to those who are customarily labeled "intellectuals." During a research project on an Indian reservation, for example, Kluckhohn invited a philosopher to participate as a field worker and was astonished by the richness of the information on ethics and other branches of philosophy that this untrained investigator obtained from a respondent whom Kluckhohn had long known but from whom he had not been able to elicit the same kind of information. Curious as to what had produced this change, Kluckhohn subsequently queried the respondent, who spoke with keen pleasure of his talks with the philosopher. What had been so rewarding for the respondent, Kluckhohn discovered, was the congeniality of the questions posed and the lines of thought which the philosopher was able to open up and pursue because of his training (1955).

For respondents who enjoy discussion and the exchange of ideas but whose daily lives lack intellectual stimulation, the opportunity to be questioned, to think about and respond to new or different topics, can be highly rewarding. An interview can be a gratifying experience for a thoughtful person who does not have enough to think about, as well as to one who does.

Previous Experience, Preconceptions, and Perceptions

The foregoing motivations do not, of course, operate *in vacuo*. Before they can produce active participation, they must be shaped by a wide variety of situational factors. But, more immediately, they are shaped by the respondent's previous experiences, direct and indirect, with interviewing and by his general style of perceiving and responding to new experiences and personal encounters.

If the respondent has had a previous interview experience—and, with the proliferation of interviewing organizations, this is not nearly so rare as it once was—this experience is likely to color his initial perception of any subsequent interviewer. If this experience consisted only of participation in bona fide research interviews, the interviewer's problem would be restricted, one would hope, to counteracting an occasional respondent's unpleasant experience. Unfortunately, with the sharp increase in the incidence of door-to-door salesmen who pose as survey interviewers,[2] and with the wide publicity given to the occasional crank who poses as a tele-

---

[2] It is interesting to note that salesmen, by adopting the role of interviewers, imply clearly that the interviewer, regardless of his subject matter, has little difficulty in gaining entrée—or at least much less difficulty than the salesman, regardless of the merits of his product.

phone interviewer of the Kinsey variety, increasing numbers of respondents have had prior experiences which have nothing to do with research interviewing but which cause them to view any interviewer negatively.

The respondent's prior experience need not have been directly personal and need not have involved an interview situation. He may well respond to what he has heard about the experiences, pleasant or unpleasant, of a friend or relative. Moreover, his preconceptions of, or prior experiences with, research or the sponsoring organization will color his initial perception. Some persons regard social research as "nonsense," as manipulative in a sinister way, or as an invasion of privacy. Others regard with hostility or indifference the sponsoring university or the research organization, which the interviewer may mention in the hope of encouraging the respondent to participate. Although for some respondents a university affiliation enhances the interviewer's prestige, others regard a university as a collection of "long-hairs," "leftists," or "absent-minded professors."

Individuals who have had no prior experience with interviews may cast the interviewer—a stranger who asks questions—into an information-gathering role with which they have had experience —a government inspector, a tax collector, a salesman, a newspaper reporter, a social worker, a truant officer—or into a role with which they have had no personal experience but some secondhand familiarity—an F.B.I. agent, an "efficiency expert," a spy, or a private detective. These mildly "paranoid" views may be strengthened by the behavior of some interviewers who, despite training, feel a certain guilt about their occupation and probably reflect this in their behavior.

PERCEPTION OF TANGIBLE REWARDS

Some respondents perceive in the interview some sort of reward or tangible gain that the interviewer has in no way promised and that is not, in fact, connected with the interview. And often the interviewer is unaware of the respondent's expectations of such reward. In a study of voting behavior, for example, the respondent may perceive the interviewer as means through which he can obtain government assistance—e.g., a tax rebate or political patronage of some sort. From an interviewer studying the amount of information respondents possess about selected diseases, the respondent may hope to get a medical diagnosis or referral. Through an industrial interviewer, he may hope to get a transfer or promotion.

If the interviewer becomes aware of such expectations, his response to them must depend on the situation and his own qualifications. In return for their participation, Kinsey and his colleagues offered respondents scientific answers (but not advice) to their questions on sexual behavior (1948, p. 37), and there is no reason why, within the bounds of professional ethics, the interviewer should not provide answers to the respondent's questions once the interview is completed. He may also suggest sources of information to the respondent or offer to carry out inquiries on his behalf. But the offer of such a *quid pro quo* in advance may provide the interviewer with a highly selected group of respondents—as may well have happened to a medical investigator who offered a free neurological examination as an incentive to all individuals who were willing to serve as subjects in a control group (Marcus et al., 1960). Moreover, the promise of a *quid pro quo* may bias the responses to certain questions.

More usually, the interviewer is incapable of satisfying the respondents' expectations of reward—and often he is unaware of them. He must remain sensitive to whether the respondents entertain such unfulfillable expectations and disabuse the respondents of them without losing them as participants.

CUSTOMARY MODES OF INTERPERSONAL RELATIONS

Although the nature and directions of respondents' preconceptions of the interviewer depend on their past experience and knowledge, as well as his explanation of purpose, the cues that respondents use to modify their initial impression depend on their customary mode of social interaction. Sociologists and anthropologists have long used terms such as *Gemeinschaft–Gesellschaft*, folk–urban, and particularistic–universalistic to contrast two broad categories of interpersonal behavior. One way, which is exemplified by small communities in which every resident knows every other, involves the assessment of individuals as total human beings —that is, as aggregates of those personal characteristics believed to be significant. The other way, which is exemplified by industrial, urban society, confines assessments within the boundaries set by specific role relationships—e.g., salesman–customer, airline stewardess–passenger, landlord–tenant—and, generally, disregards characteristics outside the requirements of the specific relationship. The respondent who is accustomed to a folk, or particularistic, view may not feel reassured about the interviewer until he has learned about his personal habits, his marital status, his political allegiances, his recreational preferences, and other characteristics which do not bear directly on the interview situation. The universalistic, or urban, respondent is more likely to assess the interviewer in terms of his competence as an interviewer—the perspicacity of his questioning, his ability to assimilate information, perhaps his articulateness and intelligence, and possibly his formal qualifications, e.g., university degrees—and to have little interest in his personal characteristics.

Although most individuals have some experience in relating to people in both styles, it is probably safe to generalize that unsophisticated, rural respondents are more likely to take a particularistic view and, hence, to assess the interviewer on the basis of his personal rather than professional behavior, whereas urban, industrial, or professional respondents—bank presidents, college faculty members, physicians—are more accustomed to segmental relationships and, hence, are more likely to judge the interviewer on the basis of his competence. One cannot, however, safely predict the style of any individual respondent; hence, the interviewer must be alert to cues to the respondent's preferred style. The interviewer who stresses his professional role may have difficulty in enlisting the participation of the particularistic respondent; so may the interviewer who strives to develop a highly personal relationship with a respondent who perceives him in a universalistic, segmented manner.

The Personal Circumstances of the Respondent

The motivations that encourage or inhibit a respondent's participation are modified by the immediate situation—the time and the setting—in which the request for participation is made. Every respondent has certain routines, activities, and preoccupations that conflict with participation in an interview. The interviewer who is aware of them can time his request to reduce such conflict to a minimum.

Many situational demands on the respondent are periodic, predictable, and consistent for some or most of the respondents in the study. Meal hours, hours of employment, the peak hours of a housewife's routine, and the scheduling of popular television programs are sufficiently predictable to enable the interviewer to avoid imposing on respondents.

Within a homogeneous group of respondents, seasonal cycles of work—harvest among farmers, tax periods among accountants, the busy season in various industries and businesses, the court calendar among lawyers—offer the interviewer favorable and unfavorable times for gaining respondent participation. Certain nonrecurring events—a strike, a hurricane, the closing of a local industry, a political controversy—may so preoccupy respondents as to make an interview seem an irrelevant imposition, whereas normally participation might be readily forthcoming.

The setting in which the interview takes place may also influence participation. Conducting the interview in a respondent's home may offer the interviewer an opportunity to supplement or check the responses by observation of the home or family relationships, but, if the home is crowded, it may not provide sufficient privacy to prevent the respondent from being distracted or to prevent family members from interrupting the interview, joining in, or in-influencing the responses.

In selecting a nonhome setting—a hospital, a family service clinic, a church, a municipal building—the interviewer should try to determine whether the site selected may have connotations for the respondent that could influence either his willingness to participate or the quality of his response. Conducting the interview in a church hall, for example, may have a negative effect on the participation of respondents who do not attend church or who belong to other denominations, and it may inhibit responses to questions concerning illicit behavior. Similarly, interviewing workers at their places of employment may inhibit responses expressing criticism of employers or working conditions. If a central location is chosen for interviewing, it may be desirable to reimburse the respondents for transportation or baby sitting if these costs seem likely to hinder or prevent participation.

Certain personal circumstances of the respondent are entirely idiosyncratic and cannot be predicted. If a request for an interview interrupts a family quarrel, a physician's visit, or some other crisis, the interviewer may perceive and understand the situation and perhaps be able to arrange for a subsequent appointment. But often he will be unable to identify the cause of a peremptory refusal. The respondent who has just been dismissed from his job, the respondent who has just received word of a death in the family, the respondent who is momentarily expecting the arrival of a process server or a prospective buyer for his house, or the respondent who is paranoid is likely to rebuff the interviewer without explanation. However, changes in personal circumstances, after a lapse of time, are sufficiently likely to make a return visit worth attempting. Occasionally, however, the interviewer will be refused persistently for no apparent reason.

THE DEMANDS OF THE INTERVIEW

The influences that we have discussed thus far can operate to a greater or lesser extent in any kind of interview, but their salience will be much influenced by the demands—in terms of time, thought, and self-revelation—made by the specific interview. The housewife may respond willingly to a fifteen-minute interview on her culinary practices but refuse to participate in three or four hours of questioning on child rearing. The corporation executive, on the other hand, may be willing to devote an hour or more to an interview on fiscal policy or labor relations but flatly refuse a ten-minute interview on his brand preferences. A professional writer may willingly spend several hours each month as a panel respondent to evaluate advertising messages but be unwilling to devote a few minutes to the census taker. Each of the demands made by an interview needs careful examination from the respondent's point of view.

TIME

Depending on its scope and depth and the pace of the respondent, an interview may range in length from a few minutes to scores of hours spread over many days or even months. The interviewer who is not concerned with standardization can never accurately predict the length of an interview, but, when he notes a lag of interest or responsiveness on the part of the respondent, he has the advantage of being able to change his subject matter or to halt the interview and resume it at another time. The schedule interview, by contrast, has a fixed number of questions in a fixed sequence; presumably, the schedule has been pretested and formulated so that the first questions capture the interest of the respondent, interest is maintained by a change of subject or pace, and the total length is reasonable. Therefore, there is little that the interviewer can do to counteract the boredom or impatience of an individual respondent or to evade his blunt initial question, "How long is this going to take?" If the interviewer stops the interview in midstream and offers to continue it at a more propitious time, he runs the risk of losing the second part of the responses and some degree of standardization.

SUBJECT MATTER

Although one cannot generalize to individual respondents, certain subjects are regarded as more interesting and others more threatening, and these qualities can strongly affect participation. A political group dedicated to reform, for example, may be eager to respond to a study about its activities, feeling that all information it provides is likely to attract support. Similarly, a population of enthusiasts in any recreational activity—sports-car racing, sailing, clock collecting—is likely to make a cooperative, almost proselytizing, response to an interviewer. On the other hand, certain populations, particularly those whose activities are illegal, socially disapproved, or under momentary attack or criticism—bookmakers, procurers, the executives of certain industries, lobbyists, certain political figures—are likely to be defensive and hostile toward inquiry into their activities.

Threatening or taboo subjects are usually defined as those subjects that are personal, intimate, and not generally the topic of public conversation—e.g., sex, religion, or financial status. A somewhat broader view of a threatening subject defines it as any area in which the respondent cannot know his status as compared to others because the subject is rarely discussed in public. Since he cannot be certain of the norms, the respondent is reluctant to give information because it may depict him as deviating from the norms.

Similarly, even a subject that is publicly discussed may be threatening to a respondent who believes that his own views or practices are deviant or status reducing. Thus, the respondent whose income is low in relation to his social class and occupation may find questions about income threatening, whereas the respondent whose income is high will not be threatened—unless he perceives the interviewer as an agent of the Internal Revenue Service.[3] Similarly, a seemingly neutral subject—government policy, for example, or health information—may be threatening to those respondents who are not well informed and who feel that "I don't know" answers will reflect badly on them. Although a sensitive topic may make interviewing difficult, the fact is that a wide variety of respondents frequently have been interviewed successfully on such subjects. Perhaps one explanation of this is that the interview is different in many ways from a social conversation (see pp. 314–319) and that respondents may perceive the interviewer as an authority on the subject and will speak freely because they do not expect to see the interviewer again.

Often the possibility of threat can be reduced by the wording or

[3] With a low-income respondent, questions about income may, of course, trigger a lengthy declamation on the injustice of it all—especially if he knows just how relatively low his income is.

sequence of the questions. But sometimes concern with the threat of the subject matter is a projection of the interviewer's own discomfort rather than a sound evaluation of the feelings of the respondents. The interviewer who himself is, or can become, comfortable with the subject matter and confident about his handling of response material and respondent resistance may find it quite possible to obtain information on what many may regard as a threatening subject matter.

One important dimension of threat involves the handling and ultimate use of response material—the basic purpose behind its collection, processing, and subsequent publication. If the respondent can be persuaded, in his own terms, that the information will be used for socially valuable purposes, that it will be handled in a professional manner and in the strictest confidence, and that the published report will completely conceal his identity, his participation will be less difficult to elicit.

Such assurances can rarely be communicated to the respondent by means of a fixed explanation. The respondent's decision as to whether or not he will trust the interviewer may depend on any one or more of a variety of factors—the interviewer's competence in his subject matter, his academic status or his institutional affiliation, his reputation among other respondents, his personal appearance, the discretion he has shown in interviews with other respondents. In some situations, the respondent will make up his mind by himself. In situations in which communication occurs among respondents and the interviewer is highly visible, the respondent may, before he is interviewed, have considerable information about the interviewer from observation and hearsay. He may have been urged or dissuaded by others and, in some cases, strongly advised or instructed as to how to react.

Respondents will also vary greatly in the time they take to make up their minds about the interviewer. In a study in which there is no communication among the respondent set, a respondent may reach a decision within the first few minutes of conversation with the interviewer. On the other hand, where there is a great deal of communication among the respondent set and where the interviewer is highly visible, the interviewer may have to spend several months among the respondents before he can gain their acceptance. A number of investigators have reported obtaining only superficial information for several weeks or months and then, rather suddenly, obtaining the sought-for level of information. If the investigator is not aware that gaining the level of participation he needs may take considerable time, he may become prematurely discouraged and frustrated.

Communication, Influence, and Power among Respondents

Between one study and another, there may be wide variation in the extent to which the respondents talk to one another about the study or attempt to influence one another toward or against participation. It is unlikely, for example, that respondents constituting a small random sample of a large city will know one another. On the other hand, if a lodge or a fraternal society in a small community is studied, each member probably knows every other member, and an interview is very likely to be discussed by the members informally or even in formal meetings.

Respondents vary, also, in their autonomy to decide whether or not to participate in an interview. Prison inmates, factory workers on the job, and school children in a classroom, for example, cannot be interviewed without the consent of those who are responsible for them. On the other hand, although the consent of those responsible is an essential prerequisite and will facilitate the study, some of the respondents may well resent their active participation being assumed and will offer only token participation unless the interviewer also solicits their individual participation. Even in less tightly controlled groups, informal leaders may exert influence and expect their followers to consult them before deciding for or against participation in certain kinds of interviewing. In other circumstances, however, each respondent will make his own decision, with little or no reference to his various affiliations, friendships, and loyalties; but, even here, his decision may be based, in part, upon something he has heard about the study—from a respondent or from someone else in the group. Because communication among respondents can crucially influence their participation, the various currents of communication in which each respondent is involved require careful examination.

ASSESSING COMMUNICATION AMONG RESPONDENTS

Obtaining an estimate of the degree of communication among respondents requires an examination of three social networks in which the respondents are situated. The first of these is the set of respondents[4]—that is, all the people who are interviewed in the course of the study. The respondents comprising the set may be in geographic propinquity to one another—e.g., the crew of a ship, the workers in a factory, or the residents of a village—or they may be quite widely separated—the Fellows of the American Sociological Association, or a set of pediatricians practicing in clinics in American cities of 50,000 population. But spatial distance between respondents need not prevent either a feeling of cohesiveness or the possibility of communication among them through common membership in regional or national organizations that conduct meetings or sponsor publications. Whether or not there is communication among some or all the members of the respondent set, the mere fact of membership can, as we shall see, have considerable influence on participation.

The second network in which each respondent is involved consists of his *social milieu*—that is, the various people in his environment who influence, and in some cases control, his behavior. In some studies, the set of respondents and the social milieu will be virtually identical—e.g., a study involving the total population of a factory or the total membership of a professional or fraternal organization. But often the set of respondents and the social milieu

[4] We have chosen to use the term "set" because terms such as "group," "sample," or "population" all have meanings and connotations we wish to avoid. We use "set" in the mathematical sense—to mean a collection of elements (in this case respondents) defined either by enumeration or by their possessing defined characteristics. In interviews for generalization, the set of respondents is usually preselected on the basis of defined characteristics. In other cases, especially in exploratory studies, the investigator may select respondents as the study develops and cannot identify the full set until the last respondent has been interviewed.

merely overlap; and sometimes they are completely separate. In a study of infantry soldiers, for example, the set of respondents may consist exclusively of privates, but the commissioned and non-commissioned officers form a crucial part of the social milieu, even though they themselves are not respondents. The officers' permission to undertake the study is necessary, and they may influence the degree and quality of participation.

The third network in which the respondent may be situated can be termed his *reference group* or his *significant others*. Even when it is not the direct subject of the study, the respondent's social class, his occupation, his aspirations, his membership in voluntary organizations, and his acquaintances can all influence his decision to participate and the quality of his participation. Thus, the participation of a Negro in a study of interracial housing, for example, can be influenced not only by the set of respondents (the other residents) but also by his attitude toward his own social status, his membership in one or another integrationist group, and his militancy on racial issues.

Each of the three networks in which the respondent is involved offers opportunity for communication. Indeed, some networks—professional organizations, for example—exist largely for the purpose of facilitating communication.

Communication is rarely an all-or-nothing phenomenon. Depending on the subject matter and purposes of the study, the respondent will select from his total social environment—relatives, friends, fellow workers, fellow members in organizations and cliques, advisors, employers, and so forth—only those individuals with whom he believes that communication about the study is likely to be meaningful and relevant; thus, in almost any study situation, communication is likely to be selective rather than total. If the respondent set is hierarchically divided—as in the case of a military unit or a corporation—the nature and amount of communication will differ both within the various levels and between them. If the respondent set is split into various subsets by factions —union–management, liberal–conservative, integrationist–segregationist—communication may be confined within each of the subsets; in any event, communication between subsets will differ from communication within them.

The interviewer must not assume that the individual respondent is equally loyal to each of the groups to which he belongs. Often, group membership is maintained out of convenience, conformity, or habit rather than strong conviction. Even in situations of strong factionalism and apparently strong unanimity, some respondents can generally be found who do not share the prevailing norms and values and whose viewpoint and perspective differ from the "party line." An awareness of this is important to the interviewer, not only in terms of the information he may derive from such respondents in the interview but also in terms of participation. He may discover, for example, that beneath the surface of apparent harmony and agreement within a friendship group, extended family, clique, or organization there may be a degree of diversity and lack of unanimity which can have a strong influence on participation. Atypical or deviant respondents may also have atypical communication channels which they may use to influence participation.

The fact that communication *can* occur does not mean that it inevitably *will*. The communication-inducing factors that we have enumerated above will not have equal salience for all respondents. Moreover, much will depend on the volume and urgency of other matters currently in the communication network. Thus, if there is little of moment occupying the communicators, or if the communicators live in a setting in which "nothing much ever happens," a mildly interesting interviewer or a minimally threatening study may occasion considerable discussion. But if the channels of communication are normally filled to capacity, a study or an interviewer would have to be highly salient in order to displace other subjects of communication.

To sum up, the interviewer should, in advance of the study and periodically while it is going on, estimate the quantity of communication, the channels through which it flows, the respondents and other significant individuals likely to be involved, and the effects of such communication on participation. To do this effectively, he must periodically attempt to identify factions, formal and informal leadership, and friendship and recreational groups and to assess the impact of the study on individual and group loyalties and interests in the light of other events in the environment. This must be a continuous concern of the interviewer because only rarely will such information be fully and accurately available to him at the outset. It is only as he becomes increasingly familiar with the respondent set that its structure and dynamics will gradually become apparent to him.

THE ABSENCE OF COMMUNICATION
AMONG RESPONDENTS

When the likelihood of communication among respondents is negligible or nonexistent—as in the case of a small random sample in a large or densely populated geographic area—the task of the interviewer is simplified in some respects and complicated in others. Unless there are ordinances prohibiting all kinds of solicitation,[5] the interviewer need not spend time and energy on clearing with the formal authorities, persuading the informal leaders about the value of the study, or determining the optimal sequence and timing of his interviews—that is, deciding whether to interview the leadership first or last or whether to use several interviewers to interview simultaneously various factions or segments of the respondent population. Where there is no communication among respondents, each interview begins *de novo*, and an unfortunate experience with one respondent will affect only that interview and have no influence on the subsequent ones. Furthermore, if the requirements of standardization do not prohibit it, the interviewer can modify his explanation of the purpose of the interview or his behavior to suit each particular respondent because variations between interviews cannot lead to misunderstanding or distortion as they are discussed among respondents.

On the other hand, there are certain disadvantages inherent in a lack of communication. The interviewer must create a favorable impression on each respondent anew; he cannot enlist the leadership to promote his efforts among its followers; and he cannot rely

[5] At the time of this writing some three hundred communities in some thirty states have the so-called Green River ordinance, which restricts any kind of door-to-door soliciting without a license or permit obtainable from the town officials, generally the police. Since this ordinance is aimed primarily at the discouragement of certain types of salesmen and fund raisers, no bona-fide interviewer is likely to be barred by it. But failure to obtain the necessary permit can result in embarrassment and delay.

on communication among respondents to help build participation or to simplify the task of explaining his purposes.

THE PRESENCE OF COMMUNICATION AMONG RESPONDENTS

When communication among respondents is possible (and, in the absence of convincing evidence to the contrary, the interviewer must always assume that it is possible), several problems confront the interviewer. They stem from the fact that, once he has made contact with the respondent set or conducted his first interview, information about him or about the study may reach respondents before he himself approaches them. In general—and particularly in the early stages of interviewing—the interviewer cannot know what is communicated about him, who shares this communication, or how it may affect participation. An unpleasant experience in an early interview can adversely affect the participation of subsequent respondents, and a satisfying experience may enhance it. His statement of purpose may be distorted as it is communicated from one respondent to the next and, thus, may alter the respondents' participation and expectations. Moreover, the interviewer may become identified with the first respondents whom he interviews, and this identification may work to his advantage or disadvantage in subsequent interviews.

Although we shall devote the next chapter to the specific tactics and techniques that the interviewer can employ to maximize participation, certain general principles can be stated here. First, since he must use a consistent statement of purpose for all respondents, the interviewer must make certain, by careful pretesting, that his statement is as simple and as distortion-proof as possible. In the nonschedule interview, it is not necessary that the statement be worded identically for each respondent, but its substance must be essentially consistent. The use of differing statements of purpose can only cast suspicion on the interviewer if these differences come to light when respondents compare experiences. The interviewer also must devote careful thought to the sequence in which he interviews various respondents. If, at the outset, he overlooks formal leaders who have considerable control over the participation of their followers, he will probably obtain little participation from the followers. If he overlooks informal leaders, they may feel slighted and try to discourage participation by their followers. If he unwittingly selects for his first interviews the members of one clique, faction, or social group, he may become identified with it and thus arouse the hostility or suspicion of other groups. Hence, he must devote thought and effort to learning as much as possible about the social structure of the respondent set and its social milieu.

It is rarely possible for the interviewer to learn all that he needs to know before embarking on the study. He will almost always learn more in the course of his interviewing. But he can usually learn enough in advance to enable him to prevent most of the serious errors that result from making contact with a respondent set and beginning the interviewing on a chance basis.

THE INTERVIEWER'S VISIBILITY AND INVOLVEMENT IN RESPONDENT ACTIVITIES

The extent to which the interviewer becomes the subject of communication among respondents depends, in part, on the degree to which he attracts notice from the respondents, and this, in turn, depends on the characteristics of the respondent set and the nature of the study. If the respondent set consists of a random sample in a metropolitan area, each respondent is most unlikely to see the interviewer either before or after the interview itself. If, on the other hand, the respondent set is situated in a small, isolated village in which every outsider is readily identifiable and becomes the subject of observation, conversation, and speculation, most respondents will learn a good deal about the interviewer, either through observation or conversation, before he approaches them for the interview. If, because of the remoteness of the community, the interviewer is forced to take up residence for the duration of the study, his place of residence will be known, and his behavior outside the interview situation—how he spends his leisure, with whom he associates, what he talks about—is likely to be observed and commented on.

Between these two extremes, the visibility of the interviewer can vary greatly, depending on the size of the respondent set, the subject matter of the study, the general level of other activities and incidents going on in the respondent set simultaneously with the study, and the degree of difference—in background, dress, appearance, and speech—between the interviewer and the respondents. The visibility of the interviewer will vary also, of course, with the individual respondent; some will see him frequently and at close range, whereas others will remain largely unaware of his presence.

The interviewer's visibility also will depend on the respondents' prior experiences or familiarity with interviewers. To respondents who have had no prior experiences, an individual who apparently earns his living by asking questions, who spends time in recording and classifying the information he collects, and, therefore, who does not seem to be engaged in any "useful" or "productive" employment is enough of a curiosity to justify considerable observation and discussion. To such respondents, the interviewer's role may be construed as that of a spy, an undercover investigator, or a government inspector; and, if the respondent set has some suspicion, well-founded or not, that it is under surveillance, it is almost certain that the interviewer will be regarded as a threat, and his presence will be widely publicized within the respondent set. The same consequence is likely to result, regardless of the respondent set's familiarity with interviewing, if the subject matter of the interview is perceived as threatening.

Closely related to the degree of the interviewer's visibility is the degree to which he becomes involved in the daily life of the respondent set. The degree and nature of his involvement are to some extent beyond his control. In most situations, for example, there are meetings, rites, and other activities from which outsiders are strictly excluded—religious exercises in some societies, labor-management negotiations in others, to cite only two examples. The outsider will not be excluded from other activities, but his presence may be resented and may even modify the nature of the activity. Thus, sometimes the interviewer's desire to become involved may be frustrated or discouraged by the respondent set. On the other hand, circumstances may require a certain amount of involvement regardless of the interviewer's preference. If the interviewer is dependent upon the respondent set for food and lodging, the mere obtaining of these necessities requires a modicum of involvement. If a community crisis or emergency occurs, his involvement may be regarded as necessary, or at least expected, by the respondent set.

Occasionally, there will be demands by some members of the respondent set for certain kinds of involvement by the interviewer. For example, when Edith M. Lentz (Burling, Lentz, & Wilson, 1956) was studying a hospital, she was asked by the hospital administrator early in the study to look over the hospital accounts, of which the administrator was very proud. Because a refusal might have seriously reduced the administrator's willingness to participate in the study, Lentz spent considerable time going over the records. They proved useful for the research purpose and provided both Lentz and the hospital administrator with an opportunity to get to know, respect, and trust each other.

Within the limits set by circumstances, however, the interviewer has some discretion in determining the extent of his involvement. A considerable degree of involvement may be highly desirable if it offers him an opportunity for observation, the examination of documents, introspection, social conversation, and other data-gathering activities that can supplement his response materials. A high degree of involvement also may enhance respondent participation by giving the respondents more opportunity to know the interviewer, enabling him to be a listener and to be more sensitive to feedback on how he is perceived or what respondents think about the study, or enabling him to repay hospitality by using skills or providing services that are in demand by the respondents.

In some situations, however, there are disadvantages to a high degree of involvement. It is rarely possible, for example, for the interviewer who becomes involved to devote his time equally to all respondents. As a consequence, his involvement may arouse resentment, jealousy, or accusations of favoritism among the respondents with whom he spends little or no time.

Combinations of Factors Which Influence Participation

In describing the various factors that influence participation, we have necessarily had to devote more attention to the more complex types of situations. Much of their complexity is produced by the occurrence of communication among respondents. If the interviewer can ascertain in advance that communication among respondents is most improbable, he can plan each interview as an independent task, and he need not consider all the ramifications that stem from communication. As a result of our not giving equal time to situations which are relatively less complex, the reader may conclude that gaining and maintaining participation is a highly involved and difficult problem. Depending on different combinations of circumstances, gaining respondent participation may be quite simple or may require considerable thought, planning, and skill. The problems that arise in gaining participation often stem from the investigator's failure to consider some part of the over-all situation or the interrelations between the parts.

The factors that influence respondent participation can most usefully be considered in terms of the following set of queries, which an investigator should keep in the forefront of his thinking in planning and executing any study:

1. What are some of the inherent characteristics of the respondents that may make the interview a rewarding experience for them? Altruism? emotional satisfaction? cognitive and intellectual satisfactions? How can these characteristics be tapped?

2. How may the previous experiences of the respondents influence their perception of the interviewer and the interview? Have they had any previous experiences with research or with interviewing and, if so, what was positive or negative? May respondents believe that they will gain some tangible reward from the interviewer? If the interviewer role is an unfamiliar one to them, with what kinds of people may they associate the interviewer? Is there a customary mode of interpersonal relations which is congenial to the respondents, and how should this in-

fluence the interviewer's plans and tactics? Do respondents appear to be more "task" or "socially" oriented?

3. Are there personal circumstances for the respondents that may influence their participation? Which of these are periodic and predictable and which more idiosyncratic? How may the setting of the interview influence participation?

4. What demands will the interview make on the respondents in terms of time and subject matter, and how may these demands affect participation?

5. How much communication is there in the social milieu of the respondents? If there is communication, what may respondents learn about the interviewer and the study before being interviewed? How may the power structure and influence of others affect any one respondent's participation?

6. How visible will the interviewer be in the respondent's environment, and how and to what extent will his activities when not interviewing influence respondent participation?

Exploring these questions—and answering them in so far as he is able—will provide the interviewer with an estimate of the circumstances and conditions which must be taken into account in gaining participation. To see how these questions can be applied to a specific study situation, let us note how they were used in two studies.

STUDY OF A PENTECOSTAL CHURCH

In the planning of a study of a Pentecostal West Indian community in a metropolitan slum near the investigator's university,[6] preliminary inquiry indicated that the religious and recreational life centered around the church and that the pastor was widely respected and liked. Almost all respondents knew one another, but, although there was a good deal of communication within the group (question 5), there was very little outside communication. First contact, therefore, was made with the pastor, who had a great deal of influence over his parishioners (question 5) and who introduced the investigators to the respondent set at a church service.

[6] Richardson participated as a student in this study, which was under the direction of Dr. Florence Kluckhohn. He is grateful to Dr. Kluckhohn for this valuable experience.

Subsequently it was learned that the pastor acted very much as a gatekeeper and that, without his approval, the investigators would have had great difficulty in gaining participation. It was found, also, that a clique of young people resented the power of the church and the pastor; their participation was gained by an interviewer who entered the study later on, who was not identified with the pastor, and who kept himself apart from the other interviewers.

The respondent set had no previous experience with research (question 2). Since the respondents were fairly recent immigrants, were colored, and belonged to a church which, though somewhat divided, held the membership together and discouraged outside social contacts (question 3), they welcomed the investigators' sincere interest in them and their church. Having low-status jobs or being unemployed, most of the men had ample time to talk. Thus, the interviewers' demands on the respondents (question 4) in terms of time could be met easily, and the subject matter—their church, their immigration to the United States, their day-to-day activities—was not threatening and was interesting to them. The respondents appeared to gain both emotional and intellectual satisfaction from being interviewed and having interviewers share in their activities (question 1). They greatly respected the nearby university from which the interviewers came, and they were eager to be of help (question 1). The interviewers were highly conspicuous in the respondents' environment (question 6), and the respondents were accustomed to a highly social, or particularistic, mode of interpersonal relations (question 2). For these reasons, the interviewers participated in a number of social events, attended church services, and accepted and subsequently proffered invitations to meals. This set of conditions produced a high level of participation. The main problems encountered by the investigators consisted in not becoming excessively involved with respondents, in terms of both time and social commitments.

STUDY OF A LOCAL LABOR UNION

In another study, in which the respondent set was the membership of a labor union local, the investigators experienced severe difficulties in gaining participation. An initial review of communication, influence, and power among respondents (question 5) indicated that members of the union worked in a plant which had long opposed recognition of the union and had yielded only after long resistance. It was clear that management would refuse permission for interviewing inside the plant and that, even if permission was granted, it would arouse suspicion among the respondents. Consequently, the investigators felt that the most favorable setting for the interviews would be the respondents' homes (question 3).

Some initial discussion of the research with the union leadership indicated that the local leaders felt insecure and threatened, not only by the plant management but by a rival faction in the union which was trying to wrest leadership from the present incumbents (question 5). After several long and difficult interviews strung out over many weeks because the union leader continually broke appointments, he offered to give the investigator a list of twenty members to interview. These interviews were held, although the investigators were quite certain that this list consisted exclusively of loyal followers of the union leader.

Another meeting was then held in an attempt to obtain a full list of the membership so that a sample would be interviewed. After discussion, the leader agreed to ask the plant personnel manager to release the names of the union membership provided a mail questionnaire was used instead of an interview. Given the circumstances, the investigators agreed, and the questionnaire study was prepared, administered, and analyzed. Although it is easy to comment on the study with the benefit of hindsight, it is clear that, had the investigators carefully reviewed early in the study the range of factors related to participation, they might have recognized that the problems involved in gaining participation were such as to make it wise to select some other union local for the study. As it was, more time was devoted to gaining and maintaining participation than to carrying out the research.

In our concern for identifying and examining the factors that influence participation, we have thus far paid relatively little attention to the role of the investigator or interviewer. We have implied, of course, that he is not a passive victim of circumstances and that his own decisions and actions can do much to improve participation even when many circumstances are adverse to it. But we have focused on situational factors because it is only when these are clearly identified that the investigator or interviewer can act deliberately and effectively. It is to this kind of action that we shall devote the next chapter.

4

THE INTERVIEWER'S ROLE AND
RESPONDENT PARTICIPATION

Once the interviewer is cognizant of the factors that may influence respondent participation, their application to a specific research situation requires the acquisition of a great deal of information about the respondents and their social milieu. Ironically, at the outset of the study, when the interviewer most needs such information, he is in the weakest position to obtain it. Even at the outset, however, and sometimes even before entering the respondents' community, he may be able to acquire sufficient information to enable him to make some estimates about participation and some tentative plans to maximize it. These estimates and plans must, of course, be continuously reviewed and modified in the light of new information which he will acquire in the course of the interviewing.

Sources of Information

Although the amount of advance information available and the most fruitful sources of such information will vary with the respondent set and with the research problem, the following sources have been used to advantage by experienced investigators.

DOCUMENTS

A substantial amount of information about a set of respondents and their social milieu can be obtained from a variety of documentary sources. If the respondents live in a community setting, information about the structure of the community, its organizations, formal leadership, and power structure may be obtained from a file of recent issues of the local newspaper, the Standard and Poor *Directory of Business* (which describes the corporate structure and identifies the officers of large businesses in the community), public records—e.g., the lists of property owners or voters—and the annual reports of public and private community organizations. In addition, census data provide valuable demographic information. For studies of organizations, such documents as membership directories, annual and financial reports, newsletters, or journals are generally available.

By using population, economic, and other demographic data in combination with maps or aerial photographs, the investigator can obtain some estimate of the size and geographic area of a community, its degree of homogeneity, its degree of isolation, and, hence, the visibility of the interviewers and the feasibility of their commuting to and from the research area for interviews or the need to establish some base of operations in the area.

Accounts of respondents' previous experiences with research or with interviewing may occasionally be found in local newspapers if their experiences were especially newsworthy. From newspapers, also, one may obtain information on current issues, interests, values, and activities which may provide clues to the immediate preoccupations of the respondents, their customary modes of interpersonal relations, and any seasonal or cyclical activities that influence the personal circumstances of the respondents.

The amount of time an investigator devotes to the examination of documents will vary enormously, depending on the nature of the study and the documents available. In considering factors that influence participation, the investigator should not ignore documents; but he should not become so preoccupied with them as to delay his

progress toward direct observation and interviewing to supplement
and complement the documents (see Chapter 1).[1]

OTHER INVESTIGATORS AND PUBLISHED STUDIES

The experience and findings of other investigators can be of
value if they deal either with the same respondent set or with a
respondent set that is similar in terms of relevant characteristics.
Certain communities have, for one reason or another, been studied
repeatedly for a variety of purposes. An investigator planning a
study in one of these communities will find the prior experience
of the earlier investigators of great value. Although some useful
information may be found in their published work, their unpublished materials and fund of experience often warrant personal
communication with the investigators. Even if the specific respondent set has never been studied before, the experience of other
investigators with similar respondent sets may be of value. The
several studies of American college faculty members, for example,
are likely to be of value to an investigator studying any professional
group. The point to be emphasized here is that, if, in reviewing the
literature prior to embarking on a study, the investigator limits
himself to studies that are relevant in terms of his subject matter,
he may overlook valuable materials contained in studies that are
relevant in terms of the respondent set employed.

OUTSIDERS AND RECENT EMIGRANTS

If the respondent set is concentrated within a limited geographic
area, there will be individuals beyond the periphery who have dealings within this area—visiting officials, salesmen, newspaper reporters, insurance agents, friends, and relatives. Some of these may
be identified through news items in the local press, and some may
have a considerable store of local knowledge.

The investigator who can locate a recent emigrant from the
respondent set can often obtain useful information about many of
its characteristics. In evaluating this information, the interviewer

[1] Lamb (1960) provides a most valuable discussion of the use of documents in
the study of a community.

must, of course, take into account the emigrant's motivations for leaving the respondent set and the degree of change that may have taken place since his departure. Despite these possible limitations, however, such respondents may be extremely valuable.

THE VALIDITY OF ADVANCE INFORMATION

The reader must not infer from the foregoing discussion that even the most diligent advance study will guarantee that he will make his first contacts with the respondent set with a large amount of accurate information and, consequently, a high degree of confidence in his understanding of the problems that confront him. At best, he can learn enough to enable him to avoid certain kinds of gross errors and to get general ideas about the structure and characteristics of the respondent set and its social environment. But most of his information must be regarded as tentative, to be used only as a general guide and to be rejected without hesitation when new evidence contradicts it.

As a consequence of the limitations of advance information and the uniqueness of the interaction between the interviewer and the respondent set, the interviewer must necessarily feel his way along as he moves into the respondent set and from one interview to the next. By the end of the study, he will undoubtedly have most of the information that would have served him at the outset.

The Interviewer's Self-assessment

Many an inexperienced interviewer mistakenly assumes that respondents will share his conception of his role as an interviewer, his view of the importance of research, and his interest in the subject matter of the study. If, instead, he attempts to see himself as respondents will see him and to determine which aspects of his over-all role and which of his personal characteristics respondents are most likely to understand and respect, his success in gaining participation is likely to increase considerably.

Even in the briefest, most impersonal type of interview, the interviewer must present something of himself that the respondent will find familiar or of interest. To put it another way, he must make an effort not to display anything about himself that is likely to provoke distaste, anxiety, or hostility in the respondent. One of the major uses of advance information about the respondent set, therefore, is to permit the interviewer to estimate his personal suitability as an interviewer in the specific research situation and to decide which aspects of himself and which parts of his behavioral repertoire to emphasize in his dealings with the respondents in order to maximize participation. This is not to imply that the interviewer should attempt to be all things to all respondents. But, within the limits of his ethics and his behavioral repertoire, he is likely to have some freedom of choice in the presentation of himself. To understand how best to use this freedom, he must make, as carefully and as objectively as possible, a thorough assessment of himself as an interviewer and as a human being.

IMMEDIATELY VISIBLE CHARACTERISTICS

Certain of an interviewer's characteristics—his age, his sex, his regional accent, his physical appearance, his ethnicity, for example —are so unalterable and so immediately apparent to the respondent that they must be regarded as givens. But, although they cannot be changed, their effect on participation will vary with the research problem and with the characteristics of the respondent set. For example, a Negro interviewer should probably not attempt to interview respondents known to be anti-Negro, although he would encounter no difficulty with a respondent set that is known to be unprejudiced. The point to be emphasized is that such unalterable characteristics must be assessed not absolutely but always in relation to the respondent set and to the nature of the research topic. If, in the light of this relationship, the interviewer's characteristics seem clearly unsuitable, the choice of a different interviewer or a different respondent set should be considered. If the interviewer is also the principal investigator and cannot be replaced, he may have to change the locale of the study. If the interviewers are hired for schedule interviewing, they should be selected for personal characteristics that seem most appropriate for the set of respondents. Mistakes in the initial assessment of interviewers can be corrected by replacing those who prove unacceptable to respondents. To reduce differences between interviewers and respondents, schedule interviewers are sometimes selected from the same social milieu as the respondents. Such interviewers also can be very useful in suggesting question wording most appropriate for the respondents.

PROFESSIONAL CHARACTERISTICS

In addition to his unalterable and immediately visible personal characteristics, the interviewer has a number of professional characteristics—the academic degrees he has earned, his professional affiliations, his grasp of the subject matter, his sponsorship, his previous experience with interviewing and with research —which he may exhibit or withhold at his discretion. If his respondent set is a professional group, which is likely to be task oriented, the interviewer's display of his professional characteristics may do much to enhance participation. Indeed, participation may be withheld by some of the respondents until they are reasonably satisfied with the interviewer's professional status and competence. To other respondent sets, however, such characteristics will have little significance, and to still others they may be actually threatening. Since these characteristics are not immediately perceptible, the interviewer can use his judgment about whether to reveal them spontaneously.

PERSONAL CHARACTERISTICS

Aside from his professional qualifications and interests, every interviewer has a wide range of personal characteristics—hobbies, interests, experiences, marital status, family background, and so forth—that he can use to enhance participation. Respondents who are not task oriented are likely to judge the interviewer on the basis of "what sort of a person he is," and they will determine this largely on the basis of those personal characteristics that he chooses to display, in addition to those that are immediately perceptible.

The extent to which he needs to display these characteristics will vary with the respondent set. Some respondents, particularly those who have had no prior experience with interviewers, will develop trust in the interviewer only after they have satisfied themselves rather fully about a wide variety of his characteristics, either through what he says about himself or through his actions and behavior when not interviewing. Other respondents may demand little or nothing; but some demonstration that the interviewer shares an interest of theirs, no matter how trivial, can enhance their participation.

THE INTERVIEWER'S USE OF HIS CHARACTERISTICS

The greater his understanding of the respondent set and its expectations, the more likely it is that the interviewer can display his characteristics appropriately. And the richer his repertoire of characteristics, the more likely it is that he will be able to display something that has significance for the respondent set. Most interviewers will discover, if they assess themselves thoughtfully, that they possess some characteristics that will enable them to enhance participation. Richardson, for example, in studying fishermen, demonstrated his background and skills as a seaman because these skills were highly respected by his respondents. Since the fishermen were of English descent (and probably mildly anti-American because their ancestors had been forced to emigrate from the United States to Canada after the American Revolution), Richardson emphasized his English origins rather than his American residence and affiliation. He spoke rarely, if at all, of his academic background and qualifications. On the other hand, in a subsequent study of physicians, he emphasized his university connection and academic interests and made no reference to seafaring. Whyte (1955), whose background was very different from that of his gang-member respondents in Cornerville, was able to share with them an avid interest in baseball and his skill and interest in bowling.

The interviewer who is excessively anxious about gaining participation may try too hard to sell himself through the use of his personal characteristics. Often the interviewer need say very little, and a gratuitous filling in of personal background may have the undesirable consequence of biasing the information he obtains from respondents. The interviewer who is anxious may be tempted, also, to go beyond his real self and present characteristics that he does not, in fact, possess. Aside from ethical considerations, this tactic is extremely hazardous because such masquerading is difficult to maintain, places additional stress on the interviewer, and can have disastrous consequences for the study if it is uncovered.

If, after assessing his repertoire of personal characteristics, the interviewer decides that they will arouse hostility or anxiety in the respondent set, or that they will have some other adverse effect, he should reconsider his plans. The research purpose may possibly be served as well with a set of respondents that would not respond adversely to his characteristics; it may be possible to employ an interviewer with more acceptable characteristics; or the interviewer may be able to proceed, cautiously, with the original set of respondents, taking due cognizance of existing circumstances and conditions. There is also the alternative of covert interviewing—that is, the assumption of a role that he believes will be acceptable to the respondent (see p. 118).

The initial estimate of what aspect of his behavior repertoire to present necessarily must proceed, first, from what the investigator can determine about the set of respondents in advance of any personal contact, through documents and through outsiders who may have known something about the respondents. Then this estimate must be modified in the light of his early experiences with respondents or other persons in the social milieu and in the light of feedback on how he is being perceived (see p. 105). He may also get more direct information about the personal characteristics his respondents judge important from the types of question they ask him about himself or his work.

The Interviewer's Approach to Formal and Informal Leadership

Advance information about the elements influencing participation may also be useful to the interviewer in the planning of his tactics for making contact with the respondent set and for the commencement of interviewing. His preliminary assessment may indicate that he should encounter little difficulty; if, for example, the interview is brief and nonthreatening, if there has been no unpleasant experience with previous interviewer-like figures, and if there is little communication among respondents, he need only determine as accurately as he can the regular routines of his respondents in order to approach them at times when they are available. Then, after checking for the existence of a licensing ordinance, he can proceed with his first interview. Indeed, if he is not highly visible, and if he can assume that the interview is unlikely to annoy any of the respondents to any extent, he may even proceed without concerning himself about the ordinance.

RESPONDENT SETS WITH GATEKEEPERS

On the other hand, the initial encounter between the interviewer and a respondent can sometimes be completely prevented by persons having power over the respondents. Some sets of respondents are, in effect, captive populations, to whom access is obtainable only by permission. Obviously, the inmates of a prison, workers in a factory, or children during school classes cannot be approached without the permission and approval of the supervisory authorities. In such circumstances, it is often possible to obtain either an introduction or some sort of sponsorship, recommendation, or endorsement by an individual or organization known to the gatekeepers —either to vouch for the interviewer or to reassure the gatekeepers that the study embodies no threat, that it is scientifically important, or that it will not be disruptive to the respondents. Richardson, in making a study of the crews of British merchant ships in foreign ports, for example, recognized that the gatekeeper of each ship was the captain; but, before approaching the captain, he visited the British consul and obtained a letter of introduction, realizing that in foreign ports the captain often turned to the consul for advice. The consul's letter of introduction exerted no pressure on the captain but merely vouched for the interviewer and the study. Similarly, in a study of a labor union, a letter of introduction to the local union officers from the national president of the union may facilitate the interviewer's entry.

In dealing with a gatekeeper, the interviewer must, of course, use the method of approach to which the gatekeeper is accustomed. Thus, although, in the case of the gatekeeper of a small or informal organization, it may be possible for the interviewer to "walk in cold" and state his business, most gatekeepers—e.g., corporation officers or school authorities—deal with outsiders by appointment only and expect a letter or telephone call in advance of a visit. This can present difficulty for two reasons: First, it is often difficult to explain even the essential details of a study within the confines of a telephone conversation or a letter. Secondly, many gatekeepers find it much easier to make a point-blank refusal through these less personal media than in a face-to-face meeting. Hence it is usually more effective for the interviewer not to attempt explanations but rather to arrange a meeting in order to discuss the study.

Even in a face-to-face meeting, the question of permission must not be broached prematurely, since the interviewer cannot know whether or not the gatekeeper needs to "clear with" anyone else before granting permission. For this reason, and because an affirmative answer requires more thought than a refusal, it is often wise to limit a first meeting to general discussion and to delay the request for permission until the gatekeeper has had sufficient opportunity to assess the interviewer and the study fully and thoughtfully.

In situations involving several levels of authority, it may be difficult to identify the actual gatekeeper in advance. In seeking access to a branch plant of a large corporation, for example, does the interviewer apply for permission to the chairman of the board, the president of the company, the executive vice president, or the general manager of the branch plant? A mistake in judgment can have two consequences: If the interviewer applies for permission to someone too low in the hierarchy, the person may be embarrassed because he does not have the actual authority to grant permission; but, if application is made too high in the hierarchy, the person having the authority may feel that the interviewer has "gone over his head" without consulting him.

One solution to this dilemma is exemplified in Richardson's approach to a school system for permission to interview a sample of pupils. Here, the question was whether to approach the board of education, the director of education, or the principal of the school. The interviewer first discussed the study with the principal of the school to obtain his reaction but not to ask for a formal decision. After the principal's interest in the study and willingness to cooperate were elicited, it was jointly decided that the director of education should be approached. At his meeting with the director, Richardson was able to report the earlier meeting with the principal. Again, the study was first discussed and the reasons why the particular school was an unusually good site for the study were enumerated.

In view of the possible reactions of parents, the question of whether clearance should be obtained through the Parent–Teacher Association was discussed. The director felt, however, that since the study was related to educational policy, the matter was within the area of his authority and discretion, and it was agreed not to raise the question with the P.T.A. The director of education informally agreed to give his cooperation but asked that a formal letter be sent him explaining the purpose of the study, the previous steps in the research, and the form and content of the interview to be used. When this was done, formal consent was given in writing.

Whether the director of education made this decision himself or whether he cleared it with the school board is not known. But, even if the final authority lay with the school board, it would have been an error to go directly to the board or one of its members instead of the appointed director of education, who might justifiably resent being passed over. Moreover, the "power behind the throne," if one existed in the school board, might have felt threatened at this indication that his power was known to an outsider.

After obtaining permission for the study, Richardson made a point of discussing the research with the classroom teachers whose cooperation was necessary and who would be somewhat inconvenienced by having each child leave the class in turn to be interviewed. Moreover, because it was never assumed that a child would participate, every child's permission was requested.

During the course of interviewing more than eight hundred children, there were one or two telephone calls to the principal and the director of education from concerned parents, but they were reassured when the study was explained to them. Unless the authorities had been well informed, they could not have dealt with these complaints. During the study, the authorities were periodically informed of the progress being made.

Elliot Jaques (1952, pp. 7–9), in his study of the changing culture of a factory, described a similar multistage approach to the hierarchy—an approach that was complicated by the necessity of dealing with both management and labor.

The Managing Director and his immediate subordinates were approached first. The purpose of the project was described and answers were given to such questions as were answerable. Although at this stage plans could only be outlined in vague and uncertain terms, he and they agreed to collaborate, in so far as it was possible for them to make any definite commitment themselves in face of the indeterminate nature of the Institute proposals.

. . .

The next step was for the matter to go to the Works Council. Certain members of the management group now became anxious lest the workers' representatives would turn the whole scheme down in view of a general trade union antipathy towards, and scepticism about, industrial psychologists and psychiatrists. They suggested that the Chairman of the Human Factors Panel should be asked personally to come down to the Works Council meeting, since the high regard in which he was held throughout the factory would lend great weight in securing approval for the project, if he would say that an undertaking of this nature between Glacier and the Institute would be commendable to him. The Institute opposed this suggestion on the grounds that persuasion of this kind would run counter to the principle of getting genuine cooperation from the factory itself—a view which was shared by the Chairman of the Human Factors Panel himself. Accordingly the Institute representative went alone to the meeting of the Works Council scheduled for the end of April, where he was given an opportunity to describe the plan for the project, pointing out that although management had agreed to collaborate, independent agreement would be required from the workers' side.

As the foregoing examples make clear, permission from one gatekeeper in a hierarchical structure is not sufficient. At best, it can produce minimal participation because it provides no opportunity for respondents or others in their social milieu to understand the basic purposes of the study. And, at worst, it may produce a deliberate attempt by the respondents to sabotage the study because of resentment at being "ordered" to participate. In brief, permission of the gatekeepers is necessary for participation, but it is by no means sufficient.

In discussing the study with gatekeepers, it is generally wise to describe it in all its stages; otherwise, it is possible that access to an important segment of the respondents may be denied to the interviewer after the study is under way. Walker and Richardson, for example, in a study of a factory, were permitted to interview management and the foremen but were subsequently prohibited from interviewing nonsupervisory personnel, although this had been their intent (F. L. W. Richardson, Jr., 1950).

RESPONDENT SETS WITHOUT GATEKEEPERS

The absence of any formal gatekeeper does not relieve the interviewer of the obligation to examine the patterns of communication, influence, and power that may influence respondent participation. Where there is communication among respondents but there is no formal leader or gatekeeper, it would be helpful for the interviewer to identify an individual who is central in the communication network, who enjoys the respect of all respondents, and who could be persuaded to encourage participation. In actuality, however, this ideal person is rarely to be found, because there is rarely only one comprehensive communication network. Instead, the interviewer can usually identify several figures who are respected and influential in various subgroups to which the respondents belong— recreational, fraternal, occupational, and so forth. Often, these influential figures can be approached and their support obtained either before the interviewing gets under way or in the first stages of interviewing. In communities without strong partisan factions, several such informal leaders can be brought together for a discussion of the purposes of the study and to guide the interviewer on the characteristics of the respondent set and on the approaches he might most effectively employ.

Unlike gatekeepers, informal leaders can neither grant nor withhold permission, but, in a number of ways, they can help or hinder the interviewer's efforts at gaining participation. In some communities, they can endorse the interviewer merely by associating with him; the fact that he is accepted by these leaders will greatly facilitate his gaining acceptance among the respondents who respect the leaders. Also, through the normal channels of business and social conversation, and even in the small talk of casual encounters, the leaders can mention or answer questions about the study or the interviewer in a favorable or unfavorable way. Often, too, the leaders can help the interviewer formulate the purposes of his study in terms that the respondent set will understand and favor. An illustration of how this can be done appears on page 105.

The interviewer will frequently find that a simple explanation of the study purpose is sufficient for many respondents whose decision to participate will depend on factors other than the explanation. This is illustrated clearly by Whyte's (1955, p. 300) experience:

I began with a rather elaborate explanation. I was studying the social history of Cornerville—but I had a new angle. Instead of working from the past up to the present, I was seeking to get a thorough knowledge of present conditions and then work from present to past. I was quite pleased with this explanation at the time, but nobody else seemed to care for it. I gave the explanation on only two occasions, and each time, when I had finished, there was an awkward silence. No one, myself included, knew what to say.

. . .

I soon found that people were developing their own explanation about me; I was writing a book about Cornerville. This might seem too vague an explanation, and yet it sufficed. I found that my acceptance in the district depended on the personal relationships I developed far more than upon any explanations I might give. *Whether it was a good thing to write a book about Cornerville depended entirely on people's opinions of me personally. If I was all right, then my project was all right; if I was no good, then no amount of explanation could convince them that the book was a good idea* [italics added].

The informal leaders can also advise the interviewer about partisan issues, transient tensions, seasonal crises, and other factors which he may not have been able to discover in his advance study of the community. On the basis of this information, the interviewer can determine more clearly not only the timing of his interviews but also the sequence, since it is generally desirable to interview first those who seem favorably disposed and to leave until later those who seem likely to be hostile.

If the informal leaders are heterogeneous—including, for example, newspaper editors, grocery store owners, factory foremen, school teachers, and unskilled laborers—the interviewer has the problem of formulating statements of purpose that will be comprehensible to a variety of individuals and, at the same time, consistent with one another. It is this problem that renders the use of newspapers and other mass media for the communication of the interviewer's purpose of dubious value. If the members of a respondent set—e.g., a professional organization, a trade association, or a special-interest group—communicate largely through such printed media as newsletters, journals, and bulletins, they are likely to be sufficiently homogeneous to respond similarly to a news story or a notice about a study. But the readership of a daily newspaper or the audience of a local radio station is inevitably so heterogeneous that any report of a study will have different meanings to different individuals; some will consider trivial what others consider significant, and some will see as threatening what others see as interesting. In dealing with news media, moreover, there is virtually nothing that the investigator can do to prevent distortion of his statement of purpose. Many newspaper reporters, in an attempt to make a good story, are prone to exaggerate or overdramatize an investigator's aims or methods, and, even if the reporter produces a thoroughly accurate account, a headline writer, or a copy reader who removes a qualifying phrase, can produce considerable distortion. For these reasons, the use of mass media as a means of communication of the investigator's purposes to the respondents may be damaging rather than helpful.

Factionalism and Partisanship

Scrutiny of the patterns of communication, influence, and power among respondents may reveal that the respondent set is split into partisan groups or factions. If there is no strong hostility between the partisan groups, the interviewer may be able to gain the respect and cooperation of both groups, even though they represent opposite interests.

Where the hostility between the factions is intense, however, it is generally unrealistic for an interviewer to attempt to maintain neutrality and to work with both groups. In such a situation, each group is likely to feel that anyone who is not for it is against it, and the interviewer who maintains what he regards as a neutral position will be seen by each group as biased in favor of the other. Each group will press the interviewer for a declaration of his sympathies, and even the most casual association on the part of the interviewer with one group is likely to alienate the other.

One solution to this problem involves the method of *dual entry*— that is, the use of two interviewers, one for each faction, working separately and independently and having no contact with each other in the environment of the respondents (Merton, 1947; Davis, Gardner, & Gardner, 1941). An alternative but less satisfactory solution involves identifying and interviewing those members of each group who are ambivalent about or not strongly loyal to the group to which they belong. Such respondents, however, because of their marginal position, may possess information and hold values that are quite unrepresentative of the faction as a whole.[2]

If the factionalism relates to the subject matter of the study, the investigator is likely to become aware of it quickly. But the factionalism that divides a set of respondents may be too subtle or too far removed from the subject matter of the study to attract the attention of the interviewer. Feuds and schisms that have long survived the actual issue, or partisanship over trivial or highly technical issues, are not uncharacteristic of certain communities. Partisanship can arise over a zoning law in a small town, over the conversational versus the literary approach among foreign language teachers, over the building of a school among taxpayers, over the conflicting interests of two extended families, and so forth.

Partisanship that is not clearly visible presents the interviewer

[2] Even in war, which is the extreme form of factionalism, there are always some individuals ready to give aid and comfort to the opposing side. But the usefulness of interviewing such people as representatives of their respective groups is, of course, questionable.

with two problems: First, he may find himself rejected by a number of respondents who, unknown to him, constitute a faction; this rejection may occur because, without his awareness, he has been seen associating with the opposite faction. Secondly, if he is doing exploratory interviewing and relying on his respondents for suggestions as to further respondents, a partisan group is likely to suggest respondents who share its own views. Thus, the interviewer may believe at some point that he has collected adequate information whereas, in fact, he has been confined to only "one side of the story."

Explaining the Research Purpose to Respondents

Respondents vary greatly in the nature and the extent of the explanation they require before deciding about their participation. Most investigators in survey research have found that, in single, short schedule interviews, an initial statement such as "There are a few questions I would like to ask you," followed immediately by the actual questions, is usually sufficient to elicit participation. Other investigators—e.g., Kinsey (Kinsey et al., 1948), Whyte (1955), and Bain (1960)—have devoted a great deal of thought to developing an explanation of the research that is meaningful and relevant to the respondents in terms of their past experiences, interests, and customary patterns of language and thought.

Some of the questions raised in the preceding chapter may help the investigator to determine the appropriate form of explanation for any given set of circumstances. Unless there is no communication between respondents and no need for standardizing the interview, the statement of purpose must be consistent for all respondents. When respondents communicate with one another, they may well be puzzled, confused, and suspicious if the explanations they have been given are inconsistent or contradictory.

Although it is unlikely that an investigator will deliberately make his explanations inconsistent, there are several ways in which inconsistency can occur inadvertently. Because exploratory interviewing may uncover new ideas and insights which could change substantially the direction or emphasis of the study, it is important that an exploratory study be described sufficiently broadly to permit some change in its ultimate direction. Otherwise, a subsequent shift in ground and a corresponding shift in the statement of purpose may result in an apparent contradiction, either to the same respondent re-interviewed later in the study or between one respondent and another when they compare their interview experiences. A seeming contradiction also can arise as a consequence of distortions of the statement of purpose as it travels by word of mouth from one respondent to another. Lengthy and complex statements of purpose are particularly susceptible to such distortion. When the interviewer tries to explain his research, some respondents are too shy or anxious to comprehend him adequately, even though the explanation would be comprehensible to the same respondent in different circumstances. After the interview, the respondent may communicate his unclear or misunderstood version to other potential respondents. If this occurs with several respondents, who each transmit a different version, confusion may result.

A number of investigators have made suggestions that can be valuable in the formulation of a statement of purpose. In developing a statement that was meaningful and relevant to respondents, Macmillan (1952) found the following technique useful:

After some initial contacts with community leaders, I found that a few of them did not really understand our purpose at all, and my initial failure to communicate resulted in mediocre relations with community members in those particular locales after our interviewing program was under way. We lost considerable time with informants, clarifying misconceptions and doing a complete review of the purposes of the project.

The mistakes did furnish a valuable experience, however, since it taught the lesson of not taking things for granted in establishing such relations. After this, I ceased to assume that I had "explained the matter adequately" and made a point of testing or checking by asking a question somewhat like this, "Well, before I say good-bye for now, I'd like for you to tell me in your own words what you feel we are trying to do in the study." In the first few trials of this technique, the range and variety of responses were astonishing. Some were "right on the nose" but others were far off. It was possible from the replies to analyze *where* and approximately *why* communication had failed, and then I rectified the matter, beginning with an apology for not making myself clear in the first place. While this kind of technique is probably not applicable in all situations, it seems clear that the field worker needs to devise some methods of "testing" what he has attempted to communicate.

This technique is valuable whether or not there is communication between respondents and whether the statement of purpose the investigator is developing is to be used in a schedule interview or in an exploratory study.

Where the customary mode of interaction among respondents is social rather than task oriented, where there is communication between respondents, and where the interviewer is highly visible, the interviewer's over-all behavior may be as important as what he says. Whyte illustrates this point in his study of street-corner society (1955, p. 300); he also notes the common error of making an initial explanation too complex and better suited to other investigators than to the respondents.

In the preceding chapter, we noted the need to consider the ways in which the organization of power and influence in the respondent milieu can affect participation. It is often necessary for the interviewer to explain and describe the study in far more detail to gatekeepers and leaders than to respondents who have no special influence and who may turn to their leaders for advice. Whyte (1943, p. vi; 1956, pp. 300-301) describes the manner in which his explanation of purpose varied with the degree of influence of his respondents, and he emphasizes the importance of early contacts with the leaders.

Since illegal activities are prevalent in Cornerville, every newcomer is under suspicion. So that I would not be taken for a "G-man," I had to have some way of explaining my presence. I began by telling people that I was studying the history of Cornerville since the beginning of the Italian immigration, but I used this story only a few times. I found that in each group I met there was one man who directed the activities of his fellows and whose word carried authority. Without his support, I was excluded from the group; with his support, I was accepted. Since he had to take the responsibility of vouching for me, I made a practice of talking with him quite frankly about the questions in which I was interested. When his friends questioned him, he knew much more about me than they did, and he was therefore in a position to reassure them. . . .

I learned early in my Cornerville period the crucial importance of having the support of the key individuals in any groups or organizations I was studying. Instead of trying to explain myself to everyone, I found I was providing far more information about myself and my study to leaders such as Doc than I volunteered to the average corner boy. I always tried to give the impression that I was willing and eager to tell just as much about my study as anyone wished to know, but it was only with group leaders that I made a particular effort to provide really full information.

Where respondents have had no previous experience with research and are shy or anxious, the initial explanation, although seemingly satisfactory, may not overcome latent suspicion, and considerable misunderstanding may remain. If the personal circumstances of the respondents change during the study, the original lack of understanding or the latent suspicion can cause difficulties for the investigator. Bain (1960, p. 150), in a study of laundry workers, apparently gained acceptance among the workers initially but later encountered difficulties.

About halfway through this study, the officials of the plant began to lay off a few workers here and there, because the volume of business had slacked off from the wartime peak. Now, here I was, watching certain workers and timing their interactions. Was I a spy from the university [to which the laundry was attached]? Was I trying to find out who talked too much, or to determine who were the least efficient employees? Logical analysis would seem to render such conclusions unlikely. . . . But these were some of the suspicions which various persons began to entertain. Hostility and suspicion on the part of certain workers became open and obvious.

In an effort to counteract this, I talked with some of the workers so concerned and tried to reassure them. Some of them, still trusting me to a certain extent, admitted that they were afraid that I might be a spy. . . .

I soon found that there was little I could do to reassure the workers so affected. Talking with them did not help. It was emotionally upsetting to me to have persons who had apparently formerly liked me and trusted me exhibit rather suddenly suspicious and hostile behavior. In the process of "reassuring" them, my own emotional state subtly appeared. Realizing this, I withdrew. In such a situation, my own problem was of little importance to them. My task was not to cry on their shoulders, but to maintain my balance and let them, if possible, cry on mine. In any event, I could not afford to become emotionally involved with them.

Accordingly, I concluded that the only thing to do was to carry on as usual and act as if I were not guilty and let it go at that. Surprisingly soon thereafter, in about five days' time, the suspicion lessened. I suspect it was through no virtue of mine. I did refrain from making matters worse, such as by acting hurt, complaining to still friendly workers about it, or accusing the hostile ones of treating me unfairly. . . . What actually improved the situation, no doubt, was simply the fact that after the initial layoffs the workers regained their equilibrium sooner than I would have predicted.

Bain suggests that suspicions might have been prevented (1960, p. 149).

. . . [One of the workers] told me that if, when I had first entered the laundry, one of the officials could have introduced me to everyone and told my purpose, the situation now would have been much better. I further learned that there had always been a slight, latent suspicion that perhaps I wasn't quite what I claimed to be. Presumably, as long as the workers were emotionally secure, these latent suspicions were of little consequence, but, once the workers became worried and upset, the suspicions came to the fore in an intensified and overt manner.

Whether a more effective initial statement of purpose would have been successful in countering the change in the attitude of the laundry workers as a consequence of the layoff is difficult to determine.

Behavior of the Highly Visible Interviewer

After the interviewer has gained the initial acceptance and support of the formal and informal leaders where necessary, or when no leaders can be identified, he must still gain and maintain the participation of the individual respondent. In any research situation, the participation of the individual respondent will still depend on the advance information the respondent has received about the interviewer, his initial perception of the interviewer, and the behavior of the interviewer in the course of the interview, as well as the more general situational factors noted in this and the preceding chapter. But in some situations—particularly if the interviewer is highly visible, or if he spends his time among the respondent set when he is not interviewing—he will be judged also on the basis of his general behavior outside of the actual interview. If, therefore, he is visible to the respondents and their environment for any length of time, he must consider carefully with whom he will associate and how intense such association should be.

THE INTERVIEWER'S ASSOCIATIONS WITH RESPONDENTS

If the interviewer is in a strange community and is dependent on the respondents for the satisfaction of his social, recreational, and maintenance needs, it is only natural that he should gravitate toward those who first demonstrate their acceptance or those whom he finds personally most congenial. But this tendency has several possible consequences that can jeopardize participation. If the community is split by factions, the interviewer is likely to be identified with the faction represented by those with whom he associates during his leisure hours. In a study of an industrial plant in a small community, for example, the interviewer may be invited into social relationships with the executives, and he may find them more congenial because their level of education and their general values are closer to his own than those of the workers. But if the workers perceive this relationship, their suspicion that the interviewer shares management's views will be aroused or reinforced and gaining the workers' participation will be made very much more difficult. A second reason for avoiding a close and exclusive association with one group of respondents is that closeness to one group is likely to lead the interviewer either to identify with the views of that group in contrast to those of the other respondents or to give these views greater significance in the study than they in fact deserve.

The question of the interviewer's relationship with the respondent set often hinges on the degree of his involvement in the activities of the respondents. And the question of involvement can pose a dilemma for the interviewer. The greater his involvement, the more he is likely to learn through observation and introspection as well as through casual conversation and informal interviewing. Yet the interviewer's becoming enmeshed in the everyday life of the respondents can seriously interfere with some of the requirements of investigation. As the study progresses and respondent participation increases, the interviewer needs increasing time for formal interviewing, writing, and organizing and reviewing data. Too much initial involvement in the lives of respondents makes it difficult to become disengaged later without hurting the feelings of some of the respondents. It is also likely to lead the interviewer into partisan association, as we have pointed out, and thus jeopardize or prevent his gaining the participation of factions, cliques, or groups with which he has not associated. The dilemma has no easy resolution. Awareness of it, however, can prevent the interviewer from hastily developing complex social relationships and trying to prove himself to the respondent set. Rather, he should feel his way cautiously and not involve himself in close social relationships without first reviewing their implications for the study.

THE INTERVIEWER'S ROLE AS STRANGER

In determining the nature and extent of his relationship with the respondent set, the interviewer must consider not only the advantages and disadvantages of various degrees of involvement with the respondent set but also the advantages and disadvantages of maintaining his role as stranger. It has long been recognized that individuals who meet as strangers and form a relationship which both know to be transitory may reveal confidences which they would not reveal to acquaintances or to anyone with whom they foresee a continuing relationship. Thus, the interviewer who is regarded as a passing stranger may elicit from respondents some extremely rich and useful material which he would be quite unable to get if his relationship with them was either more intimate or of longer duration.

Although this phenomenon can have great advantages in terms of the richness of response material, it can also have serious repercussions if the interviewer subsequently remains in contact with the respondent set and develops closer relationships with it. In such circumstances, those respondents who revealed confidences to him when he was a stranger may feel embarrassed over their lack of restraint and fearful lest their confidences be revealed to others by the interviewer. It is this reaction that explains the experiences of Richardson and others who, after a very warm and fruitful initial interview with a respondent, encountered "inexplicable" coldness and reserve on their next meeting.

If the interviewer intends to remain among the respondents only briefly, he can, without adverse effect, take advantage of the confidences that his stranger's role may produce. But, if he plans to remain for some time, it is wiser for him to discourage such confidences when they appear and to delay eliciting confidential material until the respondents have developed trust in him on the basis of his behavior in the community.

THE INTERVIEWER'S BEHAVIOR

Within the limits of his own behavioral repertoire and his values, the interviewer must be willing to conform to the customs and mores of those he studies. When interviewing business executives in their offices, for example, the interviewer would do well not to wear a sport shirt and slacks—just as he would do well not to wear a business suit while interviewing farm hands working in the fields. In a community of respondents who observe the sabbath strictly, the interviewer should not breach it ostentatiously; and in a community that frowns on smoking or drinking, the interviewer may encounter difficulty if he smokes or drinks in public.

This is not to imply that the interviewer must forsake his own values and preferences completely and conform fully to those of the respondent set. But some degree of compromise is usually necessary. Thus, in a sabbath-observing community, the interviewer would probably outrage the respondents by driving about noisily and ostentatiously in a sports car, but he probably would not outrage the respondents if he did not attend their church service. There are two points worth noting in this example. First, the deliberate and unnecessary flouting of a custom is insulting to those who value it; but the attempt to sacrifice one's individuality by "doing as the Romans do" to excess is likely to arouse suspicion or to lead to a loss of respect. Secondly, as we have noted earlier, one of the appeals that the interviewer has for certain kinds of respondents is his very difference from them in certain respects. If, therefore, he attempts to minimize these differences by "blending with the scenery," he risks losing some of the very characteristics that are most interesting to the respondents. The interviewer shares with others the possession of strengths and weaknesses, and respondents share with others tolerance for deviation and breaches of etiquette.

Each interviewer must decide for himself the extent to which he is able and willing to conform to the customs of the respondents' social milieu—in terms of both his personal abilities and his conscience. Some interviewers find it easy to eat stew with their fingers from a common pot, in the manner of some of their Arab respondents; some have no difficulty in using the pronunciation of "Nigra" for Negro, as do some of their Southern respondents. But others find these kinds of acculturations extremely difficult or refuse to conform if conformity involves practices that are abhorrent to their consciences.

It is impossible for the interviewer either to make a complete analysis of respondent customs in advance or to assess correctly the degree of conformity that the respondent population is likely to demand of him. Both these factors will come to light only in the course of the study. Hence the interviewer who is overly concerned with them in advance may exaggerate their magnitude and anticipate more difficulty than is justified.

The Use of Feedback in Gaining Participation

Even if the interviewer is aware of the differences between his self-perception and the respondents' perception of him, and even if he modifies his behavior in an effort to make the respondents' perception of him as favorable as possible, he has few cues by which to judge the effectiveness of his efforts. Obviously, if he encounters a high proportion of rejections, he can conclude that something about his presentation of himself or the study is ineffective, but he may be completely unable to identify the difficulty.

For this reason, informal leaders and other respondents who are the foci of communication in the respondent set or social milieu can be extremely useful to the interviewer by providing feedback on the effectiveness of his attempts to gain participation.

It is important for the interviewer, therefore, especially in the early stages of the study, to try out the approach he has adopted on selected individuals who will give him criticism or comment that is candid and that is representative of the respondent set. In addition to helping him formulate his approach, these individuals, if they are in a position to hear about respondent reactions to him, may be able to provide him with evaluations of his effectiveness throughout the study.

Eliciting feedback information need not, of course, be limited to the informal leaders but can also involve respondents at all stages of the study. This can be done in two ways. First, in each interview the respondent can be encouraged to ask about the study or can, at some point, be given an opportunity to take the lead in talking about or asking questions about what is on his mind. Sometimes a respondent can be asked to describe the study in his own words after the interviewer has given an explanation. What he says may be startlingly revealing and helpful to the interviewer. Often shyness or anxiety prevents the respondents' expressing their concerns early in the study and much latent anxiety remains. Bain's (1960, pp. 145–146) experience in his study involving laundry workers illustrates this clearly.

When the time came to start the sociometric study (which was about a month after I entered the plant), I felt that I still did not have enough rapport with the workers for such a study. Moreover, there were indications that some of them were getting tired of being questioned. Apparently I had not originally been explicit enough about the probable length of the research, and many had thought that it would not take more than a few weeks or a month at the most. They were beginning, I suspect, to wonder just what I was doing that should take so long a time. As I shall mention later, one of my biggest mistakes was assuming that the workers knew what "research for a Master's thesis" meant. The solution (or at least, the partial solution) to this problem was so obvious that I don't know why I didn't think of it before. The solution was to do some work for a change.

I spent the next couple of weeks working on first one job and then another, with both white and colored workers, male and female. While thus working, practically the only questions I would ask were those concerned with skillful performance of the job. I stressed that I was a beginner and that I wanted to learn how to do the job so that I could get a better idea of the operations of a laundry plant. The workers were glad to show me how to do the jobs.

It would often happen that we would work for twenty minutes at a time without saying anything. At other times, if there was a general conversation going on, I might enter into it. Working on the jobs proved to be conducive to more relaxed and informal relations. Formerly, I was constantly initiating the contacts, asking the questions. Now, as we worked side by side, the workers could, in their own sweet time, ask me whatever questions were on their minds. This often gave me the opportunity to clarify my role.

Another source of information and feedback for the interviewer is the type of individual who has been termed the *key informant*. As the anthropologists typically describe him, this individual, who is usually more sophisticated than his fellow informants, befriends the investigator, provides him with insights as well as detailed information, and acts generally as his mentor and guide for the duration of the study. Despite the apparent usefulness of the key informant, however, the information he provides must be interpreted cautiously. Since his very service as a key informant is deviant behavior, it is likely that at least some of his information will not be representative of the respondent set.

Within our own society, the interviewer may be able to divide the work of the key informant between several people, each chosen for the special knowledge he may have by virtue of his occupational or social position. Thus, in a study of a factory, an investigator might choose as key informants an individual representing the middle executive level, a foreman, a machine operator who is also the captain of the factory bowling team, a bartender in a local tavern, and the proprietor of a grocery store patronized by many of the employees. None of these individuals need be endowed with either unusual wisdom or an interest in the social sciences. But each is in a position to provide information that the interviewer is unlikely to obtain from other respondents. Similarly, each may be in a position to stimulate or encourage the participation of a specific subgroup of respondents, to advise the interviewer on the most effective way of approaching them, and to check on the interviewer's degree of success with them.

Further Methods of Gaining Participation

As we noted in the preceding chapter, the respondent will not participate in an interview unless he perceives some sort of reward or gratification for doing so. When the nature of the study seems unlikely to arouse the respondent's altruism or other inherent motivations, or when the demands of the study seem too heavy for the respondent to meet without some tangible *quid pro quo,* interviewers have resorted to offering a cash payment for participation.

Payment in return for participation is sometimes necessary. If the respondents, for example, have previously been paid for acting as respondents, or if they have heard of such an experience, they are likely to expect it. Thus, the practice, in some universities, of paying student volunteers for participation in psychological experiments may make it difficult to interview students without paying them, unless the interview serves their personal interests directly. And, in various other cultures, respondents may expect payment for the "services rendered" to the interviewer.

In order to obtain respondents who are members of nonprofit groups—e.g., fraternal organizations and churches—some investigators have offered a fixed contribution to the organization to be made for every member who acts as a respondent. In this way, the respondent can feel altruistic both for his contribution to a research study and for the contribution he makes possible to the organization of which he is a member.[3]

Payment is called for, too, if the interview seriously infringes on the work or leisure time of the respondent. In one situation, for example, a team of anthropologists found the information provided by one respondent so rich and so valuable that they placed him temporarily on the university payroll and paid his transportation expenses to and from the campus to ensure his availability for

---

[3] We are indebted to Dr. Seymour Fisher for telling us of this practice.

questioning. When, as in this situation, the respondent assumes the role of consultant, the question of payment takes on a different aspect. Similarly, if respondents are required to travel to a central location for the interview, and if such travel involves expenses for transportation or baby sitters, the interviewer should consider reimbursing them. But he should emphasize that the payment is for the reimbursement of out-of-pocket expenditures rather than for the respondents' time and efforts.

In the absence of a clear necessity for payment, however, the arguments against it should be carefully considered. It seems clear that personal payment is antithetical to altruism; a number of interviewers, having aroused the respondent's altruism, have then proceeded to destroy the altruistic satisfactions by proffering payment. Payment, moreover, cannot have the same meaning for all respondents, especially if the respondent set is a heterogeneous one. As Smith, Bruner, and White (1956, p. 50) have noted: "Although the subjects were paid, money was a real incentive for participation in only two or three cases [out of ten]. For the rest, payment was mainly an indication of our seriousness and good faith, if it served any purpose at all."

Payment certainly does not create a standard condition for interviewing. If the amount of payment is held constant for all respondents, some may perceive the payment as adequate and necessary compensation, whereas others may regard it as so small as to be insulting. On the other hand, varying the size of the payment or withholding it altogether according to the perceived needs or status of each respondent may cause resentment among respondents if they communicate; and the interviewer's estimate of the respondents' needs can hardly be accurate.

Perhaps more important, payment places a fixed price on information which may be invaluable, either in fact or in the eyes of the respondent. Some respondents feel, as one of them said to an interviewer (West, 1945, p. x), "You ain't *got* enough money to *hire* me," even though they participate willingly without payment. There is also the possibility that payment, when it is a fixed sum, may affect length of response: Respondents who have little useful information may prolong or fabricate responses in order to give the interviewer "his money's worth," whereas respondents who have rich response material may feel inclined to give the interviewer only as much information as they feel he has paid for. Perhaps the question of payment is best summed up by Kinsey and his colleagues (1948, pp. 40–41):

Payment for histories has been confined to the economically poorer elements in the population, to persons who are professionally involved in sexual activities (as prostitutes, pimps, exhibitionists, etc.) or to others who have turned from their regular occupation and spent considerable time in helping make contacts. The payment has never been large, rarely amounting to more than a dollar or two for the couple of hours involved in contributing; and equivalent amounts may be paid to persons who have helped make the contacts. . . . On the whole payment has worked well, for it has undoubtedly made it possible to secure many histories which otherwise would not have been obtainable; and it should be realized that even in the groups which are paid, men and women have contributed primarily because they respect us, because they appreciate our interest in them, and because they are willing to contribute for the sake of helping others.

THE USE OF SOCIAL PRESSURE

The enlistment of the support of formal and informal leaders, which we have described earlier in the chapter, involves the use of social pressures of a kind. The assumption is that the example set by the leaders in participating, or their recommendation of the interviewer or the study, will exert a persuasive force on other respondents. But some interviewers use social pressure more directly and forcefully. One method is to urge the respondent to participate by classifying him with a group which he respects. This approach is embodied in such statements as, "I have been interviewing a number of leading citizens and, to complete my study, I should like to ask you. . . ." or (to a physician respondent) "I am interviewing all members of the county medical society, and I'd like. . . ." Such an approach exploits the desire of the respondent to conform to the behavior of others in the reference group or, conversely, his reluctance to refuse to participate in an activity which the reference group apparently endorses or approves.

Such methods may help to effect an encounter between interviewer and respondent. But at the outset of this encounter the respondent may be totally indifferent to the interviewer and his purposes or even hostile at being thus pressed to participate. Unless the interviewer recognizes this and takes measures to increase the respondent's interest or reduce his hostility, the responses are likely to be of minimal quality, if not deliberately misleading. The interviewer's task here is to use his skills in the interview to change token participation to full and interested participation. Sometimes this may become so formidable and so time consuming as to outweigh the apparent advantages of using this kind of social pressure to get the initial guarded and limited consent of respondents.

COVERT INTERVIEWING[4]

In most research situations, the role and purpose of the interviewer, once he has begun interviewing, is reasonably clear to the respondents. Although they may neither understand nor care about the details of his methodology or the precise uses to which the information will be put, they are aware that he is collecting information for some sort of research purpose. There are some situations, however, in which the characteristics of the respondent set, the interview demands, and the interviewer combine to make the likelihood of participation so remote that the interviewer is led to consider the possibility of covert interviewing—that is, concealing his true role and collecting information by playing a role other than that of interviewer. He may, for example, try to obtain membership in the group that he is studying, or he may attempt to become an inconspicuous and innocuous part of the environment of the respondent set.

The covert investigation of social phenomena has a long—and sometimes dramatically appealing—tradition, dating back to the nineteenth century (Young, 1949, pp. 14–15).

In order to penetrate beyond the mask which people wear when interviewed by outsiders Booth took up quarters in districts where he

---

[4] Covert interviewing as we describe it here may seem, at first sight, to require undue stretching of the definition of interviewing, since it clearly precludes the use of schedule or nonschedule standardized interviewing. We regard covert interviewing as falling within our purview, however, because the broad definition of interviewing includes the collection of information by oral means, even through apparently casual conversations. The covert interviewer does, of course, also depend heavily on observation, and the term "covert observation" would be just as applicable.

could pass as a homeless stranger. As a lodger in poor workingmen's families, he shared their lives and identified himself with their interests, passions, pastimes, hopes and ideals. Little escaped his observing eye and astute mind.

Similarly, Festinger, Riecken, and Schachter (1956, p. 237), in their study of a small religious group that predicted the end of the world, noted: "In our very first contact with the central figures of the group, their secrecy and general attitude toward non-believers made it clear that a study could not be conducted openly." Hence they decided to assume a covert role.

In our investigation of the group which gathered about Dr. Armstrong and Marian Keech, our observers posed as ordinary members who believed as the others did. In short, our investigation was conducted without either the knowledge or the consent of the group members.

To conceal his true identity and purpose from the patients and staff while conducting a study of a psychiatric hospital, Dr. William Caudill, an anthropologist, agreed with the director "to enter the hospital as a 'patient.' To admit Doctor Caudill as a patient under a pseudonym was not difficult. He had only to exaggerate, as would be the case with most persons, certain aspects of normal behavior. Caudill lived on the wards of the hospital for about eight weeks. During this time, he received 'psychotherapy' from a resident, who found out only after his discharge who Doctor Caudill really was" (Caudill, 1958, p. viii).[5]

[5] These tactics are clearly different from those of investigators who were known to be researchers by the respondents but who shared in such respondent activities as nursing, fishing, or bowling, either to acquire additional information or to gain or maintain participation. A further distinction may be made usefully between covert interviewing in which the investigator plays a bona-fide role—e.g., Lentz's obtaining information as a waitress while actually working her way through college (1953), Roth's being hospitalized with tuberculosis while a graduate student (1963), or Becker's studying musicians while being himself a highly competent and recognized musician (1951)—and covert interviewing in which the interviewer masquerades in a role which deliberately deceives respondents—e.g., the Festinger and Caudill studies cited above. The investigator who plays a bona-fide role is not under the continuous stress of masquerading, and it probably matters relatively little if he reveals the dual purpose of his role. When the investigator deliberately deceives respondents by masquerading, the stress of trying to play the role, the fear of being discovered, and the ethical conflict he may experience may exact a heavy price and may well reduce the quality of the data he obtains.

Later Dr. Caudill studied the hospital with his role as an investigator known to all. As the result of these experiences, both Dr. Caudill and the director of the institution do not recommend a repetition of a study in which the investigator plays a concealed role, on ethical grounds, because acting out such a role is too stressful, and because of limitations in the value of data collected (Caudill, 1958, pp. viii–ix and xiv–xv).

Before regarding these studies as good evidence in support of covert interviewing, the reader must note certain limitations inherent in them. First, these studies necessarily involved participant observation and casual conversation rather than interviewing. Although the participant observer can learn a great deal through talking with people, he must rely primarily on what he hears, sees, and introspects, since he cannot depend on the question–answer process. If, in fact, the study requires that questions be asked, the covert interviewer is severely hampered by his role. In covert roles—e.g., factory employee, convict, musician—he cannot appropriately ask certain questions that would be perfectly acceptable for him to ask in the role of interviewer, and in any covert role he cannot ask as many questions as an interviewer can without being regarded as excessively curious or suspicious. As Roy (1952, p. 47) has noted,

The investigator is "stuck with his role" of machine operator, if such is his role; he cannot step out of that role assigned to him and expected of him without at least arousing the suspicions of fellow employees and possibly incurring disciplinary action from management. Interviewing and observation are restricted to what can be accomplished in normal work routines; an inquirer may not wander all over the plant striking up conversations whenever and wherever it suits his fancy. Even in areas where he is "supposed to be" the amount of time that he can use for conversation is limited.

And as Riecken (1956, p. 256) has pointed out,

The passive-member role greatly hampered inquiry. Unable to take command of the situation as an interviewer ordinarily does, the observers were forced to maintain constant alertness for relevant data that members of the group spontaneously brought forth and had to be extremely tactful and skillful in following up leads so as not to appear too inquisitive.

Moreover, although the interview permits a unilateral relationship in which one party is preponderantly the asker of questions and the other the answerer, the social situation in which the covert interviewer places himself demands a more reciprocal kind of relationship, as Riecken observes (1956, p. 24).

Nondirective inquiry about others, while revealing little about one's own feelings or actions, is appropriate enough behavior for a new-comer, but, if prolonged, it tends to cast doubt on either the intelligence or motives of the interrogator. In ordinary social intercourse it is reasonably expected that the members of a group will give as well as receive information about beliefs, opinions, and actions relevant to their common purpose.

Yet, if the interviewer who is also a member of the group expresses his opinions and beliefs freely, he cannot expect to avoid influencing the situation he is studying. Of course, it is possible for opportunities for nondirective inquiry to develop at any time in a study. For example, this occurred late in the study of the apocalyptic group (Festinger et al., 1956, pp. 167–168) at a critical gathering.

When 4 A.M. came without a satisfactory resolution having been achieved, another break was taken. One of the authors [of the study] walked out the front door to get some air and Dr. Armstrong, thinking he was becoming disaffected and needed bolstering, dashed out after him. The doctor proceeded to deliver an inspirational talk, an important part of which was a statement about his own situation and his own belief.

But, as this episode indicates, the covert interviewer must rely heavily upon sheer chance.

Playing a covert role can put the investigator under enormous stress unless his particular skills and background fit him for the role. And being discovered is likely to lead to serious, and possibly violent, consequences. For these reasons, covert interviewing should not be undertaken lightly.

There is, in addition, a question of ethics which each investigator must resolve for himself. He must bear in mind, however, that eventual betrayal of his respondents is almost inevitable. Even if he maintains his disguise successfully to the termination of the study, and even though he disguises his population in the published version of the work, at least some respondents may encounter the work, recognize themselves, and feel betrayed.

Dealing with Refusals in the Respondent Set

Occasionally, despite his most careful efforts to develop participation, an interviewer will encounter strong resistance on the part of a very substantial proportion of the respondent set. He may, despite seemingly influential sponsorship, meet with a refusal from the gatekeepers or with complete indifference from the informal leaders. Or, having gained the support of the leadership, he may encounter either outright refusals from the respondents or participation at so minimal a level as to render the response material of dubious value.

At such a juncture, it is important for the interviewer to suspend his efforts to gain participation and to reappraise all aspects of the study. If he has developed any sources of feedback, these may be able to provide him with clues. But, lacking feedback, he can still ask himself a number of questions:

If the study is an obviously threatening one, is there any way in which the threat can be reduced or the value of the study enhanced in the eyes of the respondents?

If the study is nonthreatening, is there any characteristic of the respondent set or any circumstance in the respondents' environment that makes it appear threatening?

Has the interviewer presented to the respondents those aspects of himself that they can understand and accept in their own terms?

Do his personal characteristics or his behavior run counter to the values or customs of the respondent set?

Has he learned enough about the routines and customs of the respondent set to enable him to reduce the intrusiveness of the interview to a minimum?

Obviously, it is more productive to pose such questions to a member of the respondent set or to someone familiar with the respondents' environment, but even a review in the interviewer's own mind may produce some tentative suggestions for modification of his approach.

If such suggestions do not materialize, or if they prove ineffective, however, there are several alternatives open to the interviewer. First, he can leave the respondent set for a period of time and then return for another attempt to gain participation. Such a procedure may permit the passage of an environmental crisis of which the interviewer is completely unaware. Wholesale refusals in an industrial community, for example, may be due to preoccupation with pending negotiation of a union contract. Refusals in a respondent set consisting of college faculty members may be due to the respondents' connecting the interview with a local controversy over academic freedom. In both these instances, the interviewer may be unaware of the relevant circumstances, but during his absence the crisis may subside and with it the refusals. A. H. Leighton (1950) has suggested that a temporary absence may serve yet another purpose. Upon their first entry into a small community, interviewers will probably be regarded as strangers. But, if they depart temporarily shortly after their arrival and then return, they are no longer considered as strangers. For this reason, a strategically timed absence may enhance participation.

In a case in which the subject matter clearly seemed to threaten the respondent set, still another tactic was used by Macmillan and Leighton (1952), which they called "entry by the periphery." Instead of directly attempting to gain access to the respondent set, they pretested the study on an adjacent group that they knew to be in contact with the respondent set. They obtained the acceptance and participation of this adjacent group and demonstrated that the study had no harmful consequences. By the end of the pretest, the actual respondent set had heard enough about the investigators and the study to be willing to participate.

Still another alternative in the face of wholesale refusal—and one that is probably adopted less frequently than it should be— is the abandonment of the intended respondent set and the searching out of another, less resistant one. In many cases, respondent refusal is perceived by an interviewer as a direct challenge to his professional competence and the situation deteriorates into a contest of wills between the interviewer and the respondents. Such a contest can be extremely expensive in terms of time, money, and energy; and, even if it is won by the interviewer, his victory may be a Pyrrhic one in terms of response quality. In such a situation, the interviewer who concedes that discretion may sometimes be the better part of valor will find another respondent set and complete his study in the time that he might have devoted to a "Pike's-Peak-or-bust" approach to the respondent set that he initially chose.

Although we have attempted, in this chapter, to offer the investigator some general guidance based on the experiences that we and other investigators have had with a variety of respondent sets, it is as difficult to learn completely about gaining the participation of respondents from a book as it is to develop a high degree of virtuosity as a concert pianist or a chess player by reading books on the subject. Benjamin D. Paul (1953, p. 431), in discussing the role of the anthropological field worker, makes the point that, beyond the first few tactics in a field situation, the alternatives proliferate so rapidly that the interviewer must rely on his own judgment, personality, and competence, as well as upon abstract principles.

In part, the field worker defines his own role; in part, it is defined for him by the situation and the outlook of the natives. His is the strategy of a player in a game. He cannot predict the precise plays which the other side will make, but he anticipates them as best he can and makes his moves accordingly. . . . Because of the frequent need to improvise, the prudent anthropologist strives to retain independence of decision and be prepared to abandon his best-laid plans in favor of what is feasible in the field. Factors of personality impose severer restrictions. Some investigators find role-playing a challenging game, others find it punishing. Some can tolerate appearing ridiculous in native eyes, others need to preserve their dignity. Some can be indifferent to aloofness, others are discouraged by diffidence.

PART III

The Question–Answer Process

5

THE CRITERIA

FOR GOOD RESPONSES

Even if the interviewer has carefully considered and wisely dealt with the issues and procedures outlined in the preceding chapters—that is, if he has chosen the most appropriate interview form, selected the most promising set of respondents, developed an effective statement of purpose, and elicited a high degree of participation—he cannot be assured of a satisfactory interview. Whether he succeeds in obtaining the information he seeks will depend entirely on the communication that takes place between him and the respondents during the interview itself—that is, in the course of the question–answer process.

The reason for this is clear enough. No matter how capable and willing he is, the respondent cannot know, in advance of the questions, the scope, the quantity, or the level of the information that the interviewer is seeking. The questioning process itself, therefore, in addition to eliciting information, must communicate to the respondent enough cues about the characteristics of the desired information to enable him to shape a response that meets the interviewer's needs and criteria. We shall devote several chapters to examining the extent to which the question may be used to shape the response; but, in order to use the relevant techniques of questioning effectively, the interviewer must have very clearly in mind the characteristics of the response that will best suit his purpose. For this reason, we must turn first to an examination of the criteria of a good response.

Whatever his experience, his purpose, or the style and type of the interview, the interviewer generally has, at the end of each interview, a reasonably clear impression of how successful the interview has been. He usually "knows" whether it has been good, bad, or indifferent. His basis for judgment is likely to be some combination of criteria that takes into account the quality and quantity of the information and the degree of cooperation he has received; but it is doubtful whether he can specify each of the criteria and score his interview with respect to each of them. His impression, although it may be quite accurate, is likely to be largely subjective.

As long as the criteria remain implicit, however, there is danger that the interviewer may give excessive weight to one or two of them at the expense of others that are equally important. In a nonstandardized interview, for example, many neophyte interviewers are so deeply concerned with gaining the respondent's cooperation and getting him to talk freely that success in achieving these outcomes causes them to evaluate the interview as highly successful. Not until they review the tape recording or their notes do they discover that much of what the respondent said was not relevant to the research purpose, that responses were superficial, or that what was relevant was insufficient or, at some points, unclear.

If, however, the criteria of a good interview are made explicit, and if the interviewer can develop an intuitive familiarity with them, two consequences are likely. First, the interviewer will have a more objective and better balanced view of the quality of the interview, not merely at the end of the interview but also on a response-by-response basis. Secondly, if he recognizes that the interview as a whole or a specific response has failed to meet certain criteria, he can take corrective action by applying specific techniques that can more or less improve its quality. To provide a background for our discussion of these techniques, let us examine some of the criteria for a good interview.

Satisfactory Respondent Participation

Although gaining and maintaining satisfactory participation is never the primary objective of the interviewer, it is so intimately related to the quality and quantity of the information sought that the interviewer must always maintain a dual concern: for the quality of his respondent's participation and for the quality of the information being sought. Often, as we shall note, these qualities are independent of each other, and occasionally they may be mutually exclusive.

A satisfactory level of respondent participation is an important criterion for several reasons. If, during the interview, the respondent is sufficiently dissatisfied with his experience, he may refuse to proceed and thus prevent the collection of further information, or he may permit the interview to continue but sharply reduce the quality of his responses. If he finishes the interview feeling dissatisfied, he may refuse to participate in further interviews, or, if there is communication among the respondents, he may use his influence to dissuade others from participating. It is generally assumed that information freely given is likely to be of higher quality than information given with indifference or reluctance. To the extent that this assumption is justified, it becomes important to put the respondent at his ease and to prevent his feeling that the interviewer is threatening him, placing him under pressure, or ignoring his interests and feelings.

The skilled interviewer is constantly aware of the degree to which the interview is meeting the criteria of participation and response quality, and he is prepared to change his tactics in order to enhance one or the other of these. If the participation of a respondent is low, the interviewer may use tactics to increase participation even if such tactics temporarily reduce the validity, relevance, and other criteria by which the response is judged. Once he has succeeded in increasing participation, the interviewer may modify his tactics so as to improve response quality, remembering that the information he received while he was concentrating on increasing participation may be of questionable quality in terms of the response criteria.

In some interviews, or in some parts of an interview, a high level of respondent participation and a high quality of response may be difficult to maintain simultaneously. Confronting a respondent with a contradiction between two of his responses, for example, may well reduce his level of participation, and yet such a confrontation may be essential to the validity of the response material. Conversely, if respondent participation becomes excessive, it is always possible that the interview will develop a social quality that may reduce the relevance of the response material. Respondent participation, therefore, must be evaluated not in absolute terms but always in relation to the quality of the response.

Response Characteristics Sought in All Interviews

VALIDITY

A primary concern of interviewers is that the responses they obtain be valid. In practice, the interviewer has three means at his disposal for evaluating response validity. He may have some dependable evidence from a source external to the interview against which he can compare the response. If the external evidence is valid and the response corresponds with it, then the response—and perhaps some related responses—can be regarded as valid. If, for example, the interviewer has attended a meeting and has made an accurate count of those attending and later asks the respondent, who also attended the meeting, about the attendance, he can check the validity of the response. In such a situation, obtaining the identical information has no intrinsic value but does provide circumstantial evidence for the validity of other information given by the respondent. In other words, external validity checks provide a gauge for estimating the validity of the respondent. If the interviewer is uncertain of the validity of external evidence, he may be able to cross check with another respondent. In many circumstances, if the two independent pieces of information agree, they are probably valid, although there is always the possibility that this kind of correspondence may indicate reliability rather than validity, since both sources may be biased.

It is relatively rare, however, for an interviewer to have valid external evidence with which to compare the response material. And there are many kinds of data—for example, the whole area of a respondent's feelings or his interpretation of others' feelings— for which no direct external evidence can be obtained. In such situations, the interviewer must rely on evidence within the interview. He may assess the reliability of the information given by the respondent. If the various overlapping, related, or repetitious pieces of information hang together and there are no inconsistencies, the interviewer has some basis for believing that the information is valid. Indeed, many interview schedules include questions designed not to elicit information but to provide a validity check on other responses.

If, through lack of planning or because of certain exigencies of the interview situation, the interviewer cannot obtain internal checks on consistency, he may assess the style or manner of the responses. If the respondent shows doubt, uncertainty, or hesitancy in his responses, the interviewer may question their validity. Interpretation of the style or manner of response, however, is not easy. A highly competent and cautious respondent may indicate, by reservation, his own uncertainty as to the validity of the information he is providing, whereas another respondent may provide information with great self-assurance and without reservation. Yet the information of the cautious respondent may in fact be more valid than that given by the self-assured respondent. Only after gaining some over-all evaluation of a respondent's style of response can the interviewer develop some basis for interpreting variation within individual styles and its relation to validity.

Finally interviewers often infer the degree of validity of response from the characteristics of the respondent. In relation to the topics of the interview, the interviewer makes some judgment about the respondent's level of knowledge, background, and experience. For example, if the responses involve the reconstruction of an event, some considerations in assessing validity will be the relationship and viewpoint of the respondent to the event and the respondent's understanding of the type of event witnessed. The more technical the subject matter, the more will the respondent's qualifications be taken into account in assessing validity.

The interviewer must be careful lest stereotypical information he holds about the characteristics of different types of people distort his judgment of the validity of their responses. For example, the interviewer may assume that the responses of a person who has a college degree are likely to be more valid than those of a person who has not completed high school.

Another characteristic of the respondent that may be related to validity is his motivation in the interview. Are there reasons why he should not give valid responses? If the information could incriminate him in any way, he may not give valid responses unless he trusts the interviewer not to reveal or misuse the information. Alternatively, if the respondent believes that the interviewer can somehow be of help to him, as in getting him a job, putting him in touch with people of power and influence, or promulgating information he wishes to broadcast, these motives may cause him to provide invalid information. Validity of response may suffer if the respondent feels impelled to give the interviewer the response he thinks the interviewer would like to hear. In psychiatric interviews, for example, patients will sometimes present "unconscious" material, including dreams, in accord with what they think the psychiatrist wants to hear.

In practice, the interviewer arrives at an over-all judgment of the validity of his data by using some combination of the criteria we have described. This judgment must be made not only for the over-all data from an interview but also for separate topics within the interview and even for each response

RELEVANCE

The degree to which the interviewer can judge whether a response is relevant to the research problem varies widely. In the early stages of exploration, the objectives of information gathering are likely to be general and the boundaries of relevance ill-defined and shifting. New information may modify and revise the investigator's original objectives, and information that originally was marginally relevant may become of central importance, whereas information initially thought important may become irrelevant. Early in the study, the respondents, if they have been selected for their knowledge of the subject matter under investigation, may be as good judges of relevance as the interviewer, if not better. As the study progresses, the interviewer gains an increasingly clear view of what is relevant. His increasing ability to focus questions on relevant subject matter may well increase the proportion of relevant responses, and, within these responses, the interviewer can better identify what is relevant.

The standardized interview, in which the information required from all respondents is predetermined, involves a much narrower concept of relevance. In such interviews, any information is irrelevant if it is not prescribed in advance. An unanticipated response may make the investigator realize he has missed a vital subtopic, but, if a majority of the respondent set has already been interviewed, it is too late to change the prescribed categories of information being sought—at least in that study.

Concurrent with the interviewer's need to keep response material relevant is his need to gain and maintain the respondent's participation. If, by restricting the respondent too sharply to information relevant to the substantive goals of the research, the interviewer ignores the respondent's interests, concerns, and feelings, the interviewer may reduce, or even lose, the respondent's participation. On the other hand, if, through excessive concern with participation, the interviewer allows the respondent's interests to govern the content of the response, the resulting material may have little or no relevance to the subject matter of the research. In practice, the interviewer must constantly maintain some balance between his concurrent concerns for relevance of responses and for respondent participation, recognizing that both elements are necessary.

SPECIFICITY AND CLARITY

If a response is general, vague, or amorphous or if it is open to more than one interpretation or cannot be interpreted in relation to the research purpose, it is of little value. Some nonspecific responses take the form of a conclusion drawn by a respondent on the basis of a wide range of experience but provide no indication of the bases for the conclusion. Narrative responses may lack dates, names, places, or quantities that are essential for adequate specificity.

A response may be specific and nevertheless be unclear by virtue of its disorganized form, the vocabulary in which it is couched, or its ambiguity. Although some responses would be regarded as unclear by any number of independent judges, the clarity of a response must, for obvious reasons, be judged ultimately by the interviewer himself. Thus, for example, a response made by a specialized professional person and couched in highly technical language must be judged unclear by the interviewer who does not understand it, even though the response might be regarded as a model of clarity by the respondent's professional colleagues. The implication is, of course, that the selection criteria for interviewers should include, if possible, the ability to maintain a level of discourse equivalent to that of the respondents. But even interviewers who meet this criterion may encounter respondents who assume that they possess more knowledge than in fact they do and hence respond in a level of discourse that is beyond their comprehension, a situation we shall further examine on page 320. In such circumstances, an admission of ignorance on the part of the interviewer, although it may increase the clarity of the subsequent responses, may also reduce the respondent's willingness to participate. Hence, in some circumstances, it may be necessary for the interviewer to sacrifice a degree of clarity in order to maintain respondent participation.

COVERAGE

A major task of the interviewer is to elicit the full range of information he is seeking. At the simplest level, this may mean that all five items of a brief schedule interview are filled with acceptable responses. At a more complex level, coverage may entail obtaining a detailed life history over the course of several interview sessions. The criterion of coverage must always be related to the specific research problem, and, like relevance, it is defined with increasing precision as the study progresses and, occasionally, even as the interview progresses.

Although coverage may be measured in terms of how completely any question is answered, such a criterion may be too limited. A skilled interviewer may recognize that a question has not been fully answered but, instead of pressing the respondent for further material at that point, he will return to the question later in the interview. Conversely, a response which at one point in the interview may strike the interviewer as giving adequate coverage may, as a result of further questioning, strike him as inadequate on the basis of the amount of information the respondent appears to have at his disposal.

Response Characteristics Required
in Certain Kinds of Interview

Whereas the foregoing criteria apply to all interviews, certain others—depth, the obtaining of unanticipated responses, and length of response—are applicable only to certain kinds of interviewing or to specific segments of an interview. These criteria cannot, however, be viewed in isolation; instead, they must be considered in conjunction with the criteria we have discussed earlier. A response that has depth, for example, is of little value if it does not have clarity, and a response that is long is useful only if it is relevant as well.

DEPTH

As a response characteristic, depth has two somewhat different meanings. In one sense, it describes responses which deal with the feelings of the respondent rather than with what he thinks, remembers, or knows (Nahoum, 1958, p. 45). In this sense, a response has depth if it refers to any kind of feeling, regardless of its intensity, its intimacy, or any other quality. In another sense, depth is used to describe a response which expresses feelings, thoughts, motives, or other material that a respondent is expected to produce only with considerable reluctance or difficulty because he may feel that discussion of such material violates his standards of etiquette (Gorden, 1956) or that it is private, shameful, or incriminating.

UNANTICIPATED RESPONSES

In some research situations, the interviewer does not know enough about the topic to be able to formulate all of the most productive questions. He may, for example, be in the initial stages of exploring a new topic with a respondent who is an expert on the topic. Or he may know in an abstract way the information he is seeking but be unable to translate the concepts into questions meaningful to the respondent. In such situations, unanticipated responses may provide information of critical importance, valuable leads for further questioning, or insights that will help him understand certain phenomena.

LENGTH OF RESPONSE

Length is not in itself a direct criterion of a desirable response. Rather it is a characteristic whereby relevance, specificity, coverage, validity, or depth may be partially measured. Certainly there is no relationship between length and quality of response. On some topics, the interviewer seeks a brief response—e.g., "yes" or "no"— or a fact—e.g., age, ethnicity, occupation, or income. But on other topics the interviewer wants a lengthy response or wishes to avoid procedures which tend ". . . to put a person in a 'yes' or 'no' frame of mind" (Roethlisberger & Dickson, 1946, p. 203). To the interviewer who is trying to get a respondent to talk freely, one- or two-word responses will be unsatisfactory, whereas to the interviewer who needs short, clear-cut answers to a large number of predetermined schedule questions, a long response to each question is unsatisfactory because it may produce irrelevant information and, by jeopardizing the completion of the interview, incomplete coverage.

Achieving the Criteria

Eliciting a response that meets the criteria we have discussed above involves a number of factors: the setting in which the interview takes place, the personal and social characteristics of the respondent and the quality of his participation, the personality and style of the interviewer, and the quality of the interaction between interviewer and respondent. In almost every interview, however, some of these factors cannot be controlled by the interviewer. A more direct method of influencing response characteristics—and one that is largely under the control of the interviewer or the designer of the interview schedule—involves the formulation of the individual question. It is to this process that we shall devote the next three chapters.

6

OPENNESS VERSUS CLOSEDNESS, ANTECEDENTS, AND QUESTION–ANTECEDENT RELATIONSHIPS

Introduction

Having outlined the criteria for satisfactory response character-istics, we can begin to examine the influence of various types of questioning procedures upon responses. There are two major approaches to this problem. One of them uses broad categories to describe the over-all style of the interviewer throughout the inter-view, in such terms as "active" and "passive" (Du Bois, 1937), "guided" and "free" (Kluckhohn, 1945), or "directive" and "non-directive" (Rogers, 1945; Roethlisberger & Dickson, 1946; Kinsey et al., 1948; Eleanor Maccoby & N. Maccoby, 1954). The other approach is to identify characteristics of a single question, e.g., "leading" or "open," and to consider the effect of these character-istics at the level of the individual question.

CHARACTERIZING THE OVER-ALL INTERVIEW

Although the terms used for the broad characterization of the interview vary, the concept central to all of them is that of direc-tiveness—that is, the degree of control which the interviewer exerts over the topic, the scope and length of the response, the pace, and other characteristics of the interview.

The concept of nondirectiveness was first formulated in detail by Carl Rogers (1942), who used nondirective interviewing in counseling and psychotherapy and later (1945) suggested that it was useful in research interviewing as a means of avoiding the biasing of responses. Here is a description of what is termed a "nondirective" interview (Roethlisberger & Dickson, 1946, p. 203).

After the interviewer had explained the [interviewing] program, the employee was to be allowed to choose his own topic. As long as the employee talked spontaneously, the interviewer was to follow the employee's ideas, displaying a real interest in what the employee had to say. While the employee continued to talk, no attempt was to be made to change the topic to one . . . [the interviewer] thought was more important. He was to listen attentively to anything the worker had to say about any topic and take part in the conversation only in so far as it was necessary in order to keep the employee talking. If he did ask questions, they were to be phrased in a noncommital manner and certainly not in the form . . . which suggested the answers.

Thus, in the nondirective interview, the interviewer plays a largely passive role and allows the respondent to determine both the topic and what he is going to say about it.

This contrasts sharply with the highly directive interview, which has been well described by Kinsey and his coworkers (1948, pp. 53–54).

In order to cover the maximum amount of material in a single interview, it is necessary to ask questions as rapidly as the subject can possibly comprehend and reply. This method has the further advantage of forcing the subject to answer spontaneously without too much premeditation. Such a rapid fire of questions provides one of the most effective checks on fabrication, as detectives and other law-enforcement officials well know. . . .

The interviewer should not make it easy for a subject to deny his participation in any form of sexual activity. It is too easy to say no if he is simply asked whether he has ever engaged in a particular activity. . . . We always begin by asking *when* they first engaged in such activity.

In this form of interview the interviewer actively moves the respondent through predetermined topics and sometimes indicates to the respondent the answer the interviewer expects.

Taking an intermediate position, Maccoby and Maccoby (1954) advocate a moderate degree of directiveness. Discussing probes to supplement the questions in an interview schedule, they agree with Rogers (1945) that the interviewer should not influence the direction of responses to particular questions. But, in contrast to Rogers and in agreement with Kinsey, they regard the interviewer as responsible for guiding the respondent to particular topics so that information will be obtained on the predetermined dimensions of the research problem.

Although there has been general agreement that the central problem of the interviewer is to avoid bias, there are widespread differences of opinion as to the degree of directiveness the interviewer should employ for this purpose. Advocates of the nondirective or minimally directive interview believe that this form is more likely to obtain deeper (and hence more valid) responses and encourages the respondent to talk more freely and thus, presumably, to present a richer and more valid response. Those who defend the highly directive kind of interview argue that, in some interview situations, directiveness discourages the respondent from dissembling, prevaricating, or distorting his response and hence produces a more valid response as well as one that is more relevant to the research purpose. Thus, Kinsey and his colleagues (1948) assumed that, when respondents are expected to be evasive, questions which direct them toward the response that they are likely to evade serve to reduce this bias.

There are, however, a number of assumptions underlying the discussions of directiveness that are questionable. The first assumption is that directiveness can be meaningfully used to describe an interview as a whole. Since the purpose of an interview is the collection of information, there are some points within the interview at which a high degree of directiveness is necessary to elicit specific pieces of information, and there are other points at which a low degree of directiveness will more effectively permit the respondent to provide the interviewer with unexpected material that gives him new ideas or insights. Even the most exploratory interview is likely to vary widely in the degree of directiveness, the interviewer occasionally having to exercise considerable direction in order to give the flow of information coherence and relevance. Hence, since a single interview can have moments of high and low directiveness, the concept has little meaning when applied to an interview as a whole. As evidence of this, we may note that such terms as "highly directive" or "nondirective" have been applied to interviews which in no way resemble one another in style, purpose, interviewer–respondent relationship, or any other characteristic.

A second assumption—perhaps strengthened by Kinsey's reference to detectives and law-enforcement officials—has been that directive interviewing must be an unpleasant experience for the respondent. For many, the term conjures up relentless cross-examination of a witness by a prosecuting attorney, or an interviewer pursuing a course of questioning without regard for the respondent's feelings. That directive interviewing need not be an unpleasant experience has been demonstrated by Kinsey and his colleagues. Cornelia Otis Skinner (1950, p. 31), after being interviewed by Kinsey, described him as "a scholarly gentleman of humor and charm. He put me completely at ease, and the interview I had dreaded proved to be as simple as it was fascinating. I came away with a high opinion of Dr. Kinsey and, I don't mind saying, a pretty good one of myself." This description corresponds with Kinsey and his colleagues' own account of his behavior during an interview (1948, p. 48).

> The subject should be treated as a friend or a guest in one's home. The tottering old man who is a victim of his first penal conviction appreciates the interviewer's solicitation about his health and his interest in seeing that he is provided with tobacco, candy, or the other things that the institution allows one who has sufficient funds. The inmate in a woman's penal institution particularly appreciates those courtesies which a male would extend to a woman of his own social rank, in his own home. The interviewer should be as interested in the subject as he is in recording the subject's history.

The fears expressed about the damaging consequences of directiveness have probably been magnified by the unfounded assumption that a high degree of directiveness is maintained by the interviewer throughout the interview.

A third assumption, that nondirective interviewing leads to good "rapport," may have prevented the recognition that nondirective-ness can arouse considerable anxiety and stress in some respondents. For example, while using a nondirective approach, Richardson noted that a respondent was becoming increasingly agitated. Finally, the respondent interrupted himself and said, "I'm sorry. I don't seem to be able to help you. If you would just tell me exactly what it is you want to know, I'll do my best to answer." It appears that there are wide variations in the degree of directiveness that is congenial to different respondents, and some respondents find a lack of structure in the interview almost intolerable.

The fourth assumption, that the main concern of the interviewer is to avoid bias, has led to much debate but to little resolution of the problem. We believe that it is more profitable to examine how the interviewer does, in fact, influence the respondent. To do this, it becomes necessary to specify what the interviewer actually does in his questioning. This is difficult to determine through use of the concept of directiveness because it is very broad and has not been translated into careful empirical descriptions of interviewer be-havior. It is limited, also, because it implies a uniformity of style throughout an interview, whereas, in practice, questioning may vary considerably during the course of the interview and may produce major variations in the response characteristics.

CHARACTERIZING INDIVIDUAL QUESTIONS

The second general approach to the study of the question–answer process—that is, the examination of the effects of individual questions with given characteristics—has been used since the turn of the century. Concerned over questioning techniques used in obtaining legal testimony, Stern (1903–1906) and other German psychologists conducted a series of pioneer studies on the effect of leading questions and on testimony obtained by cross-examination as opposed to witnesses' spontaneous reporting. Other investigators have classified questions as closed or open, according to whether they can be answered by a short or a long response and have examined the different effects of these two types. Some of the classifications and definitions of question types suggested by these investigators have influenced our thinking about the components of questioning we shall describe later in this chapter.

We have adopted this approach of examining the characteristics of individual questions because our aim is to describe the actual behavior of the interviewer and to examine empirically the effects of this behavior on the responses he obtains. We have supplemented what we could learn from the interview literature with detailed examination of a large number of interview specimens obtained through tape recording. This examination quickly made us realize that no single category such as open or closed, or leading or not leading, is adequate to describe the formulation of a question. Instead, each question must be analyzed in terms of a number of component parts to provide an adequate description.[1] The approach we have adopted will become clearer if we examine the following excerpt from a tape-recorded interview.

Q: I'd like to ask you how you first had contact with this experiment.
A: This experiment? I had my name in with a part-time employment agency, and they called me about it. And, uh, I had, wasn't doing anything, and I thought, well, okay, it sounds interesting.
Q: Uh-huh. The employment service called you.
A: Oh, yes.
Q: Uh-huh. And then who did you first talk with who was connected with this?

In the first question, the interviewer asks the respondent to *describe a specific event*. But, in addition to specifying the *content* of the response, the question has been formulated so as to cue the respondent about response characteristics other than content. For example, by using the word "how" rather than "when," "where," or "through whom," the interviewer indicates that he expects a response consisting of more than one or two words. The first question is formulated, moreover, so as to permit the respondent to make any response he chooses—that is, the interviewer in no way points to one kind of answer as the one he expects to hear.

In both of these properties, the first question differs from the

[1] The early development of the components described in this and subsequent chapters was carried out by Barbara Snell Dohrenwend, Helen Moyer, Stephen A. Richardson, and Robert J. Smith.

second. The second question calls for a brief response and indicates that it is expected to be affirmative. This question, moreover, because it refers to the preceding response as its antecedent, communicates to the respondent the fact that his answers are being listened to with attention.

In the third question, the interviewer again asks for a brief response but without indicating what he expects it to be. Further, we can see in this question another way in which the interviewer communicates to the respondent. Here, by returning to the topic of the first question, the "first . . . contact," and by failing to ask more about the employment service, the interviewer limits the scope of the answer and implies that he does not want the respondent to introduce extraneous topics.

Thus, in each of his questions, an interviewer not only asks for a specific item or kind of information but also indicates how long he would like the response to be, whether he anticipates what the response will be, whether he wants the respondent to adhere strictly to the topic of the question or not, and a number of other points concerning the quantity and quality of response wanted.

In this and following chapters, although our attention will be focused on the formulation of questions, we shall deal also with other elements of the question—answer process—silences, interruptions, and encouragements; transitions from one topic to another; the sequence in which topics are approached; and the pacing of the interview—which influence communication between interviewer[2] and respondent and which can also influence the response in the direction of the criteria we have described.

In examining the specific properties of questions that can be used to influence response characteristics, there are several points that we must bear in mind. First, although for the sake of clarity we must examine each of the properties separately, in the actual question these properties appear not singly but in combination. Thus, we must be concerned with the effects produced not only by a single property but by the various combinations of properties that

---

[2] The term "interviewer" here refers to any kind of interviewer, whether he is reading the questions from a schedule or tailoring questions to fit a particular respondent.

are embodied in every question. This is by no means an impossible task—and, in Chapter 11, we shall note the effects of various combinations—but we can best understand the effects by first examining the properties singly, even though they never occur singly in a question.

Another point to be borne in mind is that the effect of a specific question property on the response may be cumulative—that is, it may depend very heavily on the frequency with which the property is used within a single interview or a sequence of questions. For example, the occasional use of questions in which the interviewer indicates which answer he expects may have little or no effect on validity or on respondent participation; but, if this technique is used in a high proportion of questions, it may either irritate the respondent and cause him to give an invalid response opposite to that which the interviewer expects, or it may make him decide that the interviewer is not really interested in what he has to say and that he may as well give the answers suggested by the questions, whether valid or not. In either case, the validity of the responses is reduced. Similarly, if the interviewer always phrases his questions so that they are related to prior questions rather than to the respondent's answers, the respondent may gain an impression that the interviewer has little interest in his responses, since he apparently ignores the cues in the responses that indicate the respondent's interests. This impression may discourage the respondent from introducing new topics that he believes are relevant to the general subject matter of the interview.

Lastly, since we are concerned with the properties of questions in terms of their effect on the respondent rather than as a reflection of the interviewer's private intentions or his own beliefs concerning the meaning of his actions, the point of view we take is that of the respondent. Thus, for example, when we examine a question to see whether it follows the line of thinking of a prior response or, instead, picks up a topic mentioned in a prior question, we ignore antecedents which might be obvious to the interviewer but would probably be overlooked by the respondent. Or, to take another example, in deciding whether a question suggests one rather than another response, we consider how the respondent would be likely

TABLE 1. *Open and Closed Questions*

TYPE	DEFINITION	EXAMPLE
Closed question	a question which can be answered adequately in a few words	
Identification type	a question calling for the identification of person, place, group, time, number, etc., by asking who, where, when, how many, or which	I was interested in what you were saying about one person taking the lead in the discussion. Which group was he from? What was his name?
Selection type	fixed-alternative question, in which the respondent is asked to select one from the two or more possible responses offered	Were you looking forward to it or not? Did you think that either of them came out of it with a different point of view, or did you think that each girl left with her own point of view reinforced?
Yes–no type	a question which can be adequately answered yes or no, possibly supplemented by a redundant phrase such as, I think so, or I doubt it	Did this tape recorder or your note-taking bother them, do you think? I see, I take it that you knew Ruth before?
Open question	a question which may require more than a few words for an adequate response	And when you first got here, what happened? What was it about his personality that you didn't like especially?

to interpret the question rather than what the interviewer intended to convey.

In order to avoid circularity of definition, we define a property in terms of its *potential* effects rather than its *actual* effects. In this way we believe we can avoid the confusion that has developed in discussions of interviewing based almost entirely on interviewers' conceptions and recollections of their own intentions and behavior.

The general approach we employ to the question–answer process is somewhat analogous to the way in which sentences are analyzed in terms of their grammatical structure or chords in music are analyzed in terms of the notes that make them up. It is possible, of course, to speak sentences without being aware of grammar or to play an instrument by ear without any knowledge of music theory. In the same way, it is possible to ask questions without a knowledge of the properties and components of questions that we shall describe. Yet, just as knowledge of grammar increases the effectiveness of a person's use of language, and just as knowledge of theory makes a better musician, so we believe the knowledge and self-awareness that come from studying the properties of questions will make a better interviewer.

Openness versus Closedness

Every question, regardless of its length or subject matter, contains an indication of the length of response necessary for adequate coverage. The *closed* question calls for a response of a few words; the *open* question calls for a response of more than a few words. The examples shown in Table 1 distinguish this property.

In general, an interviewer may reasonably expect open and closed questions to influence length of response, and the empirical data bear out this expectation. In Dohrenwend and Richardson's study of student interviews, length of response after open and closed questions was compared by counting the number of standard lines of typescript in the response, to the nearest half line. It was found that the direction of the difference in length of response was as predicted in a statistically significant number of the interviews.

As predicted:	average length of response greater after open questions:	29 interviews
Contrary to prediction:	average length of response the same or greater after closed questions:	11 interviews

In a subsequent interview experiment in which the use of open and closed questions was carefully controlled, responses to open questions were significantly longer than responses to closed questions, averaging 8.9 standard lines of typed interview transcript as compared with 3 lines (Dohrenwend, in press). The results confirm what might reasonably be expected: open questions do elicit longer responses than closed questions.

THE USES OF OPENNESS AND CLOSEDNESS

Generally speaking, open questions are more likely to be used in the early stages of a study. At this time, the investigator may not know enough about the subject of the study to be able to formulate relevant closed questions, and the responses to open questions are likely to fill in the details of his general map of the subject area and thus reveal what is most relevant to his research questions. If, moreover, he has chosen his early respondents on the basis of their special knowledge of the subject, he is likely to gain more from them, in terms of both facts and insights, by encouraging lengthy and less structured responses through the use of open questions.

In the later stages of a study, on the other hand, when the interview is standardized and the respondents are not "experts" in the research topic, closed questions may produce responses which are more relevant and specific and, hence, may obtain the desired coverage more economically than open questions.

Respondent participation may be influenced by the relative proportion of open to closed questions asked by the interviewer. The use of such open questions as, "Would you tell me what happened at the meeting?" implies that the interviewer respects the judgment of the respondent and relies upon him to select pieces of information that are useful, informative, interesting, and—provided the interviewer has made his purpose clear—relevant. If the interviewer then asks some closed questions which demonstrate pertinence to what the respondent has said, this will indicate to the respondent that the interviewer has been listening attentively. The predominant use of closed questions, on the other hand, may give the respondent the impression that the interviewer is not really interested in a full expression of his views or in him as a person but merely wants brief responses to questions that have been fabricated in advance of the interview for use with all respondents.

The use of a preponderance of open or closed questions may, of course, have different effects on different respondents. It is possible, for example, that respondents who are particularly well informed on the topic of the interview may feel that the interviewer who uses closed questions excessively is either underestimating them or, at best, failing to make use of as much information as they could potentially offer. On the other hand, it seems likely that respondents of low intelligence, low socio-economic status, or low status in an organizational hierarchy may find it difficult to tolerate a preponderance of open questions, because they are unused to talking at length spontaneously, articulately, or coherently, or because they are uncomfortable in any unstructured situation, or because they feel that they are failing to grasp the interviewer's purpose, or for all these reasons.

With some respondents, it may be effective to begin with open questions in order to open up the general area of the interview and to follow these with closed questions for the sake of specificity. With others, however, it may be preferable to begin with closed questions for the purpose of delineating the area of interest and to follow these with open questions only after the respondent has had the reassurance of functioning in the highly structured situation that the closed questions provide.

It has been generally assumed that interviewers are flexible enough in their personal styles to be able to conduct interviews in which all questions are closed, interviews with various proportions of closed to open questions, and interviews consisting entirely of open questions. Richardson and Dohrenwend have found, however, that experienced professional interviewers are unable to conduct an interview using only open questions and that some closed questions must be used to sustain the interview.

Some recent experimental studies (Moscovici, 1963) have raised the question of whether closed yes–no questions may, under certain conditions, reduce the validity of response. There is evidence to suggest that, in response to closed yes–no questions, some people have a tendency to give yes answers irrespective of the question being asked, and others have a tendency to answer no. Do some respondents feel that the interviewer expects an affirmative answer and tend to acquiesce, whereas others have a tendency to disagree with him? Couch and Keniston (1960) have identified what they term "yea sayers" and "nay sayers" and have attempted to relate these tendencies to personality variables. Of more use to the interviewer is evidence that respondents with less education have a greater tendency toward yea-saying than those with a college education (Campbell, Converse, Miller, & Stokes, 1960), and that Negro respondents interviewed by white interviewers tend to acquiesce more than white respondents, even when the education of the Negro and white respondents is equal (Lenski & Leggett, 1960). Although further investigation is needed on the personal characteristics of respondents who tend to be yea or nay sayers before they can be identified in advance by interviewers, there is sufficient evidence to suggest caution in formulating questions for respondents with low socio-economic status and education. It is with these respondents that interviewers have reported difficulties in keeping the interview going along relevant lines without recourse to a considerable degree of directiveness, which would include a heavy proportion of closed to open questions.

Perhaps one of the reasons why respondents of less education and lower socio-economic status appear to participate more easily and willingly when the interviewer uses a heavy preponderance of closed questions is that the closed question facilitates their answering a question that they do not fully understand without revealing their lack of understanding. The less the respondent understands the questions, the more the yea-saying phenomenon may come into play.

Under certain conditions, open and closed questions may have different effects on the relevance of responses. In interviews whose purpose was to reconstruct an event, Dohrenwend (in press) found that, during the course of the interview, relevance declined in responses to open questions but not to closed questions.

OPEN AND CLOSED QUESTIONS IN STANDARDIZED AND NONSTANDARDIZED INTERVIEWS

Open questions generally play a more important role in non-standardized than in standardized interviews. When exploring an area, the interviewer generally lacks the knowledge necessary for the formulation of a preponderance of closed questions. If he does formulate them, he runs the risk of losing valuable new information and insights by the very restrictiveness that is characteristic of a closed question.

In nonschedule standardized interviews, the interviewer varies the questions so as to obtain uniformity of meaning for each respondent. In the pretest stages of these interviews, one of the tasks of the interviewer involves observing the effect of open and closed questions on the respondent. Does the respondent appear anxious if a high proportion of open questions is used and more at ease with closed questions, or does he appear increasingly irritated by closed questions and do his responses tend to go beyond what the closed question calls for and introduce new topics? From the feedback, the interviewer can gauge the ways in which he can influence various respondents through variation in the use of open and closed questions; hence, he can determine which type of question is more effective with which respondents.

In the schedule interview, questions must be held constant for all respondents, but there is no logical deterrent to the use of either open or closed questions. The use of open questions, however, presents some technical difficulties. Responses to open questions are far more difficult and expensive to record and analyze than are responses to closed questions. Furthermore, in using open questions, the interviewer expects to get a reasonably long response. If the initial response to the open question gives him inadequate information or includes irrelevant material, it is difficult to use further techniques to obtain the needed information without departing from uniformity in the wording and sequence of questions.

Our experience has shown that it is more difficult to communicate clearly the meaning and intent of an open than a closed question, especially if the respondents are heterogeneous. If this experience is found to be generally true, open questions are more likely to be misunderstood;[3] if the interviewer then has to explain the question, he once again violates the requirement of standardization.

In constructing an interview schedule, the investigator strives to order questions so that they will not break the respondent's train of thought (Kornhauser & Sheatsley, 1959, p. 572f.). With closed questions, it is possible to develop an uninterrupted train of thought in a series of questions, provided that the respondent adopts the categories of content embodied in the questions. With open questions, this is more difficult because such questions give the respondent more freedom to deviate from the response ordinarily expected. The more the respondent deviates from the expected response, the more he will find the next scheduled question a break with the train of thought he is developing.

A final practical difficulty in using open questions is related to the length of response that the interviewer is able to record in the course of a schedule interview. Few interviewers have shorthand skills adequate for the purpose, and, in any case, subsequent transcription of shorthand notes is laborious and expensive. The use of tape recorders for recording responses verbatim is, of course, feasible, but their use presents a number of practical and technical difficulties and does not eliminate the cost of transcription. For all these reasons, schedule interviews generally embody a heavy preponderance of closed questions.

Because openness and closedness is the first property of questions we have described, we have had to ignore the fact that every question or series of questions has other properties and that it is the

---

[3] It is possible that our experience has led us to a wrong conclusion. If the respondent does not understand an open question, it is difficult, if not impossible, for him to give a satisfactory answer. It is relatively easy for him not to understand a closed question and yet give an apparently satisfactory answer.

combination and interplay of these properties which, in their totality, influence the response. As we describe the other properties of questions, this will become clearer.

Antecedents of the Question

Each question in an interview may profitably be examined in terms of its antecedent—a prior part of the interview to which the topic of the question refers, either implicitly or explicitly. The antecedent of a question may be something the *interviewer* has said, either (1) in the immediately preceding question or (2) in any earlier question, or it may be something the *respondent* has said, either (3) in his immediately preceding response or (4) in any earlier response. This classification provides for four possible antecedents. For practical purposes, however, (1) and (2) can be combined as "questions derived from one of the last few questions," because we have found that respondents in nonstandardized interviews rarely recall questions that occur earlier in the interview.

Not every question has antecedents. The opening question of the interview obviously cannot have them, and any subsequent question need not have them since the interviewer is free at any time to take a new tack and enter a subject area quite unconnected with what has gone before. But the lack of antecedents is, as we shall see, also a significant property.

QUESTIONS WITH INTERVIEWER ANTECEDENTS OR WITH NO ANTECEDENTS

Questions with interviewer antecedents and questions with no antecedents have in common the fact that they place the responsibility for the selection of question content, for response cues, and, indeed, for any changes in the course of the interview in the hands of the interviewer. In short, they give to the interviewer (and remove from the respondent) a degree of control over the interview. This control may strike the interviewer as highly desirable because it appears to increase his likelihood of achieving relevance, specificity, and coverage. The data from the student interviews

Table 2. *Antecedents of Questions*

TYPE	DEFINITION	EXAMPLE[4] (In a series, the last question exemplifies the procedure.)
Question derived from one of the last few questions	Topic of the question is closer to the content of one of the preceding few questions than it is to a prior response	▸Q: I'd like to ask you how you first had contact with this experiment. A: This experiment? I had my name in with a part-time agency, and they called me about it. And, uh, I had, wasn't doing anything, and I thought, well, okay, it sounds interesting Q: Uh-huh. The employment service called you? A: Oh, yes. ⌐Q: *Uh-huh. And then who did you first talk with who was connected with this?*
Question derived from the preceding response	Topic of the question is closer to the content of the preceding response than to any other prior part of the interview	▸A: . . . I was there as an observer of a discussion between two young girls on the position of women, particularly college women, and after they had graduated, their problems. ⌐Q: *You were there to observe?*
Question derived from	Topic of the question is closer to the con-	[following the sequence above]

TYPE	DEFINITION	EXAMPLE (In a series, the last question exemplifies the procedure.)
an earlier response	tent of a response prior to the last response than to any other part of the interview	A: And, if it was necessary, to take part. Q: Oh, well, did you? A: Well, only when one girl changed her position ... [response continues on same topic] └─(Q: *These were college girls, that were doing the discussing, I mean?*
Question which breaks with the last response	Topic of the question appears to be totally unconnected with prior questions or responses	A: Well, then this girl with the independent point of view took this line and suddenly began discussing the opposite point of view deliberately, but it completely floored all of us. Ya. So that was the only time I contributed by asking a question to try and clarify. Q: *Oh, what was the physical arrangement like?*

indicate that questions with interviewer antecedents did elicit more relevant responses than questions with respondent antecedents. In these interviews, the interviewer's task was to reconstruct an event in which the respondent had participated about a week earlier and

4 The arrows indicate antecedents.

to determine his reactions to the event. A response which did not serve either of these purposes was coded as irrelevant.

> Respondent more often introduces topics ir-
> relevant to the interview after questions de-
> rived from prior responses: 27 interviews
>
> Respondent more often introduces topics ir-
> relevant to the interview after questions de-
> rived from prior questions or breaking with
> the last response: 11 interviews

But the apparent advantages of this type of question may be counterbalanced by its potential disadvantages. First, the continued use of questions which do not refer to prior responses—that is, questions with no antecedents or with interviewer antecedents— may make the interview appear to the respondent as a highly fragmented, discontinuous process in which the interviewer takes little interest in the responses, aside from recording them. In short, the respondent may come to feel that he is being used solely for the interviewer's ends. Although the interviewer may be able to prevent some of this feeling of discontinuity by a skillful management of transitions (see p. 222), he cannot avoid the possibility of the respondent's feeling that the responses (or he as an individual) have little interest for the interviewer, since they are rarely referred to in the interviewer's questions.

We have found that inexperienced interviewers in nonstandardized interviews use a preponderance of questions with interviewer antecedents or no antecedents and that this hampers them in obtaining unanticipated responses. Their infrequent use of respondent antecedents seems to stem from fear that they may run out of questions; as a consequence, they are often so preoccupied with formulating the next question that they do not concentrate on what the respondent is saying or on the possibility of basing their questions on his response. They may also be fearful of losing control of the interview. With training and an increasing awareness of how to use respondent antecedents, student interviewers do increase their use of them.

QUESTIONS WITH RESPONDENT ANTECEDENTS

Questions with respondent antecedents may relate to the immediately preceding response or to any response that has been made earlier in the interview (or even in a preceding interview, if there has been a series involving the same respondent). A primary effect of such questions relates to respondent participation. By linking his questions to what the respondent has said, the interviewer demonstrates that he has been listening to the respondent with attention and interest. This may enhance the respondent's feeling of active participation in the interview and, thus, help to increase both validity and, if it is sought, the depth of response. It encourages the respondent to develop ideas more thoroughly and, if these are relevant, it thus increases coverage. When responses lack coverage, specificity, or clarity, further questioning based on these responses may rectify their shortcomings. In addition, the use of respondent antecedents, as we have noted earlier, is likely to increase the number of unanticipated but relevant responses.

But, here again, we must not assume that these effects are inevitable. Although some respondents will react positively to references to their earlier responses, others will react negatively to what they may perceive as probing or even badgering. Moreover, as we shall note shortly, specific types of questions with respondent antecedents are, in fact, useful for confronting a respondent with his contradictory responses and for trying to resolve inconsistencies between responses—two techniques that may be useful to the interviewer but highly threatening to some respondents.

Thus far we have discussed respondent antecedents as though they were all alike, despite our earlier classification of them as involving either immediately prior responses or any earlier responses. The difference between these two categories is largely one of degree, but the interviewer who restricts himself to the immediately prior response deprives himself of several important advantages that are peculiar to the use of the entire range of responses as antecedents. First, the entire range of prior responses provides the interviewer with a broader selection of topics about which to frame new questions; moreover, he may be able to recognize and exploit relationships between two responses that are quite far from one another in the interview.

Q: Some time ago you said that the school bond issue was voted down, and just a moment ago you indicated that quite a few of the residents send their children to private schools. Was it the users of the private schools who were most active in defeating the school bond issue?

More important, he can note inconsistencies between two responses and attempt to clarify them.

Q: Earlier you said that your husband worked for an electronics manufacturer, but now you say that he is a teacher. Can you clarify this for me?

Secondly, he can use any of the prior responses as a point of departure in making a transition (see p. 222), thus avoiding an abrupt transition that is without antecedents or without respondent antecedents, either of which will strike the respondent as a break in his train of thought.

Q: Quite a while back, when we were discussing the ways in which you budgeted your income, you mentioned something about your food costs. Could we go back to that for a moment?

Thirdly, the respondent's sense of being carefully attended to will undoubtedly be increased if the interviewer makes reference to something that the respondent said fifteen or twenty minutes earlier.

The use of respondent antecedents can be especially valuable when the respondent makes an allusion to information which the interviewer would like to follow up—but not at that moment because he is pursuing another line of inquiry. Later in the interview, the interviewer may relate a question to the respondent's earlier allusion and encourage him to provide further information.

ANTECEDENTS AND OTHER COMPONENTS OF QUESTIONS

Openness and closedness are entirely independent of a question's antecedents—that is, a question without antecedents or with either interviewer or respondent antecedents can be open or closed. Since any combination of these two properties is possible, let us examine briefly the potentialities of various combinations.

As we have noted earlier, both the open question and the question with respondent antecedents give greater freedom to the respondent and less control to the interviewer, either actually or apparently. Hence, the *open* question with *respondent* antecedents presumably combines cumulatively the effects of each characteristic. Conversely, the *closed* question *without* antecedents or with *interviewer* antecedents would seem to offer the respondent least freedom and the interviewer greatest control.

ANTECEDENTS IN VARIOUS FORMS OF INTERVIEW

In the early stages of a study, when the interviewer is uncertain of what questions to ask, or when the respondent knows more about the subject matter than the interviewer, it is logical for the interviewer to give the respondent as much opportunity as possible to introduce topics and develop responses and to restrict himself to analyzing and clarifying what the respondent says. In such situations, too, the interviewer, if he has freedom to range at will over the entire sequence of responses, can perceive relationships between the responses and use these relationships as a basis for further questions. In order to realize these advantages, he is likely to use questions embodying respondent antecedents.

As the exploratory process continues, however, and the interviewer's map of the territory to be covered becomes more clearly delineated and more richly detailed, his dependence on the respondent for developing topics and giving unanticipated information decreases, and he is likely to use more questions with interviewer antecedents or no antecedents in order to maximize relevance and coverage.

In the standardized interview, the interviewer's choice of the antecedents of his questions depends entirely on whether the interview is schedule or nonschedule. In the schedule interview, in which both the sequence and the wording of questions are fixed and unalterable, questions with respondent antecedents are difficult to use. Since there is no way of accurately predicting how each respondent will answer a question, it is impossible to incorporate in the schedule a subsequent question that will infallibly refer to his response. This difficulty can be overcome, to some extent, by formulating a question so that it will refer to the prior response *most likely* to be made; but this technique will be effective only when the response made is within the intended frame of reference of the question. To such a respondent, the question will appear to have respondent antecedents but, to respondents who make unanticipated responses, it will appear to break with their prior response.

A second technique is to provide alternate sets of questions, each set to be selected on the basis of the respondent's immediately preceding response. But, strictly speaking, this technique violates the principle of standardization, in that it does not present each respondent with identical questions.

In the schedule interview, the major purpose of using questions that appear to have respondent antecedents is to heighten the respondent's participation by increasing his impression of being listened to. It need not be used for the development of insights, unanticipated materials, or the elaboration of responses, since the schedule interview is based on the assumption that the schedule clearly and completely specifies the nature and scope of the information sought. In schedule interviews, the interviewers are instructed to improve the quality of responses which lack specificity, clarity, or relevance by asking further questions. Such further questions are likely to be related to prior (unsatisfactory) responses.

In contrast to the schedule interview, the standardized nonschedule interview not only permits the use of questions with respondent antecedents but can employ them to great advantage. Indeed, perhaps the primary advantages of the nonschedule over the schedule interview for purposes of standardization stem from the flexibility provided by the use of questions with respondent antecedents. By using an immediately prior response as an antecedent, the interviewer can clarify the terminology of the response or ask for elaboration. By using a more remote response, he can not only pick up the thread of an idea but, perhaps most important, he can, at any point, drop a question that seems to threaten the respondent and return to it much later in the interview, when respondent participation has improved. The question with respondent antecedents serves this purpose in two ways: First, it enables the interviewer to use the earlier (and less satisfactory) response as a springboard for a new question; secondly, it helps to increase the respondent's sense of participation.

How Questions Relate to Their Antecedents

The ways in which a question relates to its antecedents have been discussed at considerable length in the literature of interviewing under such terms as "probe" and "reflection." But these labels have been used so variously and so generally that they have lost much of their precision. We shall avoid them and apply to the procedures they designate a set of more specific terms. These we shall classify into two major categories—antecedent questions intended to *elicit additional information* and antecedent questions intended to *clarify* an earlier response.

ANTECEDENT QUESTIONS INTENDED TO ELICIT ADDITIONAL INFORMATION

Additional information can be elicited by two types of questions which are related to prior responses—the *extension* and the *echo*.

The extension is a request for further information about something that the respondent has already said. A respondent, for example, in recounting an event in which she participated, may have described it in primarily factual terms. If the interviewer is interested mainly in her feelings and reactions to the event, he may then ask, "Tell me how you felt during all this?" The earlier responses are thus used as a springboard for obtaining further information.

The extension in this case is used to deflect the discussion toward more relevant responses; such use is generally most effective when the respondent is talking fairly freely. But an extension, particularly one referring to a response made much earlier in the interview, can also be used to get the respondent to talk more freely in order to increase the coverage of the response. If, early in an interview, a respondent shows resistance to a line of questioning, the interviewer, not knowing whether the resistance is due to the respondent's lack of information or interest or to feelings of anxiety, insecurity, or threat, may move on to another question. Later, when the respondent appears more confident and at ease, the interviewer can return to the earlier topic and, through an extension, attempt to obtain the coverage that was not obtained earlier. If the information desired is subjective, extensions may be used to increase depth by encouraging the respondent after he becomes emotionally involved with the subject matter.

A second device for eliciting new information is the echo, which is an exact or nearly exact repetition of the respondent's words by the interviewer, generally with a rising inflection at the end. For example, when a respondent, in talking about his childhood, terminates his response with "During those years I was terribly unhappy," the interviewer may echo, "You were terribly unhappy?" If used effectively, the echo makes the respondent feel that the interviewer is following him closely and sympathetically and is encouraging him to continue to express himself freely.

Unlike the extension, the echo should be employed only when the prior response is relevant to the interview, because it encourages the respondent to continue with little or no change in the subject matter of his response.[5] It is useful only when the interviewer judges that the respondent has more to say on the same subject, because if it is used when he has exhausted the question, it may sound silly or irritating and, hence, may lower the level of partici-

---

[5] The interviewer's silence (see p. 203) also can be used to uncover new information, because the respondent, after a silence, may continue talking. Like the echo, the silence has little or no effect on the respondent's line of thought. The use of encouragement (see p. 198) by the interviewer may have a similar effect.

pation. Because it has been used widely in nondirective counseling and in social work and psychotherapeutic interviewing, the echo is a relatively familiar element of interviewing, and it has often been satirized, along with the "Uh-huh," in skits or in social conversations. Unless the echo is used very sparingly and judiciously, it can, of course, quickly become ridiculous.

ANTECEDENT QUESTIONS INTENDED TO IMPROVE THE QUALITY OF EARLIER RESPONSES

The techniques discussed above are used primarily to elicit new information. Often, however, information provided in an earlier response lacks clarity, specificity, coverage, or depth. To develop these qualities in earlier response material, another set of techniques is available.

The *clarification* is a request for the clarification, specification, or elaboration of ambiguous, vague, or implicit statements made in a prior part of the interview. For example, if the respondent mentions that he was brought up in a large family, the interviewer, in order to clarify the use of the word "large," may ask, "Who was in your family?" A clarification may be open: "What did you mean when you said . . . ?" or closed: "Did you decide to go or didn't you?" A clarification may also be used to obtain depth: "Why did this upset you?"

Two kinds of clarification may usefully be distinguished. In a *direct* clarification, the interviewer specifically requests information about a general, vague, or ambiguous prior response. The examples we have cited above are direct clarifications. In an *inferential* clarification, the interviewer makes an explicit inquiry about information implicit in a prior part of the interview. The inferential clarification has been most fully discussed, perhaps, by Carl Rogers (1942) in his description of nondirective counseling. There, the interviewer pays close attention to the feelings implicit in the respondent's statements and then asks a question designed to clarify and make explicit the implicit content.

To increase the clarity, specificity, or coherence of a response or a series of responses, the interviewer may use a *summary*—a question which summarizes information previously given by the respondent and explicitly or implicitly requests confirmation or correction.

The summary can accomplish several objectives, either individually or simultaneously. It can assemble, consolidate, and synthesize a number of pieces of information which the respondent has provided in discrete responses, and, in this way, it can give significance and relevance to the response material. It can clarify ambiguities. Also, without hurting his feelings, it can cut short a respondent who tends to be garrulous or discursive. In short, it gives the interviewer a way of increasing his control over the interview.

In part, the summary gives the interviewer greater control because it is a closed question, requiring only a brief affirmative as a response. As such, however, it shares with other types of closed questions the dangers of yea saying (see p. 150). It is always easier for a respondent to agree with a summary than to disagree and then specify why he disagrees. The respondent may feel shy about disagreeing or feel that his disagreement casts aspersions on the intelligence or ability of the interviewer. This danger is particularly serious if the summary is used to clarify ambiguous information, and it may be compounded by the tendency—which we have discovered by checking tape recordings against interview reports —of some interviewers to record their own summaries (which incorporate distortions) and attribute them to the respondent.

Two procedures may prevent this kind of distortion. Since the respondent is unlikely to acquiesce to a summary containing a gross distortion (see Beezer's findings, p. 196), the interviewer, at any point at which he is doubtful about the information, can deliberately introduce a major distortion with the expectation that the respondent will correct it. The drawback to this technique is the possibility that the introduction of a major distortion may cause the respondent to perceive the interviewer as stupid, inattentive, or biased and hence may reduce the respondent's participation. As an alternative to this technique, the interviewer can formulate what he regards to be an accurate summary, prefacing it by saying that he is not sure whether he has fully understood what has been said; he can then ask for corrections, no matter how minor.

When the interviewer notes inconsistency within a response, between two discrete responses, or between a response and another source of information presumed to be accepted by the respondent, he may use a *confrontation*—that is, a question which presents the respondent with the inconsistency and asks for its resolution. The confrontation may be used in an attempt to increase validity, specificity, or clarity.

Because this technique of confronting a respondent with his inconsistencies is probably best known through fictional or factual accounts of courtroom cross-examination of witnesses, it has connotations of badgering and threatening witnesses who are compelled to answer. But, although a confrontation may be threatening and have negative influence on the respondent's level of participation, this is by no means always the case. A confrontation may be regarded as an indication of the interviewer's sincere interest and careful attention. In any situation, however, the interviewer needs to weigh carefully the consequences of a confrontation for the participation of the respondent.

Occasionally, an interviewer may use a *repetition*—that is, a question which merely repeats a question previously asked. In nonschedule interviews, this may happen inadvertently, if the interviewer has forgotten he has already asked the question. (If the respondent remembers, however, this may irritate him and suggest that the interviewer is either inexperienced or inattentive.) There are circumstances, however, in which a nonschedule interviewer may use a repetition intentionally—for example, if a respondent's answer suggests that he did not understand the question:

Q: What was the purpose of this experiment?
A: Uh, well, they were discussing women's role, educated women's role, college women's role in life.
Q: Well, that was the discussion. *What actually was the purpose of the experiment?*

In a long interview, the interviewer may feel that his early questions were answered evasively or superficially or were lacking in validity but that, as the interview progressed, the respondent has

TABLE 3. *Summary of Relationships between Questions and Their Antecedents*

TITLE	DEFINITION	EXAMPLE (In a series, the last question exemplifies the procedure.)
Extension	a request for new information related to something already said	A: There were violent reactions because Sylvia was Jewish and she—so she knew how the girl would feel. Q: *Oh, how did that become apparent?*
Echo	an exact or nearly exact repetition by the interviewer of the respondent's words	A: . . . the only thing you ever hear about sororities is bad things anyhow. Q: Ya. A: Before you get to college. Q: *Before you get there.*
Clarification Direct	a direct request for information on a vague or ambiguous prior part of the interview	Q: Well, after the experiment, you say you were going to interview these people. Uh, did you? A: I wasn't going to interview them. Q: *Oh, you weren't? I'm not quite clear on that.*
Clarification Inferential	an explicit inquiry about information implicit in a prior part of the interview	A: It was held over at CURW, you know, the religious center. Q: At Myron Taylor?
Summary	a question which summarizes information previously stated	A: Well, what I meant to say was that there wasn't too much feel-

TITLE	DEFINITION	EXAMPLE (In a series, the last question exemplifies the procedure.)
	explicitly, and explicitly or implicitly requests confirmation	ing, group feeling, between myself and my friends . . . and the other girls, until after the experiment, after we all shared this little experience, and we started talking freely with one another about it, and we started exchanging ideas, we started getting much more group feeling after we had done it. Q: *Did you feel you knew them a little better?*
Confrontation	a question in which the interviewer presents the respondent with an inconsistency between two or more of the respondent's statements or between one of the respondent's statements and another source presumed to be accepted by the respondent	A: . . . And then after they had been going just over twenty minutes they really began to state their views a little more extremely, and at one point I thought it was going to develop into, not a shindig, they weren't that type of girl. . . . . . . A: . . . we thought that the discussion didn't involve people enough in the situation because although, uh, there was a lot of, uh, were a lot of interpersonal relationships that one

TITLE	DEFINITION	EXAMPLE (In a series, the last question exemplifies the procedure.)
		could talk about, none of the people really felt involved in what they were talking about.
		Q: *You said they didn't get a great deal of involvement, and yet, at one time, they were pretty excited about the topic.*
Repetition	a question which merely repeats a question previously asked	Q: What was the purpose of this experiment?
		A: Uh, well they were discussing women's role, educated women's role, college women's role in life.
		Q: Well, that was the discussion. *What actually was the purpose of the experiment?*

become less timid and threatened, has gained self-confidence, or has increased his trust in the interviewer. By repeating one or two questions asked earlier in the interview to which responses were not satisfactory, the interviewer may increase relevance, coverage, specificity, clarity, or depth. If the interviewer judges that the respondent remembers the earlier question, he may indicate to the respondent that he is aware that he has asked the same question earlier. Repetition may also provide a check on reliability by disclosing whether the second response agrees with the first.

In general, repetitions are rarely used. Many of the purposes they serve can be served as well, if not better, by varying the wording of the questions in order to approach the earlier content of the interview from a slightly different perspective.

HOW QUESTIONS RELATE TO THEIR ANTECEDENTS IN VARIOUS FORMS OF INTERVIEW

In either the nonstandardized or the nonschedule standardized interview, any relationship between questions and their antecedents can be used without restriction. In the schedule interview, on the other hand, the use of some relationships is restricted by the fact that all questions are formulated in advance. A question with interviewer antecedents can always be incorporated in the schedule. Questions with respondent antecedents can be incorporated in the schedule only if the designer of the schedule can correctly predict the types of response that the interviewer will receive to earlier questions. Extensions can be prepared for certain answers to closed questions. If, for example, the question is "Do you own a car?" the extension "What make is it?" can be presented if the question is answered, "Yes," but can be omitted if it is answered "No."

Confrontations, summaries, clarifications, or echoes cannot be incorporated into the schedule because they depend on response material which cannot be known in advance. Often, however, the schedule interviewer is instructed to depart from the schedule and to use such relationships in certain circumstances. If a respondent does not hear or understand a question, the interviewer may be instructed to use a repetition. If a response is ambiguous or otherwise inadequate, the interviewer may be instructed to use a clarification.

Such tactics do, however, constitute a departure from standardization. To the extent that the respondent answers questions in the way that the schedule designer intended, uniformity of stimulus can be maintained. But if the respondent behaves in an unanticipated way—by introducing material not called for by the question, by refusing to answer the question, by reshaping the question, or by reversing roles and questioning the interviewer—the interviewer faces a conflict between adhering to the schedule of questions and departing from it in order to lead the respondent back to the schedule by a variety of tactics, including the use of questions with respondent antecedents. The frequency of such departures is unknown, since they are rarely reported and never taken into account in the analysis of the response material.

7

EXPECTATIONS AND PREMISES:

THE SO-CALLED

"LEADING QUESTION"

The three components of questions we have thus far described and examined—openness or closedness, the antecedents of a question, and the relationship between questions and their antecedents—are significant because they can influence certain characteristics of the response. The components to which we shall now turn, the *expectation* and the *premise*, are used by interviewers to go one step further: to indicate to the respondent the actual response they expect to receive.

The reasons why interviewers formulate questions that suggest their own answers and the effects of such suggestions on the response probably constitute the most widely discussed issues in the literature of interviewing. These discussions generally deal with what is sometimes called the "leading question." A general idea of the meanings that have been given to this term can be obtained from some of the statements on the uses and effects of leading questions, even though these statements define the leading question only by implication rather than explicitly.

Cannell and Kahn (1953, p. 346) suggest: "Questions should

be phrased so that they contain no suggestion as to the most appropriate response." Whyte (1953, p. 20) makes the following analysis of the use of a leading question in an interview which he conducted: "I raise a question, but then make the mistake of giving one possible answer to that question. This is probably quite a common error in interviewing: presenting a leading question instead of a question with the possible answers completely open." Bingham, Moore, and Gustad (1959, p. 74) formulate, as a rule for interviewing, "Avoid implying the answer to your own question." Kinsey and his colleagues (1948, p. 52) write:

In a study in which the form of the questions are not standardized, there is considerable responsibility on the interviewer to see to it that his spontaneous questions are not so phrased as to bias the subject's reply. In his tone of voice and in his choice of words, the interviewer must avoid giving the subject any clue as to the answer he expects.

The Maccobys (1954, p. 466), in summarizing techniques which are widely agreed upon by practitioners, include the following on leading questions:

The question introduced by the interviewer should in no way influence the *direction* of the response. It should seek to elicit the desired information from the respondent without in any way making it likely that the respondent will lean more in one direction than another. . . .

Although the reasons for their proscriptions are not made explicit, it is clear that these authors believe that leading questions should not be used, the implication being that they will have some kind of distorting effect on responses.

There has been no agreement on a definition of the term "leading," and it is frequently used without definition. After carefully examining the interview literature and listening to a large number of interviews, we have concluded that, in most of the uses of "leading," the components "expectations" and "premises" are contained. We shall define these components below.[1] An understand-

---

[1] A further component sometimes included in discussions of the leading question is the use of loaded words, which have positive or negative affect and may thus influence response. We shall defer discussion of this until Chapter 9, which deals with the content of questions.

ing of these components and their effects can do much to clarify the thinking and traditions that have influenced the use of leading questions.

Expectations

An expectation is that component of a question by which the interviewer indicates the response he anticipates the respondent will give (or not give). If the interviewer asks, "Are you twenty-five years old?" he does not indicate the answer he expects, and hence the question can be answered by "yes" or "no." It is not, therefore, an expectation. If, however, he asks, "You are twenty-five years old, aren't you?" he clearly indicates that he expects a "yes" answer. Such a question embodies an expectation.

An expectation can generally be identified by the syntax and logic of the question. In some cases, however, an interviewer may communicate the expectation by his intonation. For example, "Did you agree with this decision?" if asked without stress on any one word, is not an expectation. However, "Did you *agree* with this decision?" or "Did *you* agree with this decision?" with surprise or incredulity registered by the emphasis, may make it clear to the respondent that the interviewer expects him to have disagreed. (We shall deal with this and other possible consequences of the interviewer's intonation, facial expression, and nonverbal behavior in Chapter 10.)

Because an expectation communicates the response expected in specific terms, it must always be a closed yes–no type. ("You have three children, haven't you?") Closed identification questions, which ask for a number ("How many children have you?"), or closed selection questions, which ask the respondent to select one of a number of possible responses offered ("Have you fewer than two children, or two children, or more?"), are not expectations. A simple way, then, of avoiding the use of expectation, if this is desired, is to phrase a question so that it is not a closed yes–no type.

Expectations can usefully be subdivided into two categories according to the degree of certainty they embody as to the likelihood that the answer suggested will be agreed to by the respondent. A *weak expectation* indicates that the interviewer is somewhat uncertain about its correctness. "Then am I correct in assuming you did not join the group?" is weak, and hence it is relatively easy for the respondent to override it and give the unexpected response. A *strong expectation* indicates a high degree of certainty. "You certainly didn't join the group, did you?" presumably makes it more difficult for the respondent to make a response that is contrary to the expectation.

A second subclassification of expectations is based not on the form of the question but on how well informed the interviewer is on the subject matter with which the question deals. In very general terms, the more informed the interviewer, the greater is the probability that he can formulate an expectation which indicates the response the respondent would have given had the question not been an expectation. The degree of information possessed by the interviewer may vary widely, but we shall divide this range into two categories: An *informed expectation* is one that is based on the interviewer's knowledge about the subject matter contained in the question or about the respondent. An *uninformed expectation* is one that is unsupported by knowledge about the subject matter contained in the question or about the respondent.

The interviewer's knowledge may be derived from information the respondent has already provided in the interview. In these circumstances, expectations can be reliably coded as informed or uninformed by independent judges listening to a tape recording of the interview and with no other knowledge of the interviewer. The interviewer may, however, bring to bear information of other kinds—what he observes or previous knowledge of the respondent or the subject matter of the interview. In these circumstances, the degree of informedness of his expectation can be judged only by himself or by someone else through questioning him.

This classification thus provides four possible types of expectations: weak informed, weak uninformed, strong informed, and strong uninformed. It is our impression that writers who warn against the use of leading questions are thinking principally of the possible distorting effects of strong uninformed expectations rather than those that are weak *and* informed—a point that will be elaborated on later in this chapter.

Premises

It is almost impossible to formulate a question that does not depend on some kind of premise or assumption.[2] Even such questions as "What is your name?" and "How old are you?" are built on the assumption, based on the interviewer's prior experience, that people are given names and have up-to-date information on their ages and that this will hold true for the particular respondent. Within our society, many characteristics of behavior are so nearly universal that they are used as the basis for many areas of questioning. It is a very easy step, therefore, to assume that the behavior, possessions, and values that are shared by those people whom the interviewer knows will be shared by all respondents. For example, if all the people whom the interviewer knows own telephones, he may ask a respondent, "What is your telephone number?" without first ascertaining whether, in fact, he has a telephone. If the answer to the question consists of a telephone number, the premise of telephone possession is, of course, correct. But if the respondent does not have a telephone, or there is no telephone at which he can generally be reached, or there is some other reason that the premise of the question is incorrect, the respondent cannot answer the question correctly unless he addresses himself directly to the premise and points out its incorrectness.

In questions dealing with information that is unique to the respondent—e.g., his life history—or unique to a small group of respondents—e.g., an unusual experience they have shared—it is difficult for the interviewer to introduce premises derived from broad general classes of information. Rather, his premises will have to derive from information he is given by the respondent—e.g., if the respondent reports that his parents were killed while he was an infant, the interviewer may ask, "How were your

---

[2] Our use of the term "premise" is intended to include both tacit and explicit assumptions.

parents killed?" The premise that the parents were killed could not have been derived from the interviewer's general knowledge of people.

We say that a question contains a premise when it builds and depends on prior information. The prior information may consist of a single bit or several bits of information. The well-worn example, "When did you stop beating your wife?" requires considerable prior knowledge on the part of the questioner—that the respondent has a wife, that he has beaten her, and that he has stopped doing so. Unless these facts have been ascertained, the question rests on a pyramid of premises any one or all of which may or may not be true.

Because, as we have pointed out, all questions to some extent contain premises, the significance of this component depends upon whether the premise is informed or uninformed. Again, we can say that, in general, the better informed the premise, the greater the probability that it will be valid. When writers on interviewing proscribe the leading question, it is the uninformed premise that is the basis of their concern, not the one that is informed.

A question containing a premise may be either open or closed. It is reasonable to postulate that, if the premise is incorrect, it is easier for a respondent to correct an open than a closed premise question, since an open question invites a response of more than a few words and prescribes less structure to the response than does a closed question. For example, the open question "Tell me what you did during your Thanksgiving vacation?" embodies the premise that everyone has a vacation at Thanksgiving. If the respondent worked and did not get a vacation and is not fearful or embarrassed about this fact, he has little difficulty in responding, "I was working over Thanksgiving," and can then go on to tell what he did. But, if the question had been closed ("Did you visit your relatives during your Thanksgiving vacation?"), the answer "no" is correct but misleading unless the respondent goes on to say, "I didn't because I didn't have a vacation at Thanksgiving; I was working." He may, however, be reluctant to do this because it involves correcting incorrect assumptions of the interviewer and he may feel embarrassed to do so. He may well find it easier to give an honest but incomplete short response.

One general class of premises warrants especial attention: a *closed alternative* question in which only some of all possible responses are presented. If, for example, after an election in which the choices for the voter were Democrat, Republican, independent, and a write-in vote, the question to an eligible voter is, "Did you vote Democratic or Republican?" the respondent can truthfully answer the question as stated only if he voted for one of these two parties. If he did not vote, voted for the independent, or cast a write-in vote, the premise in the question is incorrect, and he cannot accurately report his behavior by using the answers offered him. The limitation of alternatives in the question can sometimes be identified on grounds of general knowledge alone. For example, "Are you married or single?" leaves out the possibilities that the respondent is widowed, divorced, or living in a common-law marriage. For many questions, however, such as the voting example above, the sufficiency of the alternative responses provided cannot be determined on the basis of general knowledge but requires knowledge of the specific situation. In such cases, unless he is informed, the interviewer may easily introduce an incorrect premise. Again, it should be noted that the delimited alternative premise causes difficulty only for those respondents who cannot use the alternatives suggested.

Combinations of Expectations and Premises

The possible combinations of expectations and premises are shown in Table 4. The least likely of these to occur is an uninformed premise together with an informed expectation—for example, if the interviewer knows that the respondent's favorite color is red but has no information on whether the respondent owns a bicycle, and nevertheless asks, "Your bike is red, isn't it?" Unless the interviewer gets carried away in trying to determine how widely the respondent's favorite color is reflected in his possessions, he would probably first determine what possessions the respondent has and then determine their color.

On the basis of our examination thus far, we can make some estimate of the probabilities with which various combinations of

TABLE 4. *Combinations of Expectations and Premises and the Probability That Question Form Influences Response*

	INFORMED PREMISE	UNINFORMED PREMISE
Informed weak expectation	1[3]	3
Informed strong expectation	1	3
Uninformed weak expectation	2	4
Uninformed strong expectation	3	5
Nonexpectation	1	3

expectations and premises influence the responses. It appears reasonable to postulate that the least possibility of distortion or misunderstanding is likely to derive from the combination of a nonexpectation with an informed premise or of an informed premise with an informed expectation, whereas the greatest possibility is likely to derive from questions that combine an uninformed premise with an uninformed expectation. The remaining combinations are likely to be intermediate in their possible distorting effect. We shall examine these effects more carefully in subsequent discussion, but at this point it seems clear that the indiscriminate grouping of all types of expectations and premises under the one heading of "leading" is an oversimplification.

Legal Testimony and the Use of Leading Questions

The literature on leading questions has been so heavily influenced by jurists' experience with legal testimony that a brief review of some of the legal literature is warranted. Wigmore (1940, p. 132), in an authoritative treatise on testimony, offers the following

---

[3] The numbers are an estimate of the probability that different combinations of expectations and assumptions have distorting effects. 1 = least probability of question influencing response; 5 = greatest probability.

definition of the leading question: "A question which suggests the specific answer desired [by the questioner]." This is very similar to the definition we have given of an expectation.

Wigmore is well aware of uninformed premises, as is shown in the following citation (1940, p. 128, sec. 71):

> 1863, Bell, C. J. . . . [A question is leading] where the question assumes any fact which is in controversy so that the answer may really or apparently admit that fact. Such are the forked questions habitually put by some counsel if unchecked as "What was the plaintiff doing when the defendant struck him?" The controversy being whether the defendant did strike. A dull or a forward witness may answer the first part of the question and neglect the last.

The uninformed premise is used here as a trick to obtain an admission of the premise without the witness' being aware that he has made an admission.

Jurists' awareness that leading questions may produce false or distorted testimony has led to the establishment of rules in an attempt to avoid distortion in the examination of witnesses. Leading questions are permitted in cross-examination on the basis of the following reasoning (Wigmore, 1940, pp. 130–131, sec. 773):

> The typical situation in which the witness's presumable bias removes all danger of improper suggestions is that of an *opponent's witness under cross-examination.* The purpose of the cross-examination is to discount his testimony and weaken its force. In short, to discredit the direct testimony; thus, not only the presumable bias of the witness for the opponent's cause, but also his sense of reluctance to become the instrument of his own discrediting, deprives him of any inclination to accept the cross-examiner's suggestions unless the truth forces him to. When an opponent's witness proves to be in fact biased in favor of the cross-examiner, the danger of leading question arises and they may be forbidden.

In direct examination, the court, at its discretion, may forbid the use of leading questions on the grounds that the witness is being questioned by someone whom he knows to be friendly and to be trying to help him present his testimony in the most favorable light. In these circumstances, a witness is likely to accept and use cues provided in premises and to agree with expectations. As Wigmore puts it (1940, p. 122), "A most important peculiarity of the interrogational system is that it may be misused by *suggestive questions* to supply a false memory for the witness—that is, to suggest desired answers not in truth based upon a real recollection."

Research into the Effects of Leading Questions

A series of psychological studies provides evidence to support the belief that leading questions produce distorted responses. The nature of these studies and the results are well described by William Stern (1938, pp. 261–262), one of the investigators.

It was one of the most important conclusions from *Aussage* experiments that *leading questions* are capable of exercising a well-nigh fatal power. If the expectant tone of the question is very impressive (e.g. "Don't you recall that the man had a stick in his hand?"), and if the person being questioned does not possess great independence and resistance, it may well happen that the inquisitor packs more of his opinions into the witness through questions than the factual recollections he elicits from him.

In experiments with children and adolescents, using the picture of the farmer's house, a dozen leading questions were interspersed in a lengthy inquiry. The coefficient of suggestibility was on the average 25 per cent, that is, every fourth leading question concerning a nonexistent object was answered incorrectly in the affirmative. The bare form of the question, "Was there not a cupboard in the picture?" "Did not the boy have on a torn jacket?" etc., sufficed to elicit the reply "yes" in many cases.

Many a "yes," to be sure, may not have been spoken in full conviction of the correctness of the statement, but more in order to satisfy the insistent questioner. Conscious lying may occur as well as half believing (perhaps with this motivation: if the person in authority who is asking questions believes that it was thus and so, then it must have been).

But once a "yes" is spoken and a quite specific idea is thereby *fixed*, it is but a short step to complete conviction of correctness. For since one has committed oneself, doubts and reflections are thrust back as far as possible. Finally the suggested idea becomes so fused with total remembrance that it acquires the same certainty as correct ideas. This stabilizing of an effect of suggestion has two important consequences.

(1) In subsequent *Aussagen* about the same factual matter, ideas that were earlier suggested are often spontaneously expressed. The inquisitor, being thus unable to refer their origin to the earlier suggestion,

concludes from the spontaneity of expression that they are especially credible.

(2) The suggested idea becomes the point of departure for *allied questions* that may lead to further falsification of the facts. In the cross-examination on the picture of the peasant's house a twelve-year-old girl had answered *in the affirmative* the suggestive question "Was there not a cupboard in the picture?"

The following questions and answers refer to this illusionary cupboard:

Where was the cupboard? "In the right corner."
What color was it? "Brown."
Did it have one or two doors? "Two."
Could you see what was in it? "Yes, clothes."
What was on top of the cupboard? "A flowerpot."

This conversation could have been continued further at pleasure. The child did not wish to lie outright, but was so given to phantasy and at the same time so suggestible, that she accepted every suggestion of the questioner and provided the necessary substantiating detail.

Whipple (1909, p. 165), another investigator, makes the following summary: "The introduction of leading or suggestive questions very noticeably decreases the accuracy of report for children and, unless the conditions of report are quite favorable, even for adults."

The reported experience of the distorting effects of leading questions in legal testimony and the supporting psychological experiments of Stern and his associates have been important contributing factors to the present widespread proscription of leading questions in research interviewing. But whether the application to research interviewing of conclusions drawn from legal testimony is warranted is a point that requires further examination.

Differences between Research and Legal Interviewing

There are many differences in circumstances and purposes between obtaining legal testimony and interviewing a respondent for research purposes. In courtroom interrogation, the lawyer is identified with either the prosecution or the defense, and his basic purpose is to obtain testimony that will either place the defendant in the most favorable light possible or discredit him. Hence, there is some basis for the belief that he will attempt to influence responses in the direction he desires. By embodying a strong expectation in a question, by emphasizing the prestige and authority of his role, and sometimes by intimidation, he may attempt to influence the response in the desired direction when the witness would have given an undesirable response had a leading question not been used. By the use of a premise, he may attempt to obtain an admission without the witness' awareness that he is making an admission. The purpose of the leading question, then, is to advance the lawyer's case; in order to do this, the question may be deliberately phrased to elicit a distorted or nonvalid response.

This intentional use of the leading question as a device for obtaining a distorted response constituted the basis of the psychological experiments on testimony. Children were asked such questions as "Was there not a cupboard in the picture?" by an interviewer who knew there was no cupboard. The prestige and authority of the interviewer were undoubtedly high, since the interviews were held between an adult and child in a German school early in the twentieth century. In both the courtroom and the school experiment, the witness might have felt he would be punished for contradicting the questioner by not accepting the suggested response.

In the research interview, on the other hand, the central purpose is to collect valid data, not to obtain a desired answer. The interviewer does not deliberately attempt to trick a respondent into the admission of a premise, and he rarely has the prestige and authority over his respondent comparable to that of a lawyer over a witness. Moreover, he has no way of enforcing cooperation from a respondent. Under these conditions, a respondent may well feel more at liberty not to accept an expectation if it is other than what he would have answered had the question not contained an expectation. He may also feel freer to point out that a premise is incorrect.

A Study of the Use and Effect of Leading Questions in Research Interviewing

Because of these differences between legal testimony and the research interview, and because recent writers have not presented good evidence to support their proscription of the leading question,

Richardson (1960) and Dohrenwend undertook an empirical study to examine the uses and effects of the leading question in research interviewing.

To accomplish these purposes, it was necessary to devise a situation in which the respondents' answers could be checked for distortion against independent and valid sources. In order to meet this requirement, respondents participated in a situation in which verbal behavior was tape-recorded, and photographic and written records were made of the physical setting and of the spatial arrangement, appearance, and manner of the participants. The subjects who participated in the event recorded did not know that they would subsequently be interviewed about it.

In the interviews, which took place a week after the event, the interviewers were instructed to reconstruct both what happened and how people felt in the event in which the respondent had participated. None of the interviewers knew the respondents before the interview or had any prior knowledge of what happened in the event they were asked to reconstruct. The interviews were neither schedule nor standardized. Each interview was tape-recorded.

Three sets of interviews were analyzed. One set of seven interviews, called "experienced," was conducted by professional field workers who had received their training at a number of universities and who were judged competent by their supervisors. The second set, called "trained," consisted of eleven interviews conducted by students who had completed four months of laboratory-type exercises, discussions, and supervised field experience. The third set, called "untrained," consisted of twenty-nine interviews conducted by students without prior training or experience in interviewing.

The following operational definition was used, because it covered many of the meanings ascribed to the leading question in the literature on interviewing and because it was formulated before we had evolved the concepts of expectation and premise (Richardson, 1960): "A leading question is one which includes, either explicitly or implicitly, the answer which the interviewer expects to receive. This expectation of the answer could not have been obtained solely from what the respondent has already said in the interview."

In terms of the components identified in this chapter, the definition specifies an uninformed expectation. It is uninformed because the interviewers had no prior knowledge either of the respondent or of the event they were to reconstruct, and informed expectations based on information received from the respondent are excluded by the definition used. No distinction was made between strong and weak expectations, because, at the time of the study, we had not yet developed this distinction.[4] It is reasonable to expect, however, that the uninformed expectation is more likely to lead to distortion than the informed expectation.

Because leading questions are always closed, comparisons were made between leading and nonleading closed questions only. Questions were independently coded by two persons, and satisfactory reliability was obtained. Questions were coded independent of responses.

When the responses were compared with the detailed record of the event in which respondents participated, about half of the objective statements could be checked for validity, the remainder being difficult to judge because they involved either generalization or interpretation. Subjective statements were evaluated, wherever possible, as consistent or inconsistent with what one would infer about the participants' feelings during the event on the basis of their behavior. Unfortunately, the number of subjective statements that could be checked in this way was too small to provide a separate analysis of the effects of subjective leading questions.

The experiment tested two widely held assumptions: (1) that competent interviewers avoid using the leading question and (2) that leading questions elicit more distortion in responses than do nonleading questions. We shall examine the findings on each of these points separately.

(1) *Competent interviewers avoid the use of leading questions (i.e., uninformed expectations).*

The extent to which interviewers with different degrees of training used leading questions is shown in Table 5. One-third of all questions asked by experienced interviewers were leading, as were more than one-third asked by the trained interviewers. This result

---

[4] For the same reason, premises and their effects were not investigated.

TABLE 5. *Frequency of Use of Leading and Nonleading Questions*

	EXPERIENCED INTERVIEWERS	TRAINED INTERVIEWERS
	Per cent	Per cent
Nonleading closed question	67	59
Leading closed questions	33	41
Total number	405	347

is very different from what the assumption would lead us to expect. Although one might suspect that the large number of leading questions may have derived from very high use by one or two of the interviewers, the use of leading questions ranged from 22 to 40 per cent among the experienced interviewers and from 21 to 69 per cent among the trained interviewers. In the interview record of even the minimum user of leading questions, one-fifth of all closed questions were leading.

To check whether the more competent interviewers used leading questions less, as might be expected from the first assumption, the trained interviewers were ranked on their skill in interviewing by their supervisors, who had worked closely with them during training. (These rankings were made without regard to the experimental interviews.) The rank correlation between frequency of use of leading questions and competence in interviewing is $r = .14$, which is insignificant.

We have, then, the unexpected finding that the experienced and trained interviewers do in fact make considerable use of leading questions, despite the proscription in the interviewing literature—which was well known to them. We also found no relationship between use of leading questions and the over-all competence of the interviewer.

(2) *Leading questions (uninformed expectations) elicit more distorted responses than nonleading questions.*

Responses were first classified according to whether they contained one or more distortions or no distortions. Each of these two groups of responses was then classified on the basis of its association with leading or nonleading questions. Because the results obtained for the trained and untrained sets of interviews were almost identical, they are combined in Table 6.[5] The results show that responses to leading questions contain no more distortions than responses to nonleading questions. This provides no support for the assumption.

TABLE 6. *The Relation of Leading and Nonleading Questions to Responses Which Do and Do Not Contain Distorted Information*

STUDENT AND UNTRAINED SETS OF INTERVIEWS	NONLEADING CLOSED QUESTIONS	LEADING CLOSED QUESTIONS
	Per cent	Per cent
Response contains distorted information	17	11
Response contains no distorted information	83	89
Total number	771	538

A more rigorous test can be made by eliminating responses which are in part correct and in part distorted. When those responses which contain *only* distortions and *only* correct answers were cross-tabulated with leading and nonleading questions, the results of the trained and untrained sets of interviews were again found to be almost identical. They are combined in Table 7. These findings, too, provide no support for the assumption that leading questions elicit more distorted responses than nonleading questions.

These results clearly require cross-validation in both similar and different sets of interviewing circumstances and conditions before it is known how widely they may be generalized. They are, however, so strikingly at odds with the widely expressed proscription

[5] The experienced interview responses were not analyzed for their accuracy because of the magnitude of the undertaking. Although the use of leading questions may be influenced by training and experience, the effects of different components of questions on responses should be independent of training. This assumption is necessary for the formulation and testing of rules about the effects of components of questions on responses.

TABLE 7. *The Relation of Leading and Nonleading Questions to Responses Which Are Only Correct or Only Distorted (Trained and Untrained Sets of Interviews Combined)*

	NONLEADING PROBES	LEADING PROBES
	Per cent	Per cent
Response contains only distorted information	11	9
Response contains only correct information	89	91
Total number	276	181

against the use of the leading question that they suggest the need for re-examining the use and possible effects of the leading question. It is possible that the general proscription against leading questions has prevented interviewers from considering whether leading questions may have some influence in increasing the desired properties of response outlined in Chapter 5. If leading questions have no positive value, it is difficult to explain why they were used so frequently by trained and experienced interviewers in the study by Richardson (1960).

A Reappraisal of the Use of the Leading Question and Its Effects

In order to consider more fully the use and possible effects of leading questions, we shall discuss the two components—expectations and premises—separately because their effects may be somewhat different.

THE INFLUENCE OF EXPECTATIONS ON RESPONSES

Although the generally anticipated effect of expectations—that they will distort the response—did not occur in the Richardson study, let us attempt to specify the conditions under which a question containing an expectation is more or less likely to cause a respondent to give an answer different from the one he would have given had the same question not embodied an expectation.

If the answer suggested in the expectation is the one which the respondent would have given if the expectation had not been included, the expectation, whether strong or weak, has no effect. In practice, of course, the interviewer can never know in advance the answer that the respondent will give to a question. If, in fact, the interviewer is so well informed that he can predict the answer with a very high probability of success, one may ask why he needs to ask the question at all. Usually, questions are asked in research interviews because the interviewer is not sure of the answer and wants to obtain new information.

The contention that leading questions cause distortion is based upon the assumption that the respondent, by going along with the answer suggested to him, will make a response he would not have made had the question not contained an expectation. But there is no reason to believe that a person will usually agree with a suggested answer if it is *not* the one he would have given. Such acquiescence is likely to occur only in the following sets of circumstances:

1. The respondent may be afraid of disagreeing with the answer the interviewer suggests. He may be afraid that he will be punished if he disagrees, or disagreement may cause him embarrassment—if, for example, the interviewer asks, "You own two cars, don't you?" and the respondent feels that he should own two cars, because all his friends and neighbors do, yet he cannot afford to.

2. The respondent may be eager to please the interviewer and therefore may give him the answer he indicates is expected, even if it is incorrect.

3. If the respondent is bored, uninterested in the subject matter, or impatient to finish the interview, he may agree with expectations even if they are incorrect. Disagreement takes more time and effort because it requires explanations. In these circumstances, a respondent is likely to agree with a *slight* distortion, feeling that

the degree of correction is not worth bothering with. If, on the other hand, the expectation contains a *major* distortion, the respondent who is reasonably conscientious may take time and trouble to correct it.

In the courtroom examination of witnesses, and probably in the experiments on legal testimony, conditions of fear and a wish to please are likely to hold. In the study we have reported, none of the three conditions above prevailed. How often they do prevail in research interviewing we do not know, but we would judge not very often.

So far we have assumed that the interviewer will use what prior information he possesses to predict the answer the respondent would have given had no expectation been included in the question. There may be circumstances, however, in which the interviewer deliberately suggests the answer that he predicts the respondent would *not* have given. This, as we have pointed out, sometimes occurs in legal testimony when the lawyer, in his attempt to make a point or to discredit a witness, seeks a particular response. This was not done in the study we have reported. In research interviewing, as we shall note (p. 196), there may be some conditions under which the interviewer may deliberately use an expectation suggesting the answer that he predicts the respondent would not give, but this will occur only rarely.

From this discussion, then, we can conclude that an expectation can introduce a distortion only if the interviewer's suggestion is not in accord with what the respondent would have answered without the expectation *and* if the respondent agrees with the distortion introduced by the expectation. This combination did not emerge in the study we have reported, and it is likely to occur in research interviewing only if the interviewer is poorly informed and if the respondent is fearful, eager to please, or bored. Thus, it appears that the fear of distortion attributable to the leading question has been exaggerated for research interviews. Yet, even if they introduce distortions only rarely, there is still merit in proscribing the use of leading questions unless we can show that expectations have some positive value.

So far we have examined the question of whether an expectation may result in a response different from the one that would have been given had the question not contained an expectation. A separate and perhaps more important question is the extent to which the introduction of an expectation influences the validity of the response. Writers who have warned against the use of leading questions have presumably based their warning on the assumption that the response would have been more valid had an expectation not been used. But we may well ask whether there are circumstances in which the response to a nonexpectation would have been invalid, whereas the addition of an expectation in the same question would increase the validity of response. If, in certain circumstances, expectations increase validity, then they serve a useful function.

Generally speaking, a respondent is likely to make an invalid response to questions about thoughts, values, and behavior that may be disparaging or incriminating to himself or to others whom he wishes to protect. Invalid responses may also be made in an attempt to discourage further questioning in areas about which the respondent feels embarrassed. To understand the effects of expectations used in such circumstances, let us note how the expectation gives the respondent added information about the interviewer. An expectation that suggests the *valid* answer (though not necessarily the answer the respondent might have given to a nonexpectation) indicates that the interviewer is either a shrewd or lucky guesser or is knowledgeable about the subject matter of the question. Furthermore, if the interviewer suggests an embarrassing, incriminating, or taboo answer with calmness, acceptance, and confidence, he indicates that he will not be critical of or shocked by responses that admit to deviant or unsanctioned attitudes or behavior.

If the interviewer correctly predicts the valid response to several questions, the impression of his being knowledgeable is increased. The interviewer conveys this information, of course, only if he anticipates the valid response correctly, but, even if one or two questions suggest responses that would be valid for most people with the characteristics of the respondent but for some reason are not valid for the particular respondent, the respondent will generally appreciate that the suggestion is a reasonable one and reflects a high level of prior knowledge. This impression is strengthened if the expectations occur early in the interview and could not reasonably have been derived from information the respondent has given to the interviewer. On the other hand, the interviewer whose expectations are repeatedly incorrect, especially if they are very wide of the mark, indicates to the respondent that he is relatively ignorant about the subject of the question. The interviewer who is unfamiliar with a subject may reinforce this impression by manifesting embarrassment and lack of confidence.

It is reasonable to believe that respondents are more likely to give valid answers to interviewers whom they regard as knowledgeable, competent, and at home in the subject matter of the interview than to ignorant, embarrassed interviewers—in part because respondents recognize that the competent interviewer can more readily detect falsehoods. Moreover, if the expectation suggests the valid answer, the respondent has only to answer "yes," whereas, if he disagrees, he may well have to give reasons for the disagreement and begin elaborating a falsehood. This may be difficult to do convincingly to a knowledgeable interviewer.

The better informed the interviewer, the more likely it is that he may increase the validity of response under the conditions we have described. Provided the response he suggests is valid, the interviewer may strengthen the effect by using strong rather than weak expectations. He may also use expectations where he is virtually certain of the valid answer in order to impress the respondent with his knowledge rather than to obtain new information.

THE INFLUENCE OF PREMISES ON RESPONSES

It is possible that the condemnation of the leading question derives more from the effects of premises than from the effects of expectations. As we have pointed out, every question contains some sort of premise. Provided the premise is correct, its use can save a great deal of time because it enables the interviewer to build on what he knows and to focus on obtaining new information.

As with the expectation, the better informed the interviewer, the greater the likelihood that his premise will be correct. If the interviewer is uninformed, there is little or no value in his using a premise based on speculation or inadequate information, and he may avoid ambiguity and misunderstanding by checking whether the premise is valid for the respondent. Instead of asking a married older man he has just met, "Have your children left school yet?" it is wiser to first ask whether he has children rather than assume their existence as a premise for the question.

In research interviewing, most incorrect premises occur because the interviewer assumes incorrectly that he is well informed. Although the tactic of obtaining an admission of an incorrect premise without the respondent's being aware he has made an admission may be used deliberately in obtaining legal testimony (see p. 179), this tactic serves no purpose in research interviewing, where the purpose is to obtain valid responses, if for no other reason than the ambiguity and difficulty of interpreting the response.

The use of informed premises may have real value in increasing validity under circumstances we have already described in connection with the expectation. When the respondent is reluctant to divulge information about himself or others, the interviewer may use premises as well as expectations to convey his prior knowledge of the subject and his willingness to discuss it openly and without embarrassment. It is this use of premises that Kinsey and his colleagues (1948, pp. 53–54) advocate in an often misunderstood passage.

> The interviewer should not make it easy for a subject to deny his participation in any form of sexual activity. It is too easy to say no if he is simply asked whether he has ever engaged in a particular activity. . . . Consequently we always begin by asking *when* they first engaged in such activity . . . and since it becomes apparent from the form of our question that we would not be surprised if he had had such experience, there seems to be less reason for denying it. It might be thought that this approach would bias the answer, but there is no indication that we get false admissions of participation in forms of sexual behavior in which the subject was not actually involved.

Because the distinction generally has not been made between the effect of the leading question in producing a response different from the one that would have been given had the question not been leading and its effect on the validity of response, there has been considerable confusion in critical discussions of Kinsey's statement. Kinsey's statement can be rephrased as follows: if the premise of participation in any form of sexual activity had *not* been used, less valid responses would have been obtained than if it had been used. The use of premises under the conditions described by Kinsey may simultaneously bias the response and increase validity.

When the interviewer wishes to maximize the information he conveys about himself and about the knowledge he possesses, he may combine one or even several premises with a strong expectation. Such a procedure, however, may well backfire unless he is very sure of his ground.

IDENTIFICATION OF EXTREME OPINIONS

Another positive function of leading questions has been suggested by Litwak (1956, p. 185), who points out that a question which tends to push respondents toward a particular response can be used to identify those with extreme opinions because of their resistance to this push. For such a purpose, the deliberate use of an expectation that gives the appearance of being uninformed seems appropriate; in fact, in this situation the nonexpectation would fail to distinguish extreme from moderate opinions in a given direction. For example, to separate respondents into pro- and anti-union groups, one might ask, "On the whole, do you think labor unions do a good job or not?" If, however, one were interested in identifying strongly anti-union respondents, more valid data could be obtained by the use of such an expectation as "Don't you think that, on the whole, labor unions do a good job?"

THE EFFECTS OF EXPECTATIONS AND PREMISES ON RESPONDENT PARTICIPATION

As the foregoing discussion indicates, the frequently expressed concern that leading questions may distort responses appears exaggerated. But, even if distortion occurs only occasionally, the use of leading questions seems unjustified. We have identified a set of conditions, however, in which leading questions—or expectations and informed premises, as we prefer to call them—may, in fact, increase validity of response. Although these conditions did not occur in the study we cited and do not occur frequently in research interviewing, experienced interviewers, both in the study we reported and in field situations, nevertheless frequently use leading questions. To further explore this phenomenon, we need to examine some of the other desired response qualities described in Chapter 5, setting aside, for the time being, the concern with bias and distortion that has dominated previous discussions of the leading question.

To learn more about how expectations are perceived by the respondent, Richardson and Dohrenwend conducted interviews in which, unannounced to the respondent, expectations were used frequently or omitted completely. When recordings of the interviews were later played back to them, the respondents reported that questions which contained expectations gave the impression of interest, friendliness, and encouragement *provided that the answers suggested in the expectation were generally the answers they were intending to give.* These feelings probably stem from the fact that the leading question plays an important part in social conversation. As Fear (1958, p. 84) has pointed out, "A normal conversation between two people consists principally of comments that anticipate a response." And, as most of us recognize from everyday experience, two people who know each other well very often can correctly predict each other's responses.

Often, however, the interviewer will have little or no advance knowledge about either the respondent or the general subject matter of the interview or both. In these circumstances, he can become informed only through what he learns directly from the respondent. But if, later in the interview, he uses informed expectations, these demonstrate to the respondent the care and attention with which he has listened. That the effect impresses respondents, we have already reported. It appears, then, that the use of informed expectations and premises has positive value in increasing the level of respondent participation. On the other hand, incorrect premises, and expectations which incorrectly anticipate the response of the respondent, may cause irritation and reduce participation.

THE INFLUENCE OF EXPECTATIONS AND PREMISES ON UNANTICIPATED RESPONSES

One of the values of the nonschedule exploratory interview is that the respondent may be encouraged to volunteer information beyond that requested by the interviewer. This is particularly valuable when the interviewer is still unfamiliar with the range of topics and is still trying to identify topic areas that are productive. In examining the effects of expectations used by experienced and inexperienced interviewers (see p. 185), Dohrenwend and Richardson (1964) found that in thirty-one of the forty interviews volunteered information was more frequently elicited by questions that embodied expectations than by those that did not.

Traditionally, it has been recommended that unanticipated responses should be obtained by the use of nondirective open questions. Empirical data show, however, that the use of such questions also causes respondents to introduce matters that are not relevant to the research topic. Expectations, by contrast, do not produce a large number of digressions from the topic of the interview—i.e., the volunteered information was usually relevant.

The findings that expectations are more likely to produce unanticipated responses than questions not using expectations and that irrelevant digressions were not introduced suggest a useful new way of obtaining unanticipated responses. The generalizability of these findings and the range of interviewing conditions under which they may hold require further investigation. It does seem profitable at this point, however, to consider the mechanisms whereby this unexpected result may have been obtained.

We postulate that there are two kinds of expectation or premise that will encourage unanticipated responses and one kind that will not. One kind of expectation that encourages unanticipated responses is the correct expectation, which creates the impression that the interviewer is paying close attention and understands what is being said. Its effect is to encourage the respondent to develop his ideas freely without fear of losing the attention or understanding of the interviewer and to feel free to go beyond the questions asked.

Another kind of expectation or premise that may elicit unanticipated information is suggested by results reported by Beezer (1956, p. 13), who found, in interviews with East German refugees, that leading questions which were deliberately naïve and unambiguously incorrect yielded more information than nonleading questions. For example, when respondents were asked, "I understand you don't have to pay very much for food in the East Zone because it is rationed," most of them tried to correct and enlighten the interviewer about general conditions in East Germany. Since such statements place the respondent in the position of expert vis-à-vis the "ignorant" interviewer, they seem to encourage the respondent to decide for himself what he should talk about. In this way, expectations which are unambiguously incorrect may also induce the respondent to introduce topics not mentioned by the apparently uninformed or confused interviewer, as in the following excerpt from a recorded interview:

Q: Mrs. C was against typing and shorthand being taught at school?
A: No, that was Mrs. K. Mrs. K is a graduate of Smith, I believe. She said you could get science in girls' schools. Mrs. C went to Cornell. I graduated from McGill. Mrs. M went to school out West. I don't know which school.

The respondent here reacts to the interviewer's error of identification by providing unrequested information which helps the interviewer distinguish the four women being discussed. Clearly, the use of a deliberately distorted premise or expectation as a way of obtaining unanticipated responses must be used sparingly, or the interviewer may create an impression of naïveté and foolishness and thus risk reducing participation.

The type of expectation or premise that does not encourage unanticipated responses is the one that is neither completely correct nor completely incorrect. Introspective reports by respondents suggest that slightly distorted or ambiguous premises and expectations imply inattention or lack of comprehension on the interviewer's part. In this case, correction of the interviewer's misconception may seem petty and difficult. Thus, such questions appear not only to fail to stimulate the respondents to talk confidently and freely but also may produce invalid responses through the respondent's failure to correct the interviewer. Thus, in the following excerpt, it is not clear whether the suggestion finally accepted by the respondent really expresses his perception:

A: The father seemed dominated by the mother . . . the mother was good. She took care of the child.
Q: She was the stronger character, is that right, would you say that?
A: Yes and no.
Q: Yes and no?
A: Well it all depends on how you mean strong and dominant, but you couldn't say she was a strong person after what she had done.
Q: I was thinking about the fact that they ended up with this kind of a [spoiled] child. Dominant was the word I was thinking of, but overprotecting explains.
A: That's right.

Here it is impossible to know whether "dominant" and "overprotecting" really express the respondent's objection to the term "stronger" or simply represent acquiescence to a suggestion seen as not being too far from the truth. Premises and expectations which are ambiguous seem not only to inhibit unanticipated responses but also to lead to distortion of response.

We suggest, therefore, that, used with proper precautions, expectations and premises may provide a useful tool for eliciting volunteered information. Provided that the interviewer has some background in the research problem on which he is working, he should be able to formulate expectations and premises which he is reasonably sure are either correct or naïvely and unambiguously incorrect. With such formulations, the danger of introducing errors is probably minimized. As a positive gain, the interviewer may find that such questions encourage respondents to volunteer information beyond that requested, without producing a large number of digressions from the interview topic.

8

ENCOURAGEMENTS, SILENCES, GUGGLES, AND INTERRUPTIONS

As the tape recording of almost any interview will clearly demonstrate, the interviewer's utterances are not confined to the posing of questions. He uses also a variety of other vocalizations—as well as periods of silence—which, although they do not constitute questions, can considerably affect the responses.

Encouragements

Encouragements are brief sounds and phrases—e.g., "Uh-huh," "I see," "That's interesting," "Good," and "Yes, I understand"—which indicate the interviewer's attentiveness to, and interest in, what the respondent is saying. Encouragements may be introduced at any time—while the respondent is speaking or during pauses.

Encouragements appear to serve several purposes. They convey to the respondent that the interviewer comprehends, is interested, and is listening carefully. They indicate that the interviewer would like him to continue speaking on the same topic. In this use, the encouragement has a function very similar to that of an extension (see p. 161), i.e., it encourages the respondent to "tell more" without specifying the scope or direction of the further response. If the encouragement is used only when the interviewer wishes the respondent to continue talking, the absence of encouragements at other responses may have an inhibiting effect.

Two types of evidence support the postulated effect of encouragement in lengthening responses. The first, derived from our experience in listening to large numbers of tape-recorded interviews, is strong but impressionistic and hence difficult to test quantitatively. The second type of evidence stems from a considerable number of psychological experiments. In a review of studies of the effects of such encouragements as "Uh-uh," "Good," nodding the head, and smiling, Krasner (1958) reports thirty positive results and only eight negative results.[1] Most of these results were obtained in studies in which the questions asked of the respondents were either minimized or eliminated by means of comprehensive initial instructions to the respondent; in this manner, verbal prescriptions during the response period were largely controlled. Following initial instructions, the respondent was allowed to speak for a time without encouragement in order to determine the initial level of the response under study; then, in a subsequent period, all or most of the responses of the chosen kind were followed by encouragements. Positive results were indicated when the rate of the chosen response was higher during the second than during the initial period. To cite an example, Quay (1959) demonstrated that reports of "family" or "nonfamily" childhood memories could be selectively increased by encouragement with a flat "Uh-huh."

Richardson (Richardson, Hastorf, & Dornbusch, 1964) has had extensive experience with the use of encouragements in interviewing children. The purpose of the interviews was to get ten- and eleven-year-old children to respond freely and fully to two standard questions: "Tell me about ——— (some child well known to the respondent)" and "Tell me about yourself." The responses were analyzed to determine the kinds of words and phrases that the children used in their characterizations. After the standard

[1] Results concerning the effects of such mechanical reinforcements as buzzers are reviewed by Krasner but have been excluded from this discussion since they do not constitute the kind of reinforcement that an interviewer might be expected to use.

initial question, no further questions could be asked, since these would have suggested categories of description—e.g., "Do you *like* Susan?" or "What sort of things does Johnny *do*?" To encourage further responses after a child had stopped talking, interviewers were instructed to use a standard set of encouragements in a pre-scribed order—e.g., "You're doing fine." Such encouragements had a significant effect in lengthening the children's responses.

Two studies suggest some of the conditions under which en-couragements are ineffective. Salzinger and Pisoni (1960) showed that respondents who received fewer than eight encouragements during a ten-minute period did not appreciably increase their rate of response, whereas those who received eight or more encourage-ments showed significant increase.

In another study which helps to explain the occasional ineffec-tiveness of encouragements (Mandler & Kaplan, 1956), the subject was not interviewed but instead was asked to say words without repeating himself. For the first one hundred words, no encourage-ments were given. During the next two hundred words, encour-agements were given following plural nouns. When interviewed afterward, all subjects reported being aware that the experimenter had been saying "Mm-hmm," and they were asked what they had thought it indicated. On the basis of their responses to this question, the subjects were divided into a positive group, which "thought that the reinforcer had positive aspects, that it meant they were doing all right, that it was encouraging them to go on," and a negative group, which "thought that the reinforcer had negative aspects, that it meant they were going too fast, giving the wrong kinds of words" (Mandler & Kaplan, 1956, p. 582). In effect, the "Mm-hmm" was interpreted as an encouragement by some but not by others, and this difference was reflected in their responses. During the first one hundred words after encouragements had begun, the positive group showed a significant rise in its rate of saying plural nouns, whereas the negative group showed a slight decrease.

Thus, although encouragements are usually effective in con-trolling the subject matter of responses, they have been shown to be ineffective in either of two circumstances: when the respond-ent's initial rate of giving the response to be encouraged is very low and when the respondent interprets the encouragement as an expression of disapproval.

In addition to affecting the length of responses, encouragements may also have an influence on their validity. A study by Hildum and Brown (1956), for example, indicates that encouragement can systematically bias responses. In telephone interviews about a general education program, these investigators used four procedures: (1) the encouragement "Good" after pro-general-education responses, (2) the encouragement "Good" after anti-general-education responses, (3) the encouragement "Uh-hum" after pro responses, and (4) the encouragement "Uh-hum" after anti responses. The encouragement "Good" influenced the direction of responses, whereas the "Uh-hum" did not. The respondents to whom the interviewer said "Good" after pro-general-education opinions gave more opinions in this direction, whereas respondents to whom the interviewer said "Good" after anti-general-education opinions gave more opinions in the anti direction.

Thus, it appears that in using encouragements care must be exercised lest they lead to invalid responses. This danger may be considerable when encouragements are being used to prescribe a particular subject matter. When an interviewer encourages every statement on a given topic, it is quite possible that his encouragements all lean in the same direction on some issue. The results of Hildum and Brown (1956) suggest, however, that, even in this circumstance, the interviewer can avoid influencing the direction of the responses by taking care to use such encouragements as "Uh-hum" rather than such obvious and definite encouragements as "Good." Although systematically biased use of encouragements may influence validity detrimentally, there seems to be no direct way in which encouragements can influence it positively.

Encouragement, possibly supplemented by indications of desired subject areas, may positively influence the extent to which respondents introduce unanticipated but relevant material. In a study by Salzinger (1956), a half-hour interview was divided into three equal periods. In the first period, the respondents were allowed to talk with a minimum of questioning and encouragements from the interviewer. In the second period, they were treated in one of three ways: They were (1) asked questions concerned with affect, (2) given encouragement whenever they made statements about affect, or (3) both asked questions about affect and given encouragement when they made statements about affect. In the third period of the interview, the respondents were again allowed to talk with a minimum of questioning and encouragement, none of which was directly related to affect. All three treatments had the same effect in the second period, increasing the number of statements about affect to about the same extent, but they produced different results in the third period. Those respondents who had been given encouragements but no questions concerning affect said the most about this topic in the third period; those who had only been asked questions about affect in the second period made the fewest statements on this topic in the third period; those who had been both questioned and encouraged ranked second in the number of affect statements they made in the third period.

These results suggest that encouragement can be used to direct the respondent to a general topic, such as affect, while leaving him free to select subtopics. Thus, the interviewer can keep the respondent on topics relevant to the interview without having to assume the entire responsibility for topic selection. Of course, if a respondent does not mention a particular topic spontaneously and the interviewer is forced to direct his attention to it by means of questions, he may also find that the respondent does not persist so long on that topic as he would have if he had mentioned it spontaneously. This conclusion follows from Salzinger's finding that encouragements and affect questions later produced fewer affect statements than encouragements alone.

Although the studies we have cited are valuable in suggesting some of the effects that encouragements may have on various response characteristics, there is need for some caution in applying their findings to any specific interview situation. As we noted in our discussion of openness and closedness, some respondents are as much hindered by a lack of structure as others are hindered by an excess. And the continued use of encouragement may produce distorted or irrelevant responses from the respondent who does not have much to say but feels obliged by the encouragement to "keep on talking."

The foregoing comments also have clear implications for the respondent's level of participation. If the respondent is initially well disposed toward the interviewer and is comfortable with the subject matter of the interview, it seems likely that encouragements will increase his level of participation; but they may not be necessary for this purpose, since participation may already be high. If the respondent feels neutral toward the interviewer and the subject matter, encouragements may increase his level of participation. But, if he feels hostile toward the interviewer or uncomfortable about the subject matter, he may well interpret an "Uh-huh" as a criticism of his response. And, if he cannot respond at length without guidance or if he tends to express himself succinctly, encouragements may make him generally uncomfortable and thus reduce his level of participation.

Fortunately, the interviewer who is sensitive to the possible effects of encouragements can benefit from the feedback he obtains from their use in an interview and, to some extent, can reduce or increase their frequency in the light of their effects on the respondent and his responses.

Silences

Perhaps the most common fear of an inexperienced interviewer in a nonschedule interview is that he will not be able to maintain a continuous flow of verbal interchange. In his anxiety to keep the question–answer process moving, he may perceive any pause or silence as a threat and a danger signal to be disposed of as quickly as possible by introducing another question. Even if the interviewer has asked a question, any hesitation or pause before the respondent answers often leads him to rephrase the same question or to pose a new one. In interviews by beginners, the following sequences are common:

　open question——brief pause——restatement of the question as
　　a closed question
　or
　respondent pauses in the middle of a response——the inter-
　　viewer interjects another question

It is only after some experience that interviewers learn that silences may serve useful purposes.

We define a silence as that period during which the interviewer waits without speaking for the respondent to begin or resume speaking. Two studies indicate that the effects of a silence depend on its length. Gorden (1954), after comparing three-second silences with those lasting ten seconds or longer in interviews about the effects of a tornado on a community, found that shorter silences produced longer responses. Similarly, Saslow and his colleagues (Saslow, Matarazzo, Phillips, & Matarazzo, 1957) found that the introduction of fifteen-second silences into one section of an interview shortened responses in that section.

Gorden (1954, pp. 175–177) found, furthermore, that the longer the silence, the more likely it was to be terminated by the interviewer rather than the respondent. As silences increased from two to nine seconds in duration, the percentage terminated by the interviewer increased regularly from slightly less than 15 per cent to more than 75 per cent and remained above 75 per cent up to fifteen seconds. Silences longer than fifteen seconds were qualitatively different, being associated with some kind of interruption in the interview. The general conclusion that emerges is that a silence, if it is short and is terminated by the respondent, is likely to produce a relatively lengthy response. Otherwise, silence is not an effective means of getting the respondent to talk at length.

Silences that are not too long may lengthen responses for a number of reasons. The respondent may require a short pause to formulate his thoughts before continuing to speak; breaking the silence by another question could inhibit the further response that would otherwise have been forthcoming. In other cases, the respondent may have finished speaking, but he interprets the silence as meaning that the interviewer wants him to continue along the same lines. Finally, the respondent may find the silence uncomfortable and may speak further on the same or a different topic in order to end it.

There is wide variation in the extent to which respondents use and are accustomed to silence in their verbal exchanges. This variation may be related to the respondent's speed of thought and general tempo of social interaction. Our very general impression is that silences during conversation occur more often—and hence are more congenial—to rural than to urban people, but this is only an impression. If the interviewer is sensitive to the function of silences in the conversational style of the social milieu of the respondents, he may, through adapting in the direction of what is congenial to them, increase their participation.

Guggles[2] and Interruptions

Although the encouragement and silence are used principally to increase the length of response, the guggle and the interruption are used by interviewers to shorten or terminate a response.

We became aware of the guggle while listening to large numbers of interviews. It occurs while the respondent is speaking and consists of short, usually staccato sounds made by the interviewer to indicate that he wants to say something. It often consists of "Ah" exclaimed singly, or doubly and triply, but also may be the beginnings of words which are not completed. If the respondent ignores them, guggles often become increasingly frequent and eventually constitute a full interruption. Most interviewers are unaware that they use guggles, and there are wide individual differences among interviewers in the frequency with which they use them. Because the guggle puts the respondent on notice that the interviewer is eager to say something, it may well have the effect of shortening responses.

The interruption is more forceful. It is used at the end of a phrase or sentence in the response (and occasionally even in the middle of a phrase) and consists in the interviewer's beginning to speak even though the respondent apparently intends to continue speaking. Although, occasionally, even an interruption is inadequate to stem the flow of speech of a determined respondent, it generally is effective.

[2] Because we had seen no previous mention of this behavior as we have defined it and knew of no existing word to describe it, we borrowed from Ko-Ko in Gilbert and Sullivan's *Mikado:* "As he squirmed and struggled and gurgled and guggled, / I drew my snickersnee!"

Beyond reducing the length of response, the guggle and inter-ruption may have very different effects depending on the fre-quency of their use, the point in the response at which they are made, and, in the case of the interruption, the purpose for which they are made. If guggles and interruptions are used sparingly, not too early in responses, and with the purpose of clarifying, elaborating, or confirming some point or idea made by the re-spondent, they are not likely to reduce participation. An inter-ruption may even have a beneficial effect if it stimulates the respondent's thinking. On the other hand, frequent and premature guggles, and interruptions which introduce subject matter un-related to what the respondent is saying or has said, may well be interpreted by the respondent as poor listening, rudeness, or lack of interest on the part of the interviewer and, hence, reduce participation.

As long as responses are relevant to the purpose of the interview and are not repetitive, there is little need for the interviewer to guggle or interrupt. Guggles and interruptions may become essen-tial when responses become irrelevant and lengthy. On such occa-sions, the timing of the guggles and the interruptions and the nature of the questions for which the interruption is made will determine their effect on participation.

9

THE CONTENT OF QUESTIONS

In the preceding chapters, we have focused attention on properties that are inherent in questions dealing with any subject matter. In this preoccupation with the formal components, however, we must not overlook the fact that the content as well as the form of the question influences the response. In the present chapter, we shall shift our attention to the content of questions—that is, what the question *asks about* and what it *asks for*.

It is more difficult to develop a useful conceptual system or typology for the content of questions than it is for their formal properties. Perhaps this is why there have been fewer systematic studies of the influence of question content on response. We shall consider some of the ways in which content may be profitably analyzed.

Prescribing the Scope of Response

At the beginning of an interview, the interviewer has in mind the general area or areas of content he wishes to explore. He may formulate a question as broadly as possible in an attempt to encompass the whole area of content he is exploring, or he may use a question that identifies only a very small part of the total area. The scope of the question is indicated by the relation of its content to the full area the interviewer wishes to cover. For example, if his purpose is to obtain a full account of what the respondent did on the preceding day, he may ask a question of broad scope—e.g., "Tell me what you did yesterday."—or a question of narrow scope—"At what time did you wake up?"

On the basis of interviews with respondents who had recently experienced a tornado in their community, Gorden (1954) devised a scheme which indicates how questions can vary in the scope of the response they call for. In Table 8, Gorden ranks the several question types in order of decreasing scope, from very broad to very narrow. The schema shown in the table offers two methods of varying the scope of a question. The first is embodied in the phrase listed in the fourth column; this varies from extreme breadth ("during the general period of the storm") through medium breadth ("before or after a certain point in the storm") to considerable narrowness (in which the response is restricted to a "specific time, place, event, or object"). A second method of varying the scope is shown in the second and third columns, in which such interrogatives as "What happened?" call for broad responses, whereas "Did you see?" calls for a narrower one.

It is noteworthy that the two narrowest of Gorden's questions are closed, whereas the broader questions are open. Although it is possible to ask closed questions about broad topics, such questions tend to be less clear and comprehensible than closed questions about narrow topics. For example, such broad, closed (identification) questions as "Where were you during the general period of the storm?" may confuse the respondent and mislead the interviewer if the respondent had not been in one place throughout the storm, whereas such a narrow closed question as "Where were you at three o'clock?" is likely to be clear. It is our impression that, although closed questions on a broad topic occur, they are rare. Thus, in practice, there are three combinations of procedures for prescribing scope: broad open questions, narrow open questions, and narrow closed questions.

Interviewers have employed different strategies for the sequence in which they use questions of broad or narrow scope. Becker (1954), in a study of Chicago teachers' relations with students from different ethnic and socio-economic groups, began his interviews with questions of broad scope about the nature of the problems the teachers encountered. In subsequent questions, he followed

TABLE 8. *Degrees of Scope*

ABSTRACT CHARACTERISTICS			
DEGREE	ASPECT	LEVEL	SCOPE
1	What	Happened	During the general period of the storm
2	What	Happened	Before or after a certain point in the storm
3	What	Do, see, feel	Before or after a certain point in the storm
4	What	Happened	Specific time, place, event, or object
5	What	Do, see, feel, or think	Specific time, place, event, or object
6	Why[1] or how[2]	Happened, do, see, feel, or think	Specific time, place, event, or object
7	Who, where when, how many	Happened, do, see, feel, or think	Specific time, place, event, or object
8	Did	see, feel, or think Happened, do,	Specific time, place, event, or object

up the implications of these responses with questions of narrower scope about matters on which the teachers would not have elaborated spontaneously—for example, racial differences. In a study of role conflicts experienced by school superintendents, Gross and Mason (1953, p. 200) felt it unwise to assume that the concept of role conflict was familiar to the superintendents. Hence, they first used a series of narrow questions about four cases in such a way as

---

[1] Here "why" denotes cause or purpose.

[2] Here "how" denotes by what means, in what manner, by what avenues, and so forth.

to elicit responses descriptive of role conflict; after these four cases had given the superintendents "a reasonably clear idea of the research frame of reference of the interviewer," questions of broader scope could meaningfully be asked about role conflicts. In summary, Becker moved from broad to narrow scope during the course of the interview, whereas Gross and Mason moved from narrow to broad.

In more general terms, it appears that questions of broad scope may usefully be employed early in the interview if the respondent is familiar with the general area of interest to the interviewer, possesses a frame of reference for thinking about the subject matter which is not too dissimilar from that of the interviewer, and is articulate and able to organize his thoughts. In such a case, an initial question of broad scope may result in a highly meaningful response which covers a good deal of the area planned for the interview. In the exploratory interview, a key respondent may function in this way. The interviewer may then, using respondent antecedents, follow up with questions of narrower scope to capitalize on responses which were suggestive, which only touched on areas important to the interviewer, or which opened up new topic areas which the interviewer had not previously recognized as significant for the study.

On the other hand, if the respondent has difficulty in grasping the interviewer's frame of reference and conception of what areas are to be covered in the interview, or if he has difficulty organizing and expressing his thoughts, the initial use of questions which have narrow scope may be the more profitable strategy to employ. If, in the course of the interview, the respondent finds a topic in which he is interested, questions of broader scope will allow him to express his interest in a way that is meaningful and relevant to him. Depending, then, on the subject matter of the interview and the particular respondent, the sequence of questions of broad and narrow scope may have to be varied, not only in order to obtain the information sought but to fit a style of questioning which the respondent finds comfortable and congenial and which, therefore, increases his interest and participation.

As long as the interview is not fully scheduled, the interviewer may use some discretion in the sequence with which he varies the scope of his questions. In the schedule interview, the sequence must be presented and used in essentially the same way for all respondents. This precludes the possibility of capitalizing on unanticipated responses through following up new ideas and suggestions. In the schedule interview, the scope of questions must generally remain narrow; otherwise, the respondent may so elaborate his responses that the schedule sequence no longer gives the impression of flowing in part from his responses. If his responses go further than the question anticipated, the next schedule question breaks with the response rather than seeming to flow from it. Finally, as a purely practical matter, precoding of response categories can be done more easily for questions of narrow scope than of broad scope.

Some of the other effects of scope on response can better be discussed in connection with various combinations of question content and form. This we shall do in Chapter 11, which deals with the achievement of various effects through combining different components of question form and content.

The Subject Matter of the Question

The subject matter of a question may be classified in terms of a particular study or in more general terms that can be applied to many kinds of interview topics. We shall confine our discussion to two such general classifications—questions which ask for an objective, a subjective, or an indeterminate response and questions in which the content is true or false.

OBJECTIVE, SUBJECTIVE, AND INDETERMINATE QUESTIONS

In training interviewers and in examining the effects of questions on the responses obtained, we have found it useful to distinguish among objective, subjective, and indeterminate questions according to the definitions shown in Table 9.

TABLE 9. *Objective, Subjective, and Indeterminate Questions*

TYPE	DEFINITION	EXAMPLE
Objective question	concerns observable characteristics of persons, places, objects, or events rather than opinions or feelings	What was his name? And when you first got here, what happened? I see, I take it that you knew Ruth before?
Subjective question	concerns opinions or feelings rather than observable characteristics of persons, places, objects, or events	What was it about his personality that you didn't like especially? Did you think that either of them came out of it with a different point of view, or did you think that each girl left with her own point of view reinforced? Did this recorder or your note taking bother them, do you think?
Indeterminate question	specifies neither observable characteristics of persons, places, objects and events nor opinions and feelings	Well, tell me something about this experiment that you just mentioned to me.

In general, the objective and subjective content of questions is independent of the components of question form. The indeterminate question, however, seems necessarily to be open and broad in scope. Richardson and Dohrenwend, in their analysis of nonschedule interviews (see p. 183), found that the subjective questions used by the experienced, trained, and untrained interviewers contained a higher proportion of uninformed expectations than did objective questions, as shown in Table 10. Bearing in mind the positive and negative functions which expectations may serve (see Chapter 7), the interviewer must particularly guard against using uninformed expectations when formulating subjective questions, not only because expectations are more likely to be uninformed with

TABLE 10. *Frequency with Which Subjective and Objective Questions Contain Uninformed Expectations*

	EXPERIENCED (n = 7)		TRAINED (n = 11)		UNTRAINED (n = 29)	
	Obj.	Subj.	Obj.	Subj.	Obj.	Subj.
Per cent of total questions containing uninformed expectations	32%	42%	40%	55%	40%	49%
Total number of questions	314	77	230	92	630	287

subjective than objective responses but also because it is far more difficult to obtain independent checks on the validity of subjective than objective responses.

In nonschedule interviews, neophyte interviewers appear to be unaware of whether the questions they formulate ask for objective, subjective, or indeterminate responses. Their interviews often contain sequences of questions in which the interviewer pursues a line of subjective questions but, as the respondent approaches greater depth in speaking about himself, the interviewer breaks abruptly with his previous line of subjective questioning and begins asking objective questions. Shortly thereafter, the interviewer resumes subjective questioning, and the same sequence is repeated. This pattern of questioning appears to be highly disturbing to the respondents. Reviewing a tape recording of the interview and classifying the content of his questions as objective, subjective, or indeterminate can make the interviewer conscious of his use of objective and subjective questions.

A great deal of the interview literature has been devoted to considerations of how best to obtain depth. Major emphasis in these discussions has focused on the form of questioning to employ—e.g., open or closed, directive or nondirective—and little attention has been given to the question content. In a controlled experiment using nonschedule standardized interviews, Dohrenwend (in press) found that more information was obtained about the respondent's values and feelings, and in their reporting of others' feelings and values, through subjective rather than objective questions. Although this is hardly surprising, the finding does need emphasis in view of the relatively little attention that has been paid to question content. When Dohrenwend further subdivided subjective questions into open and closed questions, more information was obtained about the respondent's feelings and values through closed than through open questions. In answering objective questions, the respondent may, of course, include some subjective information about himself. In the experiment, this was found to occur more often after objective open than objective closed questions.

"YOUR BAIT OF FALSEHOOD TAKES THIS CARP OF TRUTH"

At first sight, it would appear absurd that the interviewer should deliberately introduce misinformation into his questions when he is seeking the response qualities we have described in Chapter 5. When, however, we examined the use of expectations and premises (Chapter 7), we found that deliberate distortion of content may improve certain response qualities if the respondent is not afraid of disagreeing with the interviewer, is not over-eager to please the interviewer, has some interest in the topics being discussed, and is not impatient to finish the interview. Given these conditions, we concluded that: (1) In response to expectations, premises, and summaries, the respondent is more likely to correct a major than a minor distortion in the question presented by the interviewer. (2) The deliberate use of questions which push respondents toward a particular response may identify respondents with extreme opinions because they will resist the push. (3) The deliberate ascription of unsanctioned or deviant behavior to the respondent can show him that the interviewer is familiar with and not shocked by such behavior and, thus, make it easier for the respondent to admit to such behavior. (4) Expectations and assumptions which include deliberate distortion can obtain relevant and unanticipated responses if the respondent feels that he should "straighten out" the interviewer.

Although these points were made in connection with expectations and assumptions, they are applicable to any information the interviewer provides in the interview, whether or not it is in the form of a question. We can best illustrate the possible use of dis-

torted content in the interview by presenting the advice that
Polonius gives to his servant, Reynaldo, before sending him to
Paris to inquire about his son, Laertes, who is a student there
(*Hamlet*, Act II, Scene 1).

POLONIUS. You shall do marvelous wisely, good Reynaldo,
    Before you visit him, to make inquire
    Of his behavior.
REYNALDO.   My lord, I did intend it.
POLONIUS. Marry, well said, very well said. Look you, sir,
    Inquire me first what Danskers are in Paris,
    And how, and who, what means, and where they keep,
    What company, at what expense, and finding
    By this encompassment and drift of question
    That they do know my son, come you more nearer
    Than your particular demands will touch it.
    Take you, as 'twere, some distant knowledge of him,
    As thus, "I know his father and his friends,
    And in part him." Do you mark this, Reynaldo?
REYNALDO. Aye, very well, my lord.
POLONIUS. "And in part him, but," you may say, "not well.
    But if 't be he I mean, he's very wild,
    Addicted so and so"—and there put on him
    What forgeries you please. Marry, none so rank
    As may dishonor him, take heed of that,
    But, sir, such wanton, wild, and usual slips
    As are companions noted and most known
    To youth and liberty.
REYNALDO.   As gaming, my lord.
POLONIUS. Aye, or drinking, fencing, swearing, quarreling,
    Drabbing. You may go so far.
REYNALDO. My lord, that would dishonor him.
POLONIUS. Faith, no, as you may season it in the charge.
    You must not put another scandal on him,
    That he is open to incontinency.
    That's not my meaning. But breathe his faults so quaintly
    That they may seem the taints of liberty,
    The flash and outbreak of a fiery mind,
    A savageness in unreclaimèd blood,
    Of general assault.
REYNALDO.   But, my good lord——
POLONIUS. Wherefore should you do this?
REYNALDO.   Aye, my lord,
    I would know that.

POLONIUS.   Marry, sir, here's my drift,
And I believe it is a fetch of warrant.
You laying these slight sullies on my son,
As 'twere a thing a little soiled i' the working,
Mark you,
Your party in converse, him you would sound,
Having ever seen in the prenominate crimes
The youth you breathe of guilty, be assured
He closes with you in this consequence—
"Good sir," or so, or "friend," or "gentleman,"
According to the phrase or the addition
Of man and country.

REYNALDO.   Very good, my lord.

POLONIUS. And then, sir, does he this—he does—
What was I about to say? By the mass, I was about
to say something. Where did I leave?

REYNALDO. At "closes in the consequence," at "friend or so," and
    "gentleman."

POLONIUS. At "closes in the consequence," aye, marry,
He closes with you thus: "I know the gentleman.
I saw him yesterday, or t'other day,
Or then, or then, with such, or such, and, as you say,
There was a' gaming, there o'ertook in 's rouse,
There falling out at tennis." Or perchance,
"I saw him enter such a house of sale,"
Videlicet, a brothel, or so forth.
See you now,
Your bait of falsehood takes this carp of truth.
And thus do we of wisdom and of reach,
With windlasses and with assays of bias,
By indirections find directions out.
So, by my former lecture and advice,
Shall you my son. You have me, have you not?

REYNALDO. My lord, I have.

POLONIUS.   God be wi' ye, fare ye well.

REYNALDO. Good my lord!

POLONIUS. Observe his inclination in yourself.

REYNALDO. I shall, my lord.

Polonius wishes to learn whether his son engages in the kind of behavior that, although officially disapproved and illicit, is recognized as common among young men. The steps he orders Reynaldo to take in his inquiry are: (1) Find out whether the respondent knows Laertes, but find this out indirectly, without using Laertes' name. (2) Pretend to have distant knowledge of Laertes or of someone like him. (3) Make up stories about him which include the kinds of crimes and wanton behavior common to youth, but give the impression that these are natural and tolerable in a young man at liberty. (4) None of these inventions should be so gross as to dishonor Laertes.

Polonius is confident that the respondents will then tell Reynaldo the truth about Laertes, covering the kinds of topic that Reynaldo has opened up, since Reynaldo's willingness to speak of disapproved or illicit behavior makes it easier for his respondents to speak freely, knowing that their listener will not be shocked. Polonius' line of reasoning is almost identical to Kinsey's, which we quoted on page 192. Unlike Kinsey, however, Polonius adds more "bait of falsehood" by giving considerable additional information beyond questioning and thereby creating the impression of a social conversation and exchange of information rather than a question–answer process.

IO

OTHER FACTORS IN THE QUESTION–ANSWER PROCESS

Although the formulation of questions is central to the interview process, several additional factors influence response quality—e.g., the pace at which the interviewer moves the interview, how transitions are made from one topic to another, the level of discourse employed by the interviewer, his inflection, and his accent. Taken together with the kinds of questions used, these may be thought of as comprising the interviewer's over-all verbal style. Although the primary channel of communication in the interview is auditory, visual communication is also important. The respondent may be influenced by such factors as the interviewer's dress, posture, gesture, and appearance. Many of these factors have received little or no systematic consideration, but they cannot be ignored, since in certain circumstances they may be highly influential.

Pace

There are two main aspects of pace in the interview. One is the general tempo of the question–answer process. The other is the speed with which the interview moves from one topic to another or between topics that are emotionally neutral for the respondent and those about which he feels very strongly. In both of these aspects, the interviewer requires skill in sensing the pace appropriate for the respondent.

THE GENERAL TEMPO

Most interviewers are above average in intelligence and tend to associate with people to whom rapid tempo in discussion is common and acceptable. Some of them, therefore, have difficulty in recognizing that many kinds of respondents find a slower tempo more congenial. Respondents who have limited intelligence and who think slowly may be very sensitive about their slowness. The pace and characteristic thought patterns of the respondent may also be different from those of the interviewer because of the difference in their cultural or subcultural background. If the interviewer tries to hurry such respondents, they may become confused, insecure, or irritated and may have their thoughts deflected from the subject matter to the difficulties of the interpersonal relationship.

Where the thought patterns of the interviewer and respondent differ markedly, the interviewer will have to guard against imposing his own frame of reference and thought patterns, because they may well be meaningless and irrelevant to the respondent. Bartlett (1932, pp. 264–265) provides an excellent illustration of the need for an interviewer to modify his pace and accustomed way of thinking.

As everybody knows, the examination by Europeans of a native witness in a court of law, among a relatively primitive people, is often a matter of much difficulty. The commonest alleged reason is that the essential differences between the sophisticated and the unsophisticated modes of recall set a great strain on the patience of any European official. It is interesting to consider an actual record, very much abbreviated, of a Swazi trial at law. A native was being examined for the attempted murder of a woman, and the woman herself was called as a necessary witness. The case proceeded in this way:

The Magistrate: Now tell me how you got that knock on the head.
The Woman: Well, I got up that morning at daybreak and I did . . . (here followed a long list of things done, and of people met, and things said). Then we went to so and so's kraal and

we . . . (further lists here) had some beer, and so and so said. . . .

The Magistrate: Never mind about that. I don't want to know anything except how you got the knock on the head.

The Woman: All right, all right. I am coming to that. I have not got there yet. And so I said to so and so . . . (there followed again a great deal of conversational and other details). And then after that we went on to so and so's kraal.

The Magistrate: You look here; if we go on like this we shall take all day. What about that knock on the head?

The Woman: Yes; all right, all right. But I have not got there yet. So we . . . (on and on for a very long time relating all the initial detail of the day). And then we went on to so and so's kraal . . . and there was a dispute . . . and he knocked me on the head, and I died, and that is all I know.

If the interviewer is throughly familiar with the subject matter of the interview, he can easily forget that respondents who are unfamiliar with the subject may have to deal with it at a much slower tempo than is customary for him. Unless he is aware of this, he may not give the respondents adequate time to consider their answers or to think aloud in a manner congenial to them. For example, it is often very difficult for a vocational counselor to obtain from a lower-class person with little education a job history which is sufficiently detailed to provide usable information. If an interview covers several topics, the respondent's knowledge of and his interest in the topics may vary considerably and, hence, require changes in the tempo at several stages of the interview. The interviewer can make such changes if he is sensitive to changes in the respondent's tempo of response.

Although the interviewer may often need to slow the pace of the interview, he will, on occasion, encounter a highly intelligent, quick-thinking respondent whose time is extremely valuable. In these circumstances, the interviewer, moving as fast as he is able, may have difficulty in maintaining a pace congenial to the respondent. The problem may be aggravated if the interviewer has to record the response either on a precoded form or, even worse, if he is responsible for recording the gist of responses to open questions. If such respondents are identified in advance, interviewers should be selected who can work effectively at a rapid pace. One interesting approach to the interviewing of quick-thinking respondents involved the use of a team of two interviewers (Kincaid & Bright, 1957). By sharing the listening and questioning process, they felt that they were better able to obtain a grasp of what the respondent said and to identify and follow up leads in the response material. When only one interviewer can be used, the use of a tape recorder to relieve him of taking notes or having to record from memory is worth considering.

THE PACE FROM NEUTRAL TO THREATENING TOPICS

In discussing the interviewer's role in enhancing participation (Chapter 4), we noted that, if the respondent perceives the interviewer as a transient stranger who impinges on his social world only briefly, he may feel safe in divulging confidences to him. For many respondents, unburdening themselves to an interested, sympathetic listener is an unusual and rewarding experience, and their inhibitions about speaking freely are likely to be weakened if they perceive the relationship as a fleeting one. But, if the interviewer, instead of leaving the respondent's community, remains to talk with many other people, the respondent may become anxious and guilt-stricken about what he said and may become hostile to the interviewer. This state of affairs can make it very difficult for the interviewer to have useful subsequent interviews, and it can jeopardize interviews with other respondents if communication exists among them. The interviewer must, therefore, take some responsibility for restraining the pace at which the respondent may wish to move toward intimate or threatening topics.

MODIFYING THE PACE OF THE INTERVIEW

The pace that is most effective must generally be a compromise among what interviewer and respondent each find congenial and what the interviewer feels is necessary to get his job done. Although often the interviewer may chafe at the respondent's slowness and be highly conscious of the number of interviews still to be done, he may, in order to maintain a high level of participation, have to listen to a certain amount of information that is not relevant to his purpose. In other cases, however, the respondent may be under time pressure and begrudge the length of time the interviewer is taking.

In the nonschedule interview, the interviewer is free to modify his pace in the light of the feedback he obtains from each respondent. In the schedule interview, through pretesting a sample of respondents, the writer of the schedule must establish a pace, framework, and thought patterning that will meet the needs of all respondents in the study. The more homogeneous the respondent population, the more feasible this becomes.

Transitions

The interviewer, in some cases, will be able to influence response quality by the way in which he effects transitions between topics. He may wish to change the topic because he has obtained all the information he needs or because he feels that the respondent has nothing further to say. Or he may feel that the respondent is uncomfortable, embarrassed, or threatened by the subject matter to the extent that further questioning would adversely affect his participation; in such circumstances, the interviewer may return to the topic at a later stage in the interview, when the respondent seems more ready to discuss it.

Although the interviewer benefits his purpose by moving away from a subject about which the respondent does not wish to talk, in other cases, by premature shifts of topic, he may lose valuable information or irritate the respondent. Neophyte interviewers often are so concerned about covering a predetermined set of questions or topics that they move to a new topic while the respondent is evincing strong need to continue talking on the same subject. If the respondent is frequently diverted from what *he* wants to talk about, he will soon lose interest in the interview and may become antagonistic. Perhaps the kind of transition that is most damaging to the interview is the shift between topics having high and low affect for the respondent.

When the interviewer initiates the transition, he can exercise choice of the topic to which he moves and the manner in which he makes the move. Transitions between topics can be broadly categorized along a continuum from smooth to abrupt. Generally, the interviewer seeks a smooth transition and tries to make the change in topic meaningful to the respondent, frequently by alluding to something relevant to the new topic that the respondent has said earlier in the interview. This tactic has the secondary advantage of indicating to the respondent that the interviewer has been listening carefully and assimilating the responses. When there is no apparent relationship between prior topics and the new topic, the interviewer, in order to minimize the abruptness of the transition and to give the respondent a chance to "shift gears," may explain the reason for the shift of topic.

Although smooth transitions and ample preparation of the respondent for the change of topic are usually desirable, there are circumstances in which abrupt transitions may be more effective. This technique was used by Kinsey in interviewing people about their sexual behavior (see p. 192). An abrupt transition may also be useful when the respondent becomes intensely anxious and the interviewer deems it wise to move away from the topic that has provoked the anxiety.

Occasionally, it is the respondent rather than the interviewer who makes the transitions, and such transitions usually change the subject before the interviewer feels that it has been exhausted. In these circumstances, the interviewer, before deciding what action to take, must attempt to determine why the respondent made the transition. Merton, Fiske, and Kendall (1956, p. 55) have suggested four reasons why the respondent changes the topic: (1) the subject is peripheral to the respondent's interests and feelings; (2) the respondent finds the subject threatening or painful and wishes to escape to another subject; (3) another subject is more interesting to the respondent; and (4) the respondent has exhausted the subject. They suggest that, if the transition seems to be due to the respondent's need for escape, the interviewer may wish to revert to this critical ground at a later stage of the interview. If the respondent has made the change for other reasons, the interviewer may safely abandon the early topic.

The Choice of Language and Level of Discourse

In examining the assumptions underlying the schedule and non-schedule approach to standardization in interviewing (Chapter 2), we noted that language usage varies with geographic region, social background, special interests and occupations, and level of education. When there are differences in these characteristics between interviewer and respondent, the same word can mean different things, and different words can mean the same thing. We noted, also, that the denotation of words is more likely to be widely shared in the subject matter of such widely discussed public issues as politics, consumer preferences, and national pastimes than in subject matter that is not openly discussed in public. The interviewer needs to be continuously alert to the danger of using terms which denote one thing to him and another to the respondent.

Misunderstandings in language can also occur through the use of homonyms—words with the same pronunciation as others but with different meanings. In one study, even careful pretesting did not reveal the fact that one part of the sample construed the word "profit" in a question as "prophet" and responded accordingly. The context in which a word is used reduces the chance of misunderstanding but does not eliminate it. If the respondent is loath to admit that he does not understand a question, he may guess at its meaning and respond accordingly. If the interviewer assumes that the question was understood and if the misunderstanding is not uncovered in subsequent questions, the response will, of course, be invalid.

Respondents may differ from the interviewer and from one another not only in their understanding of the denotation of words and phrases but also in their ability to assimilate complex concepts and ideas. The formulation of a question that contains an abstract or complex idea so that it can be understood by respondents with limited experience, education, or verbal skill may be difficult, if not impossible. Richardson (1959), for example, in exploring the kinds of experiences that commercial fishermen had had with economic cooperation, was unable to learn much until he discovered that there had been an unsuccessful attempt to cooperate in the planning and financing of a hospital in the fishing community and several attempts to establish a fishermen's cooperative for the processing and marketing of fish. By introducing the subject of the hospital and the fishermen's cooperative in interviews, Richardson learned a great deal about economic cooperation, whereas his earlier direct questioning using the more abstract terms had been unsuccessful. Gross and Mason (1953) used a similar approach when studying role conflicts experienced by school superintendents (see p. 209).

Almost all occupational and special-interest groups evolve terms and phrases to describe their tools, techniques, and activities. In medicine, law, the theater, yachting, drug addiction, and homosexuality, for example, terms develop to communicate ideas, activities, and attitudes which have common interest to the members of the group. Often this technical language consists of abbreviation of terms to single syllables, letters, and numbers. The names of certain authorities will be known throughout the group and may be used as a form of shorthand to refer to an idea, a diagnostic procedure, or a philosophy or approach. When he is studying an occupational or special-interest group, the interviewer needs to learn its special language for several reasons. If he can demonstrate, at first through his use of extensions, clarifications, summaries, or confrontation questions, that he understands the special language, even though he may not use it himself, he communicates to the respondent that superficial responses which might satisfy outsiders are inadequate. Subsequently, the interviewer can demonstrate not only that he understands the special language but that he uses it correctly and naturally when asking questions and that he can use names of persons as shorthand for ideas, and so forth. Needless to say, the clumsy or incorrect use of special language can easily mark the interviewer as an outsider who is trying too hard and too quickly to gain acceptance by the group.

The "Loaded Question" or the Connotation of Words

In addition to their denotations, many words have connotations that can arouse emotional reactions in both the user and the listener. The recognition and exploitation of connotations has always been one of the skills of the orator. In survey research, there has long been concern over how the use of words with strong connotations may influence the over-all distribution of responses to a question. This use of "loaded questions" has often been written about in conjunction with the leading question.

Cantril (1947) classifies five types of "deviations from objective wordings" which may affect response.

PRESTIGE

In such questions as "President Johnson has said. . . . Do you agree?" or "Republican Party leaders believe. . . . What do you think?" the prestige (positive or negative) attached to the source of the opinion will undoubtedly influence the response. But two points need to be noted before one decides to eliminate such references. First, the name or source may be necessary to clarify the issue or to give it immediacy and meaning for the respondent. It is quite possible that a question about American–Soviet relations cannot be properly formulated without citing statements of the principal negotiators. Secondly, one must consider the population of respondents instead of speculating about bias in the abstract. If as many people will be biased against a Johnson statement as in favor of it, the results as a whole may not be biased.

STEREOTYPES

As Cantril (1947, p. 42) points out, "Various investigators have shown how the acceptance value of a proposition is changed if it is attached to emotionally toned stereotypes." It seems clear that such phrases as "defend our heritage," "go to war to defend," or "welfare state" are likely to produce affect that will influence the direction of the response. And a number of studies have shown that the same respondent will reply differently to the same question when it is differently loaded. But, here again, it is not sufficient to eschew the stereotype—even if we assume that we are invariably able to detect it—for, as we shall see, the stereotype has certain use in the interview.

PROPOSED LEGAL CHANGES

"The suggestion that a law must be changed in order to carry out a specified policy immediately creates a certain amount of opposition on the part of many people who would otherwise be in favor of the adoption of such a policy" (Cantril, 1947, p. 43). It is important to note, however, that although the question "Do you believe that the state law should be changed to prevent the sale of alcoholic beverages to minors?" may produce a *different* response from the question, "Do you believe that minors should be permitted to buy alcoholic beverages?" the first version of the question may not be biased but, in fact, may produce more accurate results than the second. What the first question does is bring to the respondent's mind the reality situation or the implications of his answer. The second version may elicit a much more casual answer than the first.

BIASED WORDING

"It is almost meaningless to ask whether or not opinion can be affected by biased wordings in the questions. It all depends on the issue involved. The primary use of biased wordings is to provide a method for the determination of the stability of opinion" (Cantril, 1947, p. 46). The primary difficulty in the elimination of biased wording stems from the difficulty of answering the question "Biased with respect to whom?" Obviously, a word that seems neutral to one group of respondents may seem biased to another. Even such seemingly noncontroversial phrases as "federal government" or "labor unions" will strike some respondents as biased. The word "nigger" will produce in a population of sociologists just as strong a reaction as the word "Negro" will in a population of white Deep South farmers. Aside from the virtual impossibility of constructing bias-free questions for a large population of respondents, biased wording has certain uses.

PERSONALIZATION OF THE QUESTION

" 'Personalization' in this context refers, not to the use of the so-called 'subjective' type of question, 'Do you think, etc.?' but to a form of question which requires the respondent to say whether or not he himself would carry out a specified course of action" (Cantril, 1947, p. 46). Cantril (1947, pp. 47–48) cites the following illustration of the effect of personalization:

(*A form*) In the census which the government is taking this spring, every adult in the country will be asked how much money he or she makes. Do you think people should object to giving the census taker this information about themselves?

Yes 30%   No 64%   No Opinion 6%

(*B form*) In the census which the government is taking this spring, every adult in the country will be asked how much money he or she makes. Will you have any objections to giving a census taker this information about yourself?

Yes 22%   No 77%   No Opinion 1%

The protest vote is greater on the A form, which allows the respondent to register an objection without appearing to be personally uncooperative. In trying to estimate the actual degree of opposition in obtaining the information, it would probably be more accurate to use the indirect, i.e., A form of the question. . . . Obviously not all types of issues are suited to personalization. Where one does have a choice between personalized and nonpersonalized forms, it is simply a matter of deciding which form presents the issue more realistically and which is more appropriate to the particular purposes of the investigation.

The loaded question has long been a source of concern in interviewing, but the focus of attention on words whose connotations are strong for the interviewer has hindered recognition of the fact that these same words may be neutral for the respondent. This is well illustrated in the following contrast pointed out by Dexter (1956, p. 155):

Dollard, similarly, reports: "One complaint against me: I had addressed a certain Negro woman as Mrs. . . ." Later on, however, he said to a southern white man, "I am studying personality among the niggers." The man replied, "I am glad to hear you say 'nigger.' I see you understand about that." Dollard adds that the use of the word "Negro" is evidently "the hallmark of a Northerner and a caste enemy."

In situations characterized by factionalism and partisanship, an interviewer who attempts to maintain neutrality is likely to be perceived as hostile. Gaining participation of a faction may require the interviewer to join that faction to the extent of surrendering a neutral position—especially if his appearance, background, and affiliation make it seem to a faction that he is not one of them and might easily be sympathetic to the opposing faction. When Dexter (1956, p. 155) was interviewing in a study of American business and political opinion on reciprocal trade and tariff issues, he represented two academic institutions—the Center for International Studies, at Massachusetts Institute of Technology, and American University—and academic people were thought of as supporting free trade and internationalism. To counter respondents' perception of him as favoring the internationalist free-trade view, Dexter attempted to determine and adopt the respondents' definition of neutrality and, like Dollard, to use terms neutral to *them*. He found that his use of the terms respondents themselves used, such as "free-trader" and "cheap labor," seemed to offset the impression that as an academic person he could not be trusted. He argues that,

Such questions as "Are you bothered by cheap foreign imports?" "Do they undersell you unfairly?" "Does the Defense Department nowadays apply the Buy American Act properly?" while not absolutely committing one, in case one has guessed an informant's views wrongly, help set the stage. Relevant reassurance, for example, that, because of a Massachusetts background, I knew how industries like textile and watches *suffer* from foreign competition also helps. Some of the Bricker Amendment objectors to reciprocal trade would probably have been favorably impressed by the use of terms such as "constitutional government."
The real point is not to establish neutrality for its own sake but to create a situation in which the informant will tell what is needed.

The emotional meaning of words, in some cases, may be so strong that their use in explaining the purpose of the interview can cause respondents to refuse to participate in the interview. This was well illustrated when parents of children with physical disabilities were studied to determine their expectations of a rehabilitation center service. When a pretest sample of the parents of children on the waiting list of the center was sent a letter explaining the study, a number of answers were received refusing cooperation; other parents, who had not written, either refused or were evasive when contacted. One parent explained her reason for refusal: The name of the organization making the study, which appeared on the letterhead, included the word "cripple." The parent was rather upset, saying that her child was disabled but certainly not crippled, and hence she did not wish to be included in the study. This reaction turned out to be widespread among those who had refused. When the investigator changed the letterhead to read "Studies in Child Development," the refusal rate dropped sharply (Koller, 1960).

The interviewer must be sensitive to the connotation of words and must not assume that his own reactions to words can be used to predict the reactions of his respondents. As we have seen, words that are neutral to the interviewer may have powerful connotations to some respondents and, conversely, words that have strong meaning for the interviewer may be neutral to respondents. Although some words can, on a probability basis, be predicted to arouse emotional reactions almost universally, others have idiosyncratic meanings for certain respondents which cannot be predicted. To identify these, the interviewer must depend on feedback from the respondent.

The Sequence of Topics

Recognizing that the degree of emotion or threat varies from one question to another, most writers on interviewing recommend that the more neutral questions should come early in the interview and those that elicit high affect be left until later. With a heterogeneous set of respondents, however, this sequence may vary, as was illustrated by Kinsey (see p. 49). There are circumstances, moreover, in which the general rule of sequence from low to high emotional response does not work effectively. When the interview contains subjects about which the respondent feels very strongly or with which he is preoccupied and eager to deal, the delaying of this subject can frustrate him, and it is likely that he will take the initiative in introducing the subject if the interviewer does not. Until the respondent has "talked out" this subject, the introduction of other topics is likely to be unproductive. In a study of parents of children who were physically disabled, Koller was primarily interested in their experience with diagnostic and evaluation services at rehabilitation centers, but he found it fruitless to explore this subject systematically until the parents had voiced their central concerns about the child. The parents needed the opportunity to talk to a person who was interested in their child and concerned about finding help for his disability.

Accent and Inflection

Like his choice of words, the way in which the interviewer pronounces words can sometimes reveal his place of residence and socio-economic level. The interviewer needs to be aware of this and must estimate the effect of his accent both on participation and on response quality. Like physical appearance, accent is probably noticed by the respondent most acutely when he first meets the interviewer and then diminishes in prominence as other sources and forms of information provide a wider range of cues by which the respondent can appraise the interviewer. Unless accent reveals the interviewer to be affiliated with a group toward which the respondent is hostile, it is rarely an insuperable obstacle. If it reveals a group membership that the respondent likes or admires, it may be very helpful. Interviewers vary greatly in the extent to which they can modify their accent in the direction of the accent of the person to whom they are speaking, although some can modify their speaking style and word usage to a very considerable extent. As Whyte (1955, p. 304) has noted,

When John Howard first came down from Harvard to join me in the Cornerville study, he noticed at once that I talked in Cornerville in a far different manner from that which I used at Harvard. This was not a matter of the use of profanity or obscenity, nor did I affect the use of ungrammatical expressions. I talked in the way that seemed natural to me, but what was natural in Cornerville was different from what was natural at Harvard. In Cornerville, I found myself putting much more animation into my speech, dropping terminal G's and using gestures much more actively. (There was also, of course, the difference in vocabulary I used. When I was most deeply involved in Cornerville, I found myself rather tongue-tied in my visits to Harvard.)

Consciously adopting the respondent's accent, unless it can be done with consummate skill, will probably do the interviewer more harm than good, but, for those who can do it comfortably as well as skillfully, this may be helpful in the same way as learning the word usage peculiar to a special-interest group.

In our discussion of expectations (p. 173), we noted that a question that is not in the form of an expectation may nevertheless suggest the answer expected through the intonation and inflection of the interviewer's voice. "Do you like him?" does not suggest the answer expected, but "Do you like *him*?" or "Do you *like* him?" when said with disbelief can suggest a negative response.

Among writers on interviewing, Sullivan (1954, pp. 5, 8) has probably best expressed the importance of intonation:

> Much attention may profitably be paid to the telltale aspects of intonation, rate of speech, difficulty in enunciation, and so on. . . . It is by alertness to the importance of these things as signs or indicators of meaning, rather than by preoccupation only with the words spoken, that the psychiatric interview becomes practical in a reasonable section of one's lifetime.
>
> .   .   .
>
> . . . [D]uring an interview one may learn that a person is married, and if one is feeling very mildly satirical, one can say, "And doubtless happily?" If the answer is "Yes," that "Yes" can have anything in the way of an implication from a dirge to a paean of supreme joy. It may indicate that "Yes" means "No," or anything in between.

Although Sullivan is writing about the therapeutic interview, what he says has implications for utilizing the respondent's intonation as a source of information beyond the verbal content, especially in providing clues to profitable further lines of inquiry. It also suggests the need for the interviewer to gain self-awareness of how he uses intonation. For this purpose, listening to tape recordings of one's own interviews can be very revealing.

Interviewer–Respondent Communication through Observation

Despite the widespread recognition of the importance of visual communication in the interview, very little systematic study has been devoted to what may profitably be observed during the interview and to the meaning of these observations. Perhaps if a relatively simple and inexpensive machine for making a continuous visual record had become as readily available as the tape recorder, emphasis in research on the visual components of interviewing would have been greater. One can, of course, observe an interview without hearing it by watching a television interview with the sound turned off.

We have already pointed out that the physical appearance and dress of the interviewer provide the respondent with numerous cues as to his background and status. Interviewers in a hospital, for example, may wear a white coat to show their affiliation with the hospital and possibly to suggest they are knowledgeable and of high status.[1] In many settings, there are certain expectations about the form of dress that should be worn, and it is unwise for an interviewer to overlook or violate these. In many interview situations, respondents may infer the social and economic level of the interviewer from the quality and style of his clothing.

The physical appearance of the interviewer—his facial configuration, build, and posture—provide cues for judging age, sex, and race or ethnic background, and the respondent's reactions to these characteristics may influence the quality of his participation (see chapters 3 and 4). Despite the absence of empirically based knowledge on the relationship between physical appearance and personality or temperament, there has always flourished a rich folklore on the prediction of personality from appearance; beauty is often associated with goodness, ugliness or any physical disability with evil, wide lips with passion, and thin lips with cruelty. Phrenologists, novelists, cartoonists, the stage, and the screen all contribute to and maintain the tradition. Although there is no way of predicting accurately the way in which respondents will interpret facial cues, the interviewer can call on his past experience of how people have reacted to him and can obtain some indications from early interviews with respondents.

The importance of the visual information that the interviewer can communicate to the respondent was brought home to us during an analysis of interview transcripts, in terms of the number of lines

[1] We leave as an open question the ethics of interviewers' wearing a white coat. If this leads the respondent to assume erroneously that the interviewer is a physician, the interviewer should consider the ethical question very carefully, even if he clarifies any questions about his status.

of type used respectively by the interviewer and the respondent. One interviewer–respondent ratio revealed that the interviewer said almost nothing compared to other interviewers. When we subsequently observed this interviewer, however, we noticed that she offered the respondent an almost continuous nonverbal commentary by nodding her head, gesturing with hands and arms, and changing her facial expression and posture. This commentary indicated her knowledge of subject matter and her interest, support, and understanding.

There is obviously wide variation in the kind and amount of nonverbal behavior that interviewers customarily employ. Unless an interviewer has some self-awareness of how he reacts to others as a listener, he may unconsciously provide cues that hinder the interview—indications of lack of attention or distracting mannerisms. These can often be modified when they are pointed out.

Because on-the-spot recording of responses is so customary in the schedule interview, little attention has been paid to the effects of such recording. The reading of questions and recording of responses will inevitably interfere with the interviewer's opportunities for observation during the interview, and the recording of responses will, in some cases, lead to refusal of the respondent to participate. In nonschedule interviewing, the question whether the interviewer's recording of responses or taking notes is regarded by the respondent as threatening or whether such activities help the respondent understand the role of the interviewer has long been debated. There is some consensus that, if the respondent is giving statistical or factual information which is not confidential, he is unlikely to feel threatened, and he may be somewhat surprised and even offended if the interviewer does not take down the facts and figures he presents. On the other hand, if the respondent is talking about some highly confidential matter, taking notes may distract or upset him and prevent him from giving information which he otherwise might have given. It has been found on numerous occasions, however, that respondents' initial suspicion about note-taking can be overcome and that, with time, they tend to take it for granted.

Many of the categories of information that the interviewer provides visually to the respondent apply equally to the information that the respondent provides to the interviewer. As we noted earlier, the setting in which the respondent is interviewed—his home, work place, church, club—contains many observational cues which the respondent intentionally and unintentionally provides in the presentation of himself: his dress; his belongings; his associates; the selection, style, and arrangement of his possessions; and the general physical and social environment. Often, in the course of an interview, a respondent cannot cut himself off completely from the events of his daily life. A businessman will be interrupted by telephone calls or unexpected visitors or crises; a mother at home will often be interrupted by her children asking questions, crying, or needing to be comforted or cared for. These interruptions of the interview may provide valuable opportunities for the kind of observation that was discussed in Chapter 1.

The respondent's posture and gestures are easily observable, but the interpretation of this information is problematic. Birdwhistell (1952) and others have pointed out that, because we are trained to focus on verbal communication and generally disregard nonverbal communication, we are probably far less guarded in our nonverbal behavior and may reveal information that we carefully control or censor in speech. But, because we do not depend on nonverbal behavior for communication, it is not standardized to nearly the same extent as language and has a large idiosyncratic component. Hebb (1946) and Turhan (1941, p. 118) have suggested that emotions and facial expressions may be interpreted provided, first, that deviation from normal patterns of expression takes place and, second, that there is sufficiently frequent observation of these deviations in the context which gave rise to them to permit inferences about their meaning. It is common knowledge, for example, that people who have lived together for many years can detect and correctly interpret nonverbal behavior that strangers and acquaintances cannot perceive. Unless the interviewer spends long periods of time with a respondent, there is a great deal of nonverbal behavior which he cannot interpret meaningfully. Much of the interpretation must be at a clinical, and often speculative, level, and there is wide variation in the skill of observers.

II

ACHIEVING RESPONSE QUALITY
THROUGH THE
QUESTION–ANSWER PROCESS

In the preceding five chapters, we have described and examined individual components of question form and interviewer style in order to determine how they may influence responses. In this chapter, we shall reverse our point of view in order to determine how desired response characteristics—validity, relevance, specificity, and so forth—may be influenced by variations in question formulation and interviewer style. This provides an opportunity to examine combinations of components and styles more effectively than was possible in the earlier chapters. In order not to repeat the critical evaluation we have made of each component of question form, we shall discuss the matter from the standpoint of our best judgment of what is known without always citing sources or evidence.

Response Characteristics Desired in All Interviews

RESPONDENT PARTICIPATION

Respondent participation is not a direct outcome measure by which the quality of the response material can be gauged. Yet without adequate participation there may be no interviews, and poor participation may negatively influence all the direct response or outcome characteristics the interviewer is seeking. In chapters 3 and 4, we discussed the development of participation largely in terms of setting the stage for the interview. Here, we shall review the ways in which the level of participation may be influenced within the interview itself, by question formulation and other elements of the question–answer process.

The relationship between respondent participation and the use of open and closed questions depends on the needs of different kinds of respondent. An articulate, intelligent respondent who is well informed on the subject of the interview generally prefers to share in the responsibility for topic selection and development and to express himself in the manner he considers appropriate to the topic. To satisfy this preference, the interviewer should use some open questions of broad scope early in the interview, provided that he can successfully formulate and specify through them the information he is seeking. If the respondent then continues to produce relevant, specific, information, the interviewer will need to use only encouragements, extensions, or echoes, and possibly clarifications where the respondent has not made himself clear or has been too concise.

As the respondent continues speaking, the interviewer makes mental notes of points that need expansion or clarification, allusions that are briefly made to areas that deserve to be followed up, apparent contradictions between two responses, subtopics that have been overlooked, and so on. These can be followed up with a high proportion of closed questions, some open questions of narrow scope, and early respondent antecedents in the form of clarifications, summaries, and possibly confrontations. To initiate a line of inquiry which breaks with prior content, the interviewer may use a series of questions with interviewer antecedents. In the course of such an interview, the initiative for topic selection may move between interviewer and respondent and be reflected by such changes in question form as we have noted.

For the type of respondent we have just described, certain patterns of questioning may well reduce the level of participation. If the interviewer uses too many questions with interviewer rather than respondent antecedents, if he frequently and prematurely changes the topic, and if he uses questions of narrow scope, many of which seem unrelated and do not develop some apparent line of inquiry, the respondent may well feel that the questioning does not tap what knowledge he can provide. He may feel that the interviewer is not sufficiently interested in his views to listen carefully or to pick up the leads he offers, and he may become frustrated at not being permitted to deal with the topic according to his frame of reference and at having to respond to inept questions that do not get at the heart of the matter.

The questioning techniques preferred by intelligent, articulate, well-informed respondents may, if used with other kinds of respondent, severely reduce the level of participation and even lead to refusal to continue the interview. Persons who have difficulty in organizing their ideas and in expressing themselves—because of lack of experience and opportunity, reticence, embarrassment, or a strong feeling of status difference between themselves and the interviewer—find question forms that give them scope, initiative, and freedom of response highly threatening. Strauss and Schatzman (1960), through examining recorded interviews with middle- and lower-class respondents,[1] found that the interview with lower-class respondents tended to deteriorate sharply unless the interviewer used either closed questions of narrow scope or questions derived from earlier responses. Middle-class respondents, who generally understood the purpose of the interview much more clearly, were able to provide coherent responses to open, broad questions and to extensions derived from the preceding response.

Depending on the type of respondent, the following points can be made with respect to participation.

1. To the intelligent, articulate respondent, a heavy preponderance of closed over open questions may suggest that the interviewer is not interested in him as a person or in having him express and develop his views. Other respondents find the opportunity to

[1] Lower-class respondents had an annual income of less than $2,000 and no more than elementary-school education. Middle-class respondents had an income of over $4,000 and some college education.

take the initiative burdensome and feel more comfortable when the interviewer clearly structures the interview.

2. The use of respondent antecedents, especially those referring to earlier statements, provides strong evidence of attentive listening and, hence, may increase the level of respondent participation. The lack of respondent antecedents can create the impression of lack of interviewer interest.

3. Where a question or topic appears threatening to the respondent, a change of subject through a break and a subsequent return to it by the use of early respondent antecedents may prevent the respondent from feeling threatened early in the interview and elicit a richer response after the respondent has gained confidence.

4. Under some conditions, a confrontation may be so threatening to a respondent as to jeopardize his participation. If a respondent enjoys argument, however, and does not feel threatened by the topic, a confrontation may enhance his interest in the interview, his respect for the interviewer, and, hence, his participation.

The effect of expectations and premises on participation seems to depend on whether the expectation correctly predicts what the respondent would have answered had the expectation not been used and whether the premise is correct from the viewpoint of the respondent. The expectation or premise used in this way and derived from earlier responses constitutes strong evidence of the interviewer's attentiveness and, hence, is likely to increase participation. Incorrect expectations or premises, especially if they occur repeatedly, can annoy or irritate the respondent and, hence, reduce participation.

The use of encouragements appears to help participation if the respondent is interested in the subject matter and is talking fairly freely and if he does not construe encouragement as criticism.

The effect of guggles and interruptions appears closely tied to the frequency and purpose of their use. If used sparingly and only to clarify a response or to make a connection between two points made by the respondent, they demonstrate that the interviewer is listening attentively. The interruption (prefaced, if necessary, by a guggle) should occur at an appropriate juncture and not while the respondent is trying to develop a point or idea. Used clumsily, the interruption may reduce participation.

Frequent alternation of objective and subjective questions appears to be highly disturbing to respondents and damaging to participation. In recorded interviews, it is not uncommon to hear the interviewers begin a line of inquiry about the respondent's feeling and then, apparently fearful that he is getting in too deep, move abruptly to an objective question. Then, in the midst of the objective topic, the interviewer returns suddenly to a subjective topic. In such circumstances, participation is likely to deteriorate.

Some discrepancy between the styles of the interviewer and respondent in pace, choice of language, level of discourse, and appearance can generally be tolerated by the respondent and will not affect participation adversely. In fact, too strenuous an effort on the part of the interviewer to become like the respondent may lead to his becoming suspect. It is only when differences in style seriously hamper communication that participation may suffer.

VALIDITY

Validity of response is fundamental to the interview. Without validity, there is no value in participation, relevance, depth, or any other of the desired response characteristics. Certain other response conditions are necessary for validity but do not ensure it. Without participation, for example, there will be no interview, and many interviewers believe that the more freely the respondent participates, the more valid his responses are likely to be. However, unless responses are relevant to the interviewer's purpose, their validity is worthless, and, unless they are specific and clear, their validity will be difficult to determine. Similarly, if depth or unanticipated responses are sought, validity is irrelevant unless these response characteristics are obtained.

To the extent, then, that the interviewer can influence these other response characteristics, he is providing the necessary, although not sufficient, conditions for achieving validity. Despite its fundamental importance, however, we know very little about how we can *directly* enhance validity through manipulating question techniques. We know somewhat more about how some forms of questions reduce or interfere with it.

Although they have generally been condemned as reducing validity, the components of the leading question may, in certain of its forms and under certain conditions, increase validity both indirectly and directly. Their use in increasing participation—and hence, indirectly, validity—has been noted earlier in this chapter.

Expectations and premises may directly improve validity when respondents are asked about thoughts, values, and behavior that may be incriminating to themselves or to others they wish to protect or when respondents attempt to evade content areas which they regard as embarrassing. Under these conditions, a question which does not contain an expectation or a premise may elicit a less valid response than one containing an informed expectation or premise. An expectation or premise which is correct indicates that the interviewer is knowledgeable about the subject matter of the question and that he can accept the premise or the answer suggested by the expectation calmly and without embarrassment. This makes the respondent feel that an evasive or invalid answer will not be acceptable and that any unsanctioned or embarrassing thoughts or behavior that he admits to are likely to be familiar and unembarrassing to the interviewer. The effect of correct premises and expectations is probably strongest if they occur early in the interview.

The extent to which expectations and premises reduce validity seems to have been considerably exaggerated. Under many conditions, a respondent will feel free to reject the answer suggested in an expectation or an incorrect premise. He appears likely to accept an incorrect expectation or premise when he is afraid of disagreeing with the interviewer, eager to please or impress the interviewer, or uninterested in the interview and impatient to finish. Under these conditions, an interviewer should avoid using expectations unless he is so well informed that he can formulate correct ones with virtual certainty.

With all respondents but particularly with those who are fearful, eager to please, uninterested, or impatient, the interviewer may increase validity by bearing in mind the following points.

1. The respondent will be more likely to correct a major than a minor distortion contained in summaries, expectations, and premises.
2. The deliberate use of questions which push the respondent toward a particular response serves to identify respondents with extreme opinions, since they are more likely to resist the push.
3. The deliberate nonjudgmental ascription of unsanctioned behavior to the respondent or the person under discussion can communicate to the respondent that the interviewer is familiar with and not shocked by such behavior. A realization of this may encourage the respondent to give a valid rather than a socially acceptable answer.

Two forms of antecedent may on occasion contribute to validity —the confrontation and the repetition. If two of the respondent's statements appear contradictory or inconsistent, a confrontation which points out the discrepancy may increase validity either directly or indirectly through increasing specificity or clarity. A repetition can be useful when the interviewer is skeptical about the validity of the response. If he receives the same response to a repetition of the same question later in the interview, however, he can be certain only of its reliability rather than its validity. If a different response is given, a confrontation may be used to explore the discrepancy.

Encouragements may under certain conditions reduce validity. If the interviewer encourages every response on a given topic and these responses lean in the same direction, respondents may increase the number of their responses in the direction encouraged—presumably to please the interviewer (Hildum & Brown, 1956).

The use of closed alternative questions in which only some of all possible responses are presented may reduce validity. Delimited-response questions of this kind—sometimes called "forced choice" questions—are usually employed to classify all respondents into a few categories—for example, to identify those who are for or against a political party and those who have no opinion. Responses to such questions are invalid only if they lead to a misclassification of a respondent, but some experienced research workers believe that, particularly on complex issues, misclassification is quite likely to result from such a straightforward, either-or approach to the respondent. By failing to elicit the respondent's qualifications of his opinion, the argument runs, such questions invite only superficial, unthoughtful responses which would, if elaborated, actually be so altered as to change the classification of the individual. There is evidence to support this criticism under one very important condition—namely, when respondents are being asked for opinions which they have not clearly formulated. For example, Cantril (1947, p. 37, pp. 48–49) reports that when respondents were asked, "About how soon do you think we will be in the [Second World] war?" 12 per cent of the respondents estimated two months or less. When, however, comparable respondents were asked, "Do you think we will be in the war within two months?" 25 per cent responded "yes." From data such as these, Cantril concludes that uninformed opinions are guided by the alternatives offered.

Closed alternative questions in which only some of all possible responses are presented need not impair validity if they are employed properly. Only if they are used indiscriminately, without consideration of either the investigator's purpose or the probable state of respondents' opinions, would we expect them to produce consistently invalid responses.

RELEVANCE

The general impression that open questions elicit less relevant response material than closed questions may well stem from the fact that open questions are more difficult to formulate than closed ones and that they generally elicit longer responses. The need for a more carefully qualified statement about the relation between relevance and openness or closedness is suggested by the results reported by Dohrenwend (in press). In a controlled experiment, she found that two interviewers obtained a higher proportion of usable response material with open questions, whereas two others obtained a higher proportion with closed questions. Furthermore, the proportion of usable material declined in the course of the interview in response to open questions but not in response to closed questions. In this experiment, both interviewers and respondents were well informed on the subject of the interview.

The effect of open and closed questions on relevance, therefore, may depend on the clarity with which the subject matter is formulated in the question and the amount of knowledge that both interviewer and respondent possess about the topic of the interview. If the interviewer knows a good deal about the topic and the respondent does not, closed questions may obtain more relevant responses than open questions because the respondent may lack the frame of reference necessary to judge relevance or the conceptual ability to organize responses to open questions. If, on the other hand, the respondent is better informed on the topic than the interviewer, he may be better able to give relevant responses to open questions than the interviewer is able to formulate a large number of closed questions. If interviewer and respondent are equally well informed, the effect of open or closed questions on relevance may, as Dohrenwend's experiment suggests, depend on the interviewer—possibly on his skill in formulating open questions that are meaningful and relevant to the respondent. When the subject matter is threatening, a high proportion of closed questions may be effective in preventing evasive—and, hence, irrelevant—responses. Dohrenwend found that, in eliciting responses that dealt personally with the respondent, closed questions produced more relevant material than open.

If the subject matter is difficult or threatening, too sustained or heavy pressure by the interviewer to obtain a high proportion of relevant data may reduce both validity and participation. In such circumstances, the respondent may occasionally need to rest or to speak about something that is important to him, even if it is not relevant to the interviewer's purpose; if he is not permitted these digressions, his responses may deteriorate or he may attempt to terminate the interview.

If his responses begin to drift away from the topic, a number of techniques can be used to bring the respondent back to what is relevant: clarification of an earlier response that was relevant, a summary of what the respondent has said that was relevant, and, if necessary, the guggle and interruption.

Maintaining relevance while seeking unanticipated responses presents a particular problem. We have found that expectations elicit more unanticipated responses than nonexpectations and that such responses contain a higher proportion of relevant material. We suggest that a grossly uninformed expectation, which indicates clearly that the interviewer "doesn't know what he's talking about," makes the respondent want to "set him straight" and enables the respondent to adopt the role of teacher vis-à-vis the interviewer. The apparent naïveté of the interviewer is so striking to the respondent that it clearly establishes the topic for him.

SPECIFICITY

Specificity of response is perhaps most directly related to the scope of the question. Experienced interviewers seem to expect questions of narrow scope to yield more specific answers than questions of broad scope, but we can find no published studies or evidence from our own work to support this belief.

Experienced interviewers have suggested that specificity is more likely to be elicited by less directive than more directive procedures (see Merton, Fiske, & Kendall, 1956, p. 15). In the nonschedule interviews we studied, we examined the effect on specificity of open questions, clarifications, respondent antecedents, and nonexpectations, and we found that none of these yielded a higher degree of specificity. This suggests that specificity may not be very sensitive to indirect control. The interviewer may obtain greater specificity directly: by remaining alert for responses that lack specificity and then asking for further clarification or for the evidence underlying inferences made by the respondent. If the lack of specificity appears to derive from incomplete understanding of the question, it may, then or later, be reformulated.

CLARITY

Clarity differs from specificity in that it represents a failure of the interviewer to understand what is said because the respondent uses unfamiliar vocabulary or a rambling and disorganized style. Lack of clarity may also occur because the response contains insufficient information, perhaps because the respondent overestimates the interviewer's background of knowledge.

If lack of clarity is due to ambiguity in the response or to the interviewer's difficulty in comprehension, the interviewer may use respondent antecedents in the form of an echo or a direct or inferential clarification. He may also use a repetition of the question. He may restate his understanding of what the respondent has said in the form of a summary, inviting correction and indicating his uncertainty, or he may use a manifestly incorrect summary in order to give the respondent an opportunity to correct it. If the interviewer is thoroughly confused by a response, he may have to use an interruption. If lack of clarity is due to incompleteness of response, the interviewer can ask for an extension of the last response, or he can use an echo, silence, or encouragement. Unfortunately, we know of no research relating question form to clarity. In the interviews we studied, the respondents were articulate, fewer than 2 per cent of all responses being unclear.

Experienced research workers generally believe that the less directive procedures—open questions, respondent antecedents, extensions, echoes, and silences—are more likely to produce clarity than the more directive procedures, on the grounds that lack of clarity is often due to the respondent's attempts to express himself in the interviewer's terms rather than his own. According to this line of reasoning, encouraging the respondent to focus inward, on his own thoughts and feelings, rather than outward, on the interviewer's demands and definitions, permits him to organize and express his thoughts clearly and coherently. Unfortunately, as we have already indicated, we have no data that can be used to test this belief.

There is great variation in the degree to which the interviewer knows in advance the territory he wishes to cover with a respondent. Early in the development of a study, it is necessary to translate the general concept underlying the study—for example, desegregation, migration, urbanization, or role conflict—into component parts, to determine the territory to be covered in the interview, and to define progressively both the limits and the specific information to be gathered. In this development phase, the interviewer will not standardize the content and will select respondents who can be helpful in defining the coverage. If respondents are selected for their special knowledge, the interviewer will share with them, or may largely delegate to them, responsibility for topic selection and coverage. He will achieve this through using a fairly high ratio of open to closed questions, especially early in the discussions of a topic. He will use more respondent antecedents than interviewer antecedents, in the form of extensions and, where necessary, clarifications, some echoes, and possibly occasional confrontations. Silences and encouragements will occur more frequently than interruptions, and in opening up a topic, questions of broad rather than narrow scope will be used.

When the investigator decides to use a standardized interview, his choice between schedule and nonschedule interview will depend on the assumptions he supports, the nature of the subject matter and the respondent set, and practical considerations (see Chapter 2). In the schedule interview, both coverage and the sequence of questions to be employed must be determined in advance. Closed questions are used much more frequently than open questions, not merely because they are more easily coded but also because the schedule is designed to create the impression that the questions are formulated from the respondent's preceding answer. Since this impression can be maintained only if the respondent answers in the manner requested, closed questions predominate because their answers are more predictable than those to open questions.

In order to obtain maximal coverage from respondents who

differ in the amount of usable material that they have to contribute, series of cafeteria, or contingency, questions can be used. In such a series, depending on the response to the first question, the interviewer is instructed to ask or omit further questions in the series.[1] This device not only permits the use of questions with respondent antecedents but also avoids the use of questions containing false premises. If, for example, the interviewer is interested in the kinds of social and recreational activities in which husband and wife participate jointly, the schedule should first present a question to determine whether the respondent has a wife or husband with whom he or she is living. If the answer is "yes," the next question might be, "Do you have any hobbies or sports that you engage in together?" If the answer is "no," a series of questions can be omitted. If, instead, a series of questions is asked with the premise that husband and wife do have joint recreational activities, the respondent may get a strong impression that the interviewer feels that this is desirable. And, if the respondent is fearful, eager to please, or bored, he may give some "yes" answers to meet the expectation implied by the premise contained in the questions.

Although questions in the schedule can be designed to give the appearance of having as antecedents the respondent's immediately prior response, it is very difficult to write schedule questions with early respondent antecedents because the schedule cannot anticipate the points at which respondents will provide useful unanticipated responses that may later be profitably followed up. For the same reason, echoes cannot be used, since they depend on how the respondent ends his response (generally to an open question), and this is not predictable. Confrontations also cannot be used because they cannot be incorporated into the schedule in advance. Designers of schedule interviews differ in their use of clarifications: some instruct interviewers to "probe" when the coverage of responses is inadequate; others feel that this reduces standardization. Because it is difficult to standardize encouragements and silences as a means of extending coverage, these are rarely incorporated into the schedule, but there is no doubt that schedule interviewers often

[1] The instruction may read, "If *yes,* ask Questions 10–14. If *no,* skip to Question 15." An example of such a series appears on page 39.

use these techniques at their own discretion, even though, strictly speaking, this reduces standardization.

In the nonschedule standardized interview, because he can tailor his questioning to each respondent, the interviewer can employ a wider range of question forms to obtain coverage. Instead of covering a topic with a series of closed questions, he may use an open question to delineate the topic and then give the respondent some freedom in the manner in which it will be covered, provided the respondent produces largely relevant information. Even though it introduces some irrelevant material, giving the respondent a certain degree of latitude may be necessary when the frame of reference, language, and idiom differ between interviewer and respondent. To complete the coverage that the respondent fails to produce in his early responses, the interviewer can ask a series of closed questions of narrow scope and will be able to use early respondent antecedents as transitions, if he deems this desirable. Through giving the respondent some freedom to develop a topic or subtopic, the interviewer can learn a great deal about his level of discourse, pace, choice of language, and thought patterns and use this as a basis for tailoring later questions. If the respondent balks at or seems threatened by certain questions, these can be dropped and raised again at a later point in the interview, when the respondent may have gained more confidence in the interviewer.

Response Characteristics Required in Particular Interviews

The response characteristics we have examined thus far are desirable in any interview, regardless of its purpose or subject matter. Three further characteristics—depth, unanticipated responses, and length of response—are desirable only for certain interview purposes.

DEPTH

Before we examine questioning techniques that can be used to get at the respondent's feelings and motives and to overcome the barriers that prevent his giving information freely, let us note that there is a close relationship between the attainment of depth and the level of respondent participation. In a research interview, the respondent is under no compulsion, and he generally participates on the basis of interest and good will. If, in the course of the interview, he encounters areas of questioning that are painful, embarrassing, or threatening, he is free openly or deviously to avoid answering. Hence, the extent to which depth is obtained in an interview may depend to a considerable extent on the factors influencing participation which were described in chapters 3 and 4 and earlier in this chapter.

In dealing with questioning techniques, it is necessary to separate the two components of depth: (1) eliciting feelings and motives and (2) overcoming respondent resistance. In connection with eliciting subjective responses, we have demonstrated that the content of the question influences the respondent (i.e., that more subjective statements about the respondent's values follow subjective than objective questions). Obvious though this may seem, it requires emphasis, because the verbal prescription of what subject matter is expected from the respondent is generally ignored in attempts to devise procedures for depth interviewing.

Encouragements have been shown to increase the type of response encouraged and, hence, may be used to increase the proportion of the response material devoted to feelings and motives. The interviewer must note, however, that some respondents perceive encouragements as criticisms and that systematically encouraging the direction of the response may reduce validity. Prerequisite to the use of encouragements, of course, is the presence of enough responses that reveal feelings and motives to make encouragement effective.

Once the respondent becomes interested and involved in discussing his motives and feelings, the interviewer can use, in addition to encouragements, echoes, extensions, and silences provided the silences do not become too long.

For achieving the second component of depth—the respondent's willingness to tell the interviewer things which are generally embarrassing or self-incriminating—two very different strategies have been advocated. The better known, and perhaps majority, opinion is that less directive procedures should be employed. The interviewer should use minimum guidance and allow the respondent to focus on himself, thus inducing him to give self-referred and self-revealing facts and feelings (Merton, Fiske, & Kendall, 1956, pp. 99–101). In terms of the components of questions, this viewpoint suggests that interviewers should use open questions of broad scope. Questions should emphasize respondent antecedents, both early and most recent, and questions unrelated to respondent antecedents should be avoided in order not to break the train of thought. The respondent should be encouraged to give unanticipated responses, and the interviewer should avoid expectations and uninformed premises.

This approach is not intended, however, simply to allow the respondent to ramble on about whatever he chooses to discuss. Rather, the interviewer must attempt, particularly through the use of clarifications, to identify topics which seem likely to yield data in depth. Becker (1954) used this technique in the study of school teachers to which we have already referred, beginning with open questions of broad scope and later following up the implications in the responses which the respondent would have preferred not to state openly—e.g., feelings about racial differences.

Of the two minority positions concerning eliciting depth, the better known has been most completely described by Kinsey and his colleagues (1948).[2] They believe that the most effective way to prevent the respondent from withholding information is to cross-examine him, putting pressure on him to give certain responses and keeping him off balance and unsure of what is coming next (see p. 139). Their approach implies that the interviewer should use closed questions of narrow scope, that he should use extensions as well as clarifications and confrontations, that he should assume the major responsibility for topic selection, and that he should use expectations and premises. With these relatively directive procedures, it is assumed, the interviewer can effectively put pressure on the respondent to reveal information which he might withhold if given freer rein.

[2] Kinsey and his colleagues were collecting objective data (facts about the respondent's history) rather than subjective data (about his feelings). Nevertheless, the fact that they were concerned with overcoming resistance makes their recommendations relevant to the problem of depth.

Evidence of the effectiveness of procedures which apply pressure is provided by a study of paratroopers' reactions to training jumps (Windle, McFann, & Ward, 1955). All respondents were asked, "The first time you went up in the mock tower, were you scared to jump?" Those who denied fear were then asked one of three questions:

(*Surprise*): What? You mean you weren't scared the first time?

(*Amplified agreement*): You mean you felt the same way the first time in the tower that you did when making a two-foot jump?

(*Disagreement*): You can't help being scared. Everybody's scared. Now, how did you really feel the first time you went up in the tower?

Clearly, the last question puts the greatest pressure on the respondent, and it is this one that was found to elicit by far the highest number of admissions of fear from those who had previously denied it.

It should be noted that the use of pressure emphasizes the problem of the respondent's unwillingness to give information rather than his inability to express his feelings. In contrast, most discussions which recommend the less directive procedures for eliciting depth are concerned with overcoming both unwillingness and inability to provide personal data. Thus, the use of pressure is directed at a more specialized problem than is the majority recommendation for depth interviewing.

The second minority approach to eliciting depth—that of Link (1943)—involves the use of a moderately directive schedule interview. Link begins with "informal" interviews. In the course of eight rounds of pretest interviewing of fifteen to forty-three respondents per round, he developed a schedule of questions to determine opinions in depth on a particular topic. The topic of his illustrative study, carried out during World War II, was United States participation in world affairs after the war. His procedure was to elicit first an immediate, superficial commitment to United States participation, then to ask questions about the respondent's willingness to accept various costs of this commitment, and, finally, again to elicit a statement about willingness to have the United

States participate in world affairs after the war. Of this last step he writes (1943, pp. 273–274):

The climax of this depth interview . . . is the final measure of isolationism and internationalism. In questions 2 and 5 over 80% of those interviewed expressed themselves in favor of U.S. participation in world affairs. Then, after a series of questions defining the nature, cost, and possible result of such participation, we asked:

After this war do you think that America should: (*a*) Join with England in policing (with troops) the world peace———? (*b*) Set up a World Government which all countries, including Germany and Japan can join———? (*c*) Let every country work out its own salvation———? (*d*) Other plan (quote)?

Less than a quarter, 21%, answered "Let every country work out its own salvation," which is a strictly isolationist attitude, whereas 72.5% favored some form of world participation. Thus, after picturing internationalism almost entirely in terms of its cost, the large majority still remained internationally minded. Surely here is some measure of the validity of this result, or should we say an indication of the depth and permanence of this conviction.

In terms of prescriptions, Link advocates that the interviewer use closed questions of narrow scope and extensions and repetitions rather than other forms of antecedents, that he assume responsibility for topic selection, and that he avoid expectations.

Although the three approaches advocated for depth interviewing differ in verbal procedure, there is no indication that they differ in nonverbal procedure. This similarity is somewhat unexpected in view of the contrast between the minimal control characteristic of the conventional approach and Kinsey's cross-examination. Minimal control clearly implies the use of silences and encouragements and the avoidance of interruptions and guggles. In practice, Kinsey's interviewers apparently do the same, even while carrying out a cross-examination (Cochran, Mosteller, & Tukey, 1954, p. 20):

Direct questions are put rapidly in an order which seems to these respondents hard to predict, so that it is difficult to tell what is coming next. Despite the air of briskness, we did not receive the impression that we were being hurried if we wished to reflect before replying. . . .

Although the technique of using falsehoods to overcome resistance as well as to increase validity must obviously be used with great caution, it is, as noted on p. 214, not unlike Kinsey's use of premises that assume the behavior under question.

The verbal procedures for depth interviewing proposed by the majority of research workers, by Kinsey and his colleagues, and by Link are summarized in Table 11. The sharpest contrast exists between the majority approach and Kinsey's, since these two have

TABLE 11. *Three Recommended Sets of Procedures for Depth Interviewing*

QUESTION COMPONENT	SOURCE OF RECOMMENDATION		
	Majority of research workers	Kinsey et al.	Link
Openness or Closedness	Open questions	Closed questions	Closed questions
Scope of question	Broad questions	Narrow questions	Narrow questions
Antecedents	Respondent antecedents	Interviewer antecedents and breaks	Interviewer antecedents
Form of antecedent	Procedures other than extensions (clarifications, echoes, etc.)	All procedures	Extensions and repetitions
Expectations	Nonexpectations	Expectations	Nonexpectations

no procedures in common. Link's interview falls between the others, employing many of the same procedures as Kinsey's but excluding those for which Kinsey has been most severely criticized —namely, factual delimitations, expectations, and questions which break with the last response.

To summarize, we have described three combinations of procedures which experienced research workers have used and recommended for eliciting depth. This variety contradicts the general view that there is only one accepted approach to this problem— that presented here as the majority recommendation. The single significant result with respect to the indirect effects of prescriptions of depth of response in our student interviews does not seem sufficiently solid, however, to provide support for one or another of the three procedures. Rather, in view of the fact that all three have actually been used and reported as satisfactory by their proponents, it is probably best to assume that there may actually be different ways to interview which vary in effectiveness with the nature of the research problem and the characteristics of the respondent. Clearly, more needs to be learned about the comparative merits of these three approaches.

UNANTICIPATED RESPONSES

Depending on the interviewer's purpose, unanticipated responses may be either welcome or annoying. In the initial phases of exploration, when the investigator is learning about the subject area, he may encourage knowledgeable respondents to suggest and open up subtopics which he could not have identified in advance. When the investigator does not know enough to ask the right questions, unanticipated responses are valuable, provided they have relevance or help define relevance for the study. On the other hand, when an interview has been developed to the point that it has been standardized, unanticipated responses have no immediate use.

The devices most generally recommended for obtaining unanticipated responses are open rather than closed questions; broad rather than narrow questions; respondent rather than interviewer antecedents; the use of echoes, extensions, and clarifications; and the use of silences and encouragements. The disadvantage of these techniques is that the responsibility for topic selection they permit the respondent may lead to his producing a great deal of irrelevant material. The recommended techniques are probably most effective when the respondent has gained a firm grasp of the general subject areas in which the interviewer is interested.

An alternative technique for obtaining unanticipated responses which does not seem to have the undesirable side effect of producing irrelevant responses involves the use of expectations. In Chapter 7 we suggest that expectations that are deliberately and heavily distorted can elicit useful unanticipated response material. Although the effectiveness of this technique rests only on the evidence we have presented, it seems sufficiently promising to justify further study.

Richardson and Dohrenwend's experimental data indicate that in objective questioning respondent antecedents elicit more unanticipated responses than interviewer antecedents. This difference did not appear, however, in subjective questioning.

LENGTH OF RESPONSE

Length of response is not in itself a desirable outcome, but it provides a means whereby other outcome characteristics may be influenced or achieved. At various times, the interviewer may desire long or short responses, but these are desired only because length is related to such response characteristics as validity, relevance, specificity, or depth. Long responses may be sought in an effort to elicit unanticipated material or depth, whereas short responses may be sought to increase relevance, clarity, or specificity. Control of the length of response may be important, also, in dealing with respondents who are generally garrulous or reticent or who become interested and involved in a subtopic and continue to talk after the interviewer has obtained all the information he needs.

The length of response is probably most directly controlled through the use of open and closed questions, open questions obtaining longer answers. Objective open questions obtain significantly longer responses than subjective open questions (Dohren-wend, in press), possibly because respondents resist subjective questions more than objective questions or because the differential effect of open and closed questions is greater for objective than subjective questions. There is need to examine also the sequential effect of various ratios of open to closed questions. A long series of closed questions may, as Roethlisberger and Dickson (1946, p. 203) have suggested, tend "to put a person in a 'yes' or 'no' frame of mind."

The use of silence in increasing the length of response appears effective if the silence does not exceed about three seconds in length. Longer silences are less likely to be effective. Guggles and interruptions, although not invariably successful in bringing a response to a close, generally will have this effect. Although it is reasonable to suppose that encouragements will lengthen responses, we have no direct evidence to support this belief.

The components described above may reasonably be expected to have their primary effects on length of response. The other components—antecedents, form of antecedents, expectations, and assumptions—will affect length of response less directly. It is generally believed that the forms of these components that are associated with a low degree of control, such as clarifications, respondent antecedents, and nonexpectations, will obtain longer responses, but we have been able to find no published studies or results in our own analysis which support this general belief. This absence of evidence, taken together with the positive results concerning the primary effects of open and closed questions, silences, and interruptions, suggests that length of response is most effectively controlled by these directly related procedures.

Until we had attempted to examine systematically the extent to which the interviewer can achieve desired response characteristics through his questioning procedures, we could not evaluate how much is known. At the conclusion of this examination, it is clear that, although we have much useful knowledge, there are numerous issues that require further study. Perhaps most striking

—in view of the fact that the achievement of validity is a central concern of interviewers—is the paucity of our knowledge about achieving validity by the use of question procedures. At present, it seems as though validity can best be approached indirectly through techniques which influence such other characteristics as participation. It appears, too, that the widely held proscription against the use of expectations and uninformed premises has prevented recognition of their positive values.

The Components of Questioning and the Form of the Interview

For the reasons outlined in the opening pages of Chapter 6, we have examined the question–answer process in terms of individual questions and their components rather than over-all style—e.g., degree of directiveness. Having taken our analysis as far as possible in the light of present knowledge, we can now examine its implications for the general form of the interview as a whole (Dohrenwend & Richardson, 1963).

THREE FORMS OF INTERVIEW IN CURRENT USE

We shall limit this discussion to three types of standardized interview that are currently used; and, instead of concerning ourselves with such broad and necessarily vague terms as directiveness or with the issue of standardization, we shall attempt to describe the three types of interview in terms of the question components to which we have devoted the preceding five chapters. The first type is exemplified by the opinion survey and will be labeled, for reasons to be explained below, the *limited-response* interview. The second goes under a variety of names, e.g., "semi-structured" (Argyris, 1960), "informal" (Bingham, Moore, & Gustad, 1959), and "clinical" or "nondirective" (Nahoum, 1958). We shall call this the *free-response* interview. The third is the directive type used by Kinsey and his colleagues (1948) and by Smith, Bruner, and White (1956) under the title "stress interview." This we shall call the *defensive-response* interview.

Limited-Response Interview The labels we have given to the three interview designs indicate the general task assigned to the respondent by means of prescriptions in the questions. In the limited-response interview, the respondent is expected to fill in a more or less detailed outline, drawn by the interviewer, without challenging the shape of that outline. In an opinion survey using this type of interview, for example, the respondent is asked to give his opinions on issues defined by—and, generally, in terms specified by—the interviewer, but the respondent is not to determine which of his opinions are relevant to the interviewer's inquiry.

The interviewer defines this task, first, by prescribing the length of response. Although the composition of limited-response interviews in terms of open and closed questions varies, we include in this category only interviews in which closed questions predominate over open questions. Our examination of published interviews shows a range of about two closed questions for each open question (Gurin, Veroff, & Feld, 1960) to as high as fifteen closed questions for each open question (Berelson, Lazarsfeld, & McPhee, 1954) in the main body of the interview, excluding closed background questions. So-called poll interviews may consist entirely of closed questions. Thus, although limited-response interviews are not homogeneous in their use of closed and open questions, they can be characterized as having a high proportion of closed questions.

The limited-response interview restricts the respondent's role in the selection of topics. Generally, the interviewer has a prepared list of questions which he asks in a predetermined order. Thus, most, although not necessarily all, of the interviewer's questions appear to the respondent to be concerned with a topic which the interviewer has introduced in a recent question or with a new topic. In a prepared schedule, a question can appear to assign responsibility for topic selection to the respondent only when it is so phrased that the respondent may be uncertain whether it was one of the interviewer's prepared questions. In the interview used by Gurin, Veroff, and Feld (1960) to study mental health, we find that about 6 per cent of the questions could prescribe that the respondent take responsibility for topic selection.

When the interviewer is allowed some freedom to change the wording and sequence of questions, the proportion of questions which appear to assign topic selection to the respondent may be as high as one-third (Dembo, Leviton, & Wright, 1956), but, in interviews of the limited-response type, such questions are clearly in the minority.

In the limited-response interview, the great majority of questions implicitly instruct the respondent to limit the length of his response to a few words and to limit the content of his response to the topic designated by the question. Previous work (Dohrenwend & Richardson, 1964) has shown that both these prescriptions are generally observed by respondents. Thus, the limited-response interview can be characterized as one in which, in line with the interviewer's prescriptions, respondents tend to restrict themselves to short responses on topics designated by the interviewer.

Although writers (e.g., Kornhauser & Sheatsley, 1959) have generally indicated that limited-response interviews should be free of premises and expectations, Litwak (1956) has convincingly argued that such questions are, in practice, employed to good use under such labels as "preference measure" or "extreme item." Therefore, although they are not the dominant form of question in limited-response interviews, both premises and expectations are used when they suit the investigator's measurement needs.

Free-Response Interview   In the free-response interview, the respondent's task is to build a picture around one or more points of orientation provided by the interviewer. In contrast to the limited-response interview, the free-response interview does not explicitly define boundaries for the respondent. He is expected, however, to maintain contact with the central focus or foci of the interview.

The free-response interview differs from the limited-response interview with respect to both prescription of length of response and prescription of responsibility for topic selection. For prescribing the length of response, the interviewer uses more open than closed questions. Published descriptions of interviews of this type indicate, in one instance (Adorno, Frenkel-Brunswik, Levin-son, & Sanford, 1950), a rate of about four open to three closed questions and, in another instance (Argyris, 1960), a ratio of three to two among questions prepared before the interview. Supple-mentary questions are guided by instructions to minimize the use of closed questions (e.g., Argyris, 1960).

Although they are in the minority, closed questions are never-theless used quite frequently in the free-response interview. This conclusion is based on our having observed, in interviews in which open questions were supposed to be used exclusively, that experi-enced interviewers were unable to avoid introducing closed ques-tions. The problem seems to be that open questions provide insufficient feedback to the respondent about the interviewer's comprehension of his responses and thus tend to make the re-spondent feel insecure. For this reason, some free-response inter-views may contain no more than a bare majority of open over closed questions.

Descriptions of free-response interviews stress that the inter-viewer helps the respondent to describe his experiences and feelings in a context that is meaningful to the respondent (e.g., Merton et al., 1956). In terms of prescriptions, the rule in these inter-views is that as many questions as possible prescribe that the re-spondent take responsibility for topic selection. Unfortunately, this type of question creates a problem because of its secondary effect on responses (Dohrenwend & Richardson, 1964). When the respondent takes responsibility for topic selection, he tends not only to volunteer information relevant to the purpose of the inter-view, as desired, but also to introduce irrelevant digressions. In the free-response interview, therefore, the interviewer faces the problem of minimizing irrelevancies without discouraging the re-spondent from taking a large measure of responsibility for topic selection.

Thus, the questioning procedure in the free-response interview prescribes that the respondent should feel free to give lengthy re-sponses on topics which he develops from those introduced by the interviewer. This interview differs from the limited-response interview in being designed to give the respondent a large measure of freedom and responsibility for the formulation of his responses.

Defensive-Response Interview   In the defensive-response interview, the respondent is faced with an interviewer who tries to force him into a particular position in each of a number of topic areas. The respondent is expected to defend himself against being forced into any position which, in fact, does not fit him. For example, if asked when he first engaged in a particular activity, he is expected to say that he never did if this is actually the case.

There are few published examples of the defensive-response interview in research. Kinsey, Pomeroy, and Martin's (1948) description of their interview suggests, however, that a major weapon in the interviewer's attack on the respondent is the correct premise. In addition, incorrect expectations are probably effective in developing the argumentative quality attributed by Smith, Bruner, and White (1956) to their stress interview. Thus, the defensive-response interview is characterized by restriction of the respondent's freedom of choice of response.

Another characteristic of this interview is suggested by the report, concerning the Kinsey interview, that questions were asked "in an order which seems . . . hard to predict, so that it is difficult to tell what is coming next" (Cochran, Mosteller, & Tukey, 1954, p. 20). That is, the interviewer prescribes that he, rather than the respondent, should take responsibility for topic selection. The respondent is simply expected to deal with each topic as the interviewer introduces it.

PURPOSES OF THE THREE FORMS OF INTERVIEW

Comparison of the purposes of the three forms of interview has been somewhat confused by the almost exclusive emphasis on the question of which type most nearly attains standardization. At this stage of our knowledge, however, there is no evidence to support the choice of any of the three forms on the grounds of optimal standardization of responses.

The defensive-response interview has been attacked (Wallin,

1949) as unsuitable for research purposes because the cross-examination technique it employs is regarded as antithetical to the informal, permissive interviewer–respondent relationship generally considered essential to good research interviewing. The fact that the interviewer conducts a cross-examination, however, need not imply that he treats the respondent as an accused malefactor. He may suggest that the respondent has done something or holds a particular belief without indicating that the act or belief is reprehensible. Furthermore, as we noted earlier, Kinsey's respondents regarded their interview experience as thoroughly pleasant. The defensive-response interview need not, therefore, be different in tone from any other form of research interview.

The essential differences in purpose among the three forms of interview are revealed by the different tasks set for the respondent by the types of questions employed.

In the limited-response interview, the respondent's task is to fill in an outline provided by the interviewer's questions. This task is accomplished, for the most part, by brief responses such as "yes," or "fairly strongly," or "three years," which obviously have no meaning apart from the questions. If these responses are to be valid, the questions must mean to the respondent exactly what they mean to the interviewer. The limited-response interview appears, therefore, to be appropriate when interviewer and respondents share a common vocabulary relevant to the issues and alternatives to be included in the interview.

The most obvious use for the limited-response interview, and one for which it is recommended by experienced research workers (e.g., Albig, 1957), is the study of opinions on public issues such as elections and major political policy questions (e.g., Berelson et al., 1954; Lazarsfeld & Thielens, 1958). It is used also, however, for studies concerned with less clearly articulated issues and alternatives, but here some investigators question its adequacy. For example, a reviewer of *Americans View Their Mental Health* (Nunnally, 1961, p. 264), although accepting the basic value of the study, noted the problem of interpretation raised by "variations in meanings of terms like *happiness, worry, personal problems,* etc." That is, these crucial terms in the interview may not have had the same meaning for the interviewers and all their respondents.

The free-response interview is intended to help the respondent with the task of examining and reporting on the meaning of his experiences and feelings (e.g., Merton et al., 1956). Thus, this type of interview is designed to overcome the weakness which some research workers attribute to the limited-response interview. By enabling the respondent to describe the meanings of his experiences to the interviewer, it avoids the assumption that the interviewer can understand them without explanation. It appears, therefore, to be designed for the very topics for which the limited-response interview is most likely to be considered inappropriate—that is, ambiguous public issues or private matters.

The defensive-response interview, on the other hand, is designed to break down the respondent's resistance to reporting certain experiences or expressing certain opinions. This kind of interview has been offered as an approach to topics entangled in strong social taboos and norms of what is acceptable, notably by Kinsey, Pomeroy, and Martin (1948).

Many investigators (e.g., Argyris, 1960; Maccoby & Maccoby, 1954) argue, however, that Kinsey and his colleagues were wrong in assuming that the defensive-response interview is needed to overcome resistance. They suggest that the incorporation of indirect questions, particularly projective questions, into the limited-response interview or the free-response interview is sufficient to deal with problems of resistance.

Since both positions involve problematical assumptions, we are not prepared to choose between them. The use of indirect questions presents the obvious problem of interpreting, and possibly misinterpreting, the meaning of the responses. On the other hand, the use of the defensive-response interview must assume an absence of suggestibility in the respondent, an assumption made questionable by recent evidence that in some individuals this characteristic cannot be eliminated by manipulating situational factors (Hovland & Janis, 1959; Stukat, 1958).

All three of the interview designs we have discussed are controversial in one way or another. Implicit in these controversies, however, is agreement that the objective of any interview is to produce reliable and valid responses. The disagreements concern the question of effective means for achieving this end. To resolve these, we must return to further examination of the uses and effects of various components of questions. We need research to further clarify the influence of questioning procedures on validity and other desired response characteristics. Ultimately, we must return to the fact that, in actual interviews, the various components of questions operate simultaneously and must be examined in combination as well as separately.

The interview forms in current use involve varying only a restricted number of combinations of question components, and we know almost nothing about either the feasibility or usefulness of combinations outside this range. Imaginative experimentation is needed to develop and test questions involving new combinations of components.

There is need, also, to question the widely held tacit assumption that an entire interview must embody the same general form or strategy. There are various ways and various sequences in which the three forms we have just discussed and others may be combined within a single interview.

Finally, and perhaps most important, we must attempt to assess the relative influences that are brought to bear on the desired response properties by the questioning procedures, the circumstances and conditions surrounding the interview, and the personal characteristics of the interviewer and respondent and their interaction. It is to the last of these elements that we shall devote the remaining chapters.

PART IV

Interviewer and Respondent

12

SOME CHARACTERISTICS

OF INTERVIEWERS

Although the interviewer has been a key element in each of the foregoing chapters, it was useful to defer a discussion of his personal characteristics until his tasks, responsibilities, and various work settings had been described. At this point, it is clear that the wide variety of interview situations calls for a wide variety of interview forms and styles, which in turn calls for a wide variety of skills and personal characteristics. Moreover, our description of the interviewer's task in terms of gaining and maintaining participation and in using the question–answer process effectively should provide a background against which his skills and personal characteristics may be viewed.

Some Obstacles to Assessment

A number of obstacles stand in the way of a clear-cut definition of the characteristics desirable in an interviewer, the measurement of his performance, and the development of techniques for selecting interviewers or for predicting the success of a candidate for training as an interviewer. Because of these obstacles, relatively little research has been done on the problem; and, as a consequence, much of our existing information is based upon the impressions of experienced interviewers. Information relevant to certain kinds of interviewer is sometimes unjustifiably applied to other kinds of interviewer or generalized as applicable to "the interviewer."

WHO IS THE INTERVIEWER?

As the foregoing chapters imply, the research interviewer may be any of a variety of people. His responsibilities may range from the relatively routine task of asking the questions set forth on a schedule to the complex conceptualizing necessary to plan and pretest the interview, to gain insights from response materials, and to maintain respondent participation under varying and sometimes difficult conditions. This wide variation in task raises the question whether it is more useful to attempt to set up interviewer criteria for each type of interview or to seek common denominators that are desirable in "the interviewer" regardless of the nature and context of his task.

Even if we possessed well-tested criteria for selecting interviewers for specified tasks, there is often only a small number of interviewers from whom selection can be made, or funds may be inadequate for obtaining interviewers with the level of skills ideally required. Except for the schedule standardized interview, it is important to select persons who are well trained in a research discipline related to the research purpose. Where the number of candidates available as interviewers is limited, it may be more important to use training techniques to develop the person's potential interviewing abilities as far as possible. However, the fact that a shortage of qualified applicants often makes it impossible to apply selection procedures should not discourage systematic study aimed at identifying the personal characteristics that contribute to interviewer effectiveness.

THE EVALUATION OF PERSONAL QUALITIES

A second difficulty in evaluating the characteristics of interviewers involves identifying the significant personal qualities that are related to competence in various types of interviewing. Although the quality of the responses may be judged by the criteria suggested in Chapter 5, it is difficult to determine the extent to which, in a specific interview, these qualities are a consequence of the interviewer's personal qualities, the knowledge and articulateness of the respondent, the nature of the subject matter, or the particular relationship between the interviewer and the respondent.

Those responsible for evaluating interviewers have often had to depend largely on their evaluation of the written records made by the interviewer—field notes or coded or written responses to prepared questions. Such materials can be evaluated for their coverage, relevance, specificity, and other criteria described in Chapter 5. Fuller evaluation can be made by observing interviews or listening to tape recordings. These methods make the behavior of the interviewer accessible and, thus, enable the evaluator to obtain information on what actually happened. But, in these processes of evaluation, it is difficult to analyze the intricate relationship among the methods used by the interviewer, the interaction of interviewer and respondent, the interview context, and the quality of response materials; hence, it is difficult to isolate the influence of the interviewer's personal characteristics.

Little systematic research has been done to isolate the personal variables that contribute to interviewers' effectiveness in different forms of interviewing or the variables that contribute to their potentialities for becoming effective through a program of training. In the absence of such research, experienced field workers have, at various times, attempted to construct profiles of the "ideal" interviewer, but such profiles—listings of desirable characteristics —have some basic shortcomings. First, there is not a high degree of consistency between one such list and another, perhaps because each compiler had in mind a specific type of interview situation. Secondly, the various elements comprising the profile are unlikely to be found in a single individual. As one investigator (Bronfenbrenner, 1951) remarked after reviewing a series of such profiles, "In short, God's perfect creature without God's problems." Thirdly, experienced interviewers are thinking about highly varied research situations and forms of interviewing. Despite these limitations, however, it may be useful to review the task of the

TABLE 12. *Skills Required in Different Types of Interview*

SKILLS REQUIRED BY INTERVIEWER	NON-STANDARDIZED	STANDARDIZED					
		Nonschedule			Schedule		
		Exploratory	Pretest	Interview	Exploratory	Pretest	Interview
Knowledge of subject matter	H[1]	H (General)	H (General)	H (Specific)	H	M[2]-H (Specific)	L[3]
Conceptual and analytical ability	H	H	M	L	H	M	L
Translation of concepts into content areas and questions	H	H	M	M	H	M	L
Gaining and exploiting new ideas and insights during the interview	H	H	M	L	H	M	L
Formulating questions during the interview	H	H	H	H	H	M	L
Selecting respondents	H	H	H	L	H	H	L
Gaining the participation of respondents	H	H	H	H	H	H	M (*With assistance of study director*)
Recording data from the interview	H	H	M	M	H	M	L

[1] H = High level of skill.
[2] M = Moderate level of skill.
[3] L = Low level of skill.

interviewer in various forms of interview and to consider the interviewer's personal characteristics that have been found (or conjectured) to be desirable for each.

The Task of the Interviewer

Table 12 presents, in "job description" form, the skills required in the three basic forms of interviewing now in current use. In examining the table, however, one must bear in mind that the several stages of the same form of interview are not necessarily carried out by the same person and, hence, that not all the skills need be embodied in one individual.

The nonstandardized interview, for reasons pointed out in Chapter 2, must be carried out by the principal investigator alone or with one or more colleagues. The nonschedule standardized interview can, once it has been developed and pretested, be carried out by assistants, although the skills required for interviewing of this type generally dictate that the interviewers be of a caliber closely approaching that of the principal investigator; that is, the interviewer is usually either a colleague or an assistant who has been given lengthy and rigorous training. The development and pretesting of the schedule interview, on the other hand, are essentially the responsibility of the principal investigator, but, after the schedule has been developed, he can delegate the data collection to interviewers with considerably less training and skill who have been trained only in the use of the particular schedule. The various degrees to which tasks can be delegated or shared have, as we shall note, strong implications for the skills required by interviewers for different forms of interviewing.

Knowledge of the subject matter, the ability to conceptualize and analyze, skill in the formulation of questions, and the ability to translate concepts into questions and response material into meaningful data and insights constitute a rare combination of skills that is likely to be found only in the principal investigator or a colleague. It is for this reason that neither exploratory interviewing nor the development and pretesting of any kind of standardized interviewing can generally be delegated to others. Although the nonschedule standardized interview does not demand the same degree of conceptualizing and analytic skills, it requires sensitivity to the social and educational characteristics of the respondent, flexibility of behavior, and the ability to keep in mind and to elicit a standard body of information by means of a very wide variety of question formulations and interviewing styles. In brief, in terms of the range of skills he must have, the nonschedule standardized interviewer stands midway between the nonstandardized interviewer and the interviewer who works from a schedule that others have prepared. He must have some of the former's understanding of the broad purposes of the study and the subject matter as well as all the skills of the latter.

In theory, at least, the schedule interviewer requires little understanding of the subject matter (beyond the meaning of the questions) or of the relationship between the study and the schedule from which he asks the questions. In practice, however, it has been found that in some situations the interviewer's understanding of and interest in the study increases his effectiveness. Thus, a schedule interview on the subject of, say, American foreign policy might require an interviewer with a higher level of education than one on the subject of cigarette-brand preferences.

Aside from this issue, however, certain readily definable skills are demanded of the schedule interviewer, and these skills are required in a rather considerable degree because his behavior is so closely restricted by the requirements of the schedule of questions. Most of these are skills in interpersonal interaction. The schedule interviewer must maintain an appearance of spontaneity and interest with each new respondent, even after having used the schedule in scores of earlier interviews. In every interview, he must maintain painstaking attention to accuracy and detail in asking the questions and recording and coding the responses; he must gain and maintain participation, using as closely as possible a standard statement of purpose; he must tolerate the difficulties of locating respondents and sometimes encountering refusals and rebuffs; finally, he must have sufficient self-confidence to initiate contacts with one stranger after another and not display anxiety and hesitancy lest this be sensed by the respondents and lead to a refusal to participate.

There is no necessary relationship between the skills of conceptualization, knowledge of subject matter, insight, and analysis, on one hand, and the skills of questioning, gaining participation, and sensitivity to language and idiom, on the other. The skills of interviewing and obtaining participation, however, are unlikely to be productive in research without concepts, analytic skill, insight, and subject matter. The research investigator who is a poor interviewer but has conceptual and analytic powers is likely to turn to the schedule standardized interview and hire interviewers, whether or not this may be the most appropriate type of interview. Alternatively, he may employ the methods of observation and documents, in which he may have greater facility.

The diversity of skills required in the various forms and stages of the interview not only reduces the probability of their being embodied in a single individual but also implies that the individual highly suited to one form of interview may be thoroughly unsuited to another. This point should be borne in mind in the following discussion of specific interviewer characteristics, since most of the information we present derives from the study of a specific kind of interviewer, often in a specific study situation, and may or may not be applicable to other kinds.

Ways of Characterizing Interviewers

"DEMOGRAPHIC" CHARACTERISTICS OF THE INTERVIEWER

Studies of schedule interviewers have focused largely on such variables as age, sex, ethnicity, level of education, and social class rather than personality or modes of interaction, for two reasons. First, such data are readily available to the investigator. Second, the severe restrictions set on his freedom of behavior in a schedule interview provide little opportunity for the interviewer to show the more idiosyncratic aspects of his personality. Since the interviewer–respondent relationship is short-lived and tends to be superficial, the respondent is likely to evaluate the interviewer in terms of these easily ascertainable, visible characteristics. In the nonschedule interview, where a more personal relationship is likely to develop between interviewer and respondent, a great many other qualities of the interviewer will be involved in the respondent's judgment of him, and the visible characteristics, which were initially important, may diminish in importance.

Reviewing studies of these kinds of variables in schedule interviewers, Hyman (1954, p. 293) concludes:

... [T]he general profile which emerges of the better interviewer as female, 35–44 years old, possessing superior education, experience, and intelligence, with introversion tendencies is in general agreement with the findings of other investigators already cited. It will be remembered that the Guest studies showed a high positive association between intelligence and interviewing performance, with a suggestion of a negative correlation between social orientation and performance, and that the Sheatsley labor market study found that women, those in the 30–40 age group, those with superior education, and those whose background was in the non-persuasive occupations, obtained better interviewer ratings.

In line with these findings on interviewer intelligence, Guest and Nuckols (1950) found, in a laboratory experiment, that the interviewer's intelligence was correlated with his accuracy in recording response material.

In a schedule-interview study on mental health, Benney, Riesman, and Star (1956) found that the least inhibited communication occurred when both interviewer and respondent were young people of the same sex, and the most inhibited when they were of the same age and opposite sex. Whereas Hyman focused on the interviewer alone, Benney and his colleagues examined the dyadic relation between interviewer and respondent. This raises the question, which is examined further in Chapter 14, whether interviewers can be selected effectively without reference to the subject matter of the interview and the personal characteristics of the respondents.

STATUS RELATIONSHIPS PREFERRED BY THE INTERVIEWER

One of the significant interaction characteristics of the interviewer is the degree to which he can function with respondents of all social, economic, and educational levels. There is, unfortunately, no evidence to support the belief that interviewers can function equally well with all types of respondents. Our impression, derived from our training of interviewers for nonstandardized interviewing, is that the effectiveness of some interviewers depends very heavily on whether they perceive the status of the respondent as equal, superordinate, or subordinate to their own. Some interviewers function well with respondents whom they regard as having higher status than themselves but, when interviewing respondents whom they perceive as having lower status, behave in such a way that the respondents complain of the interviewers' arrogance, discourtesy, or inconsiderateness. Conversely, other interviewers, identifying perhaps with the "underdog," appear to function more effectively with people whom they regard as subordinate to themselves in status. Although novelists, playwrights, psychologists, and other observers of human relationships have observed these phenomena, we know of no empirical studies relating them to interviewer effectiveness.

The superordinate–subordinate dimension is only one of several that require study and, ultimately, consideration in the selection of interviewers when the characteristics of the respondent set are known. Whether an interviewer works more effectively with respondents who are older or younger, of his own or the opposite sex, quick-thinking and articulate or slow-thinking and inarticulate, garrulous or taciturn are all questions that might profitably be considered.

PERSONALITY CHARACTERISTICS

A number of investigators have recognized the demands made by various kinds of research in terms of the personality or temperament of the investigator. As Kluckhohn (Gottschalk et al., 1945, p. 110) noted:

. . . [There] is some real conflict between the type of temperament and training required for doing ethnography successfully and that which a superior worker in personal documents ought to possess. For example, the gentle techniques which promote a free flow of spontaneous reminiscence are often incompatible with getting the specific details and the cross-checking of data required in good ethnographic work.

And the use of personality factors for the selection of interviewers —at least for nonstandardized interviewing—has been suggested (Kluckhohn, 1945, p. 124).

A whole monograph could, and probably should, be written upon the personality trends which characterize social anthropologists and ethnologists as a group and upon those personality trends prominent in "successful" and "unsuccessful" field workers. Of their deeper motivations and of the major emotional distortions or blocks in their personalities anthropologists, like most human beings, seldom have minimal awareness. And yet the interviewer must understand and handle himself as well as his subject and interpreter.

But this suggestion has not stimulated much systematic study and, as a consequence, most of the information available consists of the impressions of experienced investigators, of which the following, by Sidney and Beatrice Webb (1932, p. 140) is typical.[4]

Without such an atmosphere of relaxation, of amused interest on both sides, it will often be impracticable to get at those intimate details of daily experience which are the most valuable data of the sociologist. Hence a spirit of adventure, a delight in watching human beings as human beings quite apart from what you can get out of their minds, an enjoyment of the play of your personality with that of another, are gifts of rare value in the art of interviewing, and gifts which are, perhaps, more frequently characteristic of the woman than the man.

To elicit further impressions about the personality characteristics desirable in nonschedule interviewers, Richardson questioned fifteen experienced field workers. The composite list, reproduced in the Appendix on pp. 332–334, assembles an awe-inspiring array of virtues. As the listing indicates, the nonschedule interviewer is commonly held to be a "good" person who can get on well with all sorts and conditions of men. There is a heavy emphasis on interpersonal skills, the maintenance of equanimity in the face of provocation and personal stress, powerful self-discipline, and control of feelings.

On the basis of this listing, Richardson developed an experimental study using personality measures adapted from the Thematic Apperception Test, a projective test in which subjects make

[4] Although they do not specify the type of interview, the Webbs probably have in mind nonstandardized interviewing.

up stories about a standard set of pictures. Measures of interviewing performance were obtained from tape recordings of nonstandardized interviews, the purpose of which was to reconstruct an event in which the respondent had participated. These personality and interview-skill measures were obtained for the experimental group both before and after intensive training in nonschedule interviewing. A control group was given no interview training but was tested twice, at the same times as the experimental group (a full description of the study appears in the Appendix).

The personality measures did not change as the result of training, but skills in interviewing did increase. Personality measures were unrelated to the initial level of skill in interviewing before the subjects were given training. However, the following personality measures, obtained before training, were positively related to skill in interviewing after training.

Human relations: Insights into the complex of feeling relationships between the people depicted in the stories
Symbolic aggression: Emotional and verbal: to hate, be angry, engage in a verbal quarrel; to curse, criticize, or ridicule
Affiliation: To seek or form friendly relations with a person or persons; to enjoy persons of either sex
Intraggression: To blame, criticize, reprove, or belittle oneself for wrongdoing, stupidity, or failure; to suffer feelings of inferiority, guilt, remorse; to punish oneself physically, to commit suicide

The positive relationships between human relations and affiliation were in the predicted direction, the prediction being based on the belief that the nonstandardized interview generally requires a particularistic rather than universalistic relationship.[5] With respect to symbolic aggression and intraggression, there was no clear rationale for making predictions. It is generally felt that the competent interviewer is one who can closely control his aggression and who can release aggression either symbolically in fantasy toward others or—less satisfactorily, perhaps—toward himself.

[5] It is for a different form of interview, requiring different skills—the schedule interview—that Hyman (1954) and Riesman (1958) prefer a more universalistic or impersonal relationship.

From this reasoning, a positive prediction was made for symbolic aggression, and this was confirmed. A negative prediction was made for intraggression, based on the hunch that a person who in a TAT could exhibit only intraggression would have difficulty in releasing aggression in a way which would not be harmful for himself or others if his stay in the field was lengthy and stressful. The prediction was contradicted by the results, but the rationale for the prediction was not tested because the experiment did not incorporate a measure of ability to withstand field stress. Without replication of this study with variation of the type of interview and subject matter, it is impossible, of course, to know how generally applicable the results may be.

ABILITY TO WITHSTAND STRESS

In our discussion of gaining respondent participation (Chapter 4), we noted that interviews vary enormously in the degree of stress they place on the interviewer. Although, traditionally, the anthropologist has been most concerned with the problem of stress, there is no logical reason why any of the three major forms of interview may not be highly stressful. Hence, to the extent that it can be predicted, ability to withstand stress is an important factor in the selection of interviewers. In some situations, stress can affect the interviewer's effectiveness in two ways: not only can it reduce the level of his own skills and activities but, if it visibly reduces his self-confidence, it may make respondents less willing to participate or may reduce the quality of their participation.

There are no empirical studies on the relationship between interviewer competence and the ability to withstand stress. The study by Richardson (see Appendix) offers indirect evidence that personality characteristics which field supervisors assume make a field worker most vulnerable to the stresses inherent in the role are the same characteristics that predict competence in observation. To state this in another way, the person who is a competent observer is the one who is most sensitive to the stresses of field work and may be least able to withstand them. This finding is relevant to interviewing because it has long been assumed that a good observer is also a good interviewer, and this assumption has been used in the selection of interviewers. In the study by Richardson, no relationship between the skills of observation and interviewing was found.

THE INTERVIEWER'S CHARACTERISTIC MODE OF INTERACTION

Although we have discussed the personal–impersonal, particularistic–universalistic dimension of interpersonal interaction as a characteristic of respondents (Chapter 4), interviewers may also be characterized in these same terms. We do not know the extent to which variation in this dimension may be achieved through conscious effort or whether one mode or the other is more effective for interviewing generally or for specific forms of interview.

Riesman (1958, pp. 345–346) discusses the schedule interviewer's preferred modes of interaction under the terms "bluestocking" and "market researcher," a distinction closely related to the personal–impersonal dimension of interpersonal interaction we have used.

We could divide the interviewers along a number of dimensions that would bear some relevance to their performance. . . . But I want to concentrate on the market researcher and the bluestocking because the image many respondents had of the survey was influenced by the relative sociability of the one type of interviewer, the relative intellectuality of the other.

The bluestocking is characteristically a young, college-educated housewife with small children who wants a part-time job that continues her connection with the larger world and intellectual pursuits—a job that can be managed at her own pace and to suit her children's hours. She is eager to contribute to intercultural understanding, and to her own; she is interested in the opinions people have concerning current affairs (and has become used to finding them often unenlightened and widely variant from her own—or, worse, finding them nonexistent). Her persistence and gradual professionalization in the arduous and often anxiety-provoking task of interviewing is sustained, less by her personal attachment to her agency, than by her interest in and devotion to the subject matter of the surveys she works on, be it mental health, civil liberties, or opinions on foreign affairs (the bluestockings invariably jumped at the chance to work on the Teacher

Apprehension Study). Her alternative pursuits are likely to be social work or personnel work or other occupations involving a combination of technical and personal concern; and when her children are older, she is not likely to continue interviewing, or she may become a supervisor.

In contrast, the "market researcher" interviewer has a less psychological orientation, and enjoys the exercise of her social as much as of her intellectual skills. It would not be quite correct to say she likes to meet people, rather than to meet opinions and ideas; indeed, many interviewers who had primarily done market research declared that they had enjoyed the Teacher Apprehension Study more than any they had ever worked on. But this, I suspect, was at least as much because their respondents were, in the better colleges, alive, idiosyncratic and even eccentric, while the topic brought the interviewers (as election polls do also) into the public spotlight, the glamorous area of the Cold War, of national affairs. Or, to put it in another way, just because the orientation of the market researchers is social rather than intellectual, they were frequently able to appreciate the tone if not the content of their novel contacts with academicians.

The market researcher is typically older and less well educated (both formally and in terms of reading and adult education) than the bluestocking. Vivacious and enjoying relations with people, she finds interviewing a way of remaining active after the children no longer need close attention, and of earning a modest addition to the family income; if she were not interviewing, she might be running an inn, or selling in a specialty store, or in the real estate business.

Hyman (1954), although he does not provide systematically contrasting descriptions, compares "task-oriented" and "socially oriented" schedule interviewers. The task-oriented interviewer "does not feel privately irritated by a respondent's views" and does not regard the interview "as an affect-laden experience." Such interviewers "report that they only occasionally or hardly ever would enjoy staying on to chat with their respondents." Some of them report "as their chief *failing* the fact of their social '*over-involvement*' in the interview situation . . . [italics ours]. They say: 'I'm too sympathetic. I like people too much.' " They "develop a professional attitude toward their work so that they seldom become fully *ego*-involved in the situation."

The "socially oriented" interviewer, by contrast, reports frequently making friends with the respondent and regards the interview as affect-laden. Some of them demonstrate what Hyman (1954, p. 50) terms "a kind of *intrusiveness* of the interviewer, a tendency to want to enter deeply into the respondent's affairs." As one such interviewer describes herself (Hyman, 1954, p. 51):

I'm a very friendly soul. I never go anywhere without someone speaking to me. I enjoy it. . . . If I had to go out and get me a job, I'd try to get into personnel work. I like to speak to people—hear their ideas—analyze the different types. . . . I'm just genuinely interested in human nature—human beings—their behavior—what makes them think as they do.

Both Hyman and Riesman express a preference for the impersonal, universalistic mode but they base this preference on the use of the schedule interview and do not indicate whether they maintain it for all forms of interview. Hyman prefers the less intrusive interviewers because he believes they produce less response bias. It is noteworthy that writers about schedule interviews are always fearful of the negative bias the interviewer may introduce in using a schedule of questions. They say little or nothing about the positive contribution the schedule interviewer may make—e.g., using skill and charm to persuade respondents to stick with a schedule of questions that they may find thoroughly uncongenial.

Although we shall return to the personal–impersonal dimension in our discussion of the interviewer–respondent relationship (Chapter 14), two points are worth making here. First, no systematic attempt has been made to construct measures or indicators of this dimension. Secondly, with the increasing prominence of this concept in the literature of interviewing, research is needed to clarify and test a number of issues. Is the recent increasing preference for interviewer impersonality simply a reaction against the concept of the warm, friendly "rapport" between interviewer and respondent that dominated earlier thinking? Or is it an idealization stemming directly from the demands of standardization in the schedule interview, since impersonal interviewer behavior is more easily standardized than a more personal approach? How realistic is it to expect interviewers whose behavior is highly restricted by the demands of the schedule not to seek, as one of the few rewards, some of the satisfactions of interpersonal relations with respondents whom they find congenial? Are there measurable differences between people in their need to display something of themselves in their first encounter with strangers and their need to focus some attention on themselves? Do increasing differences in the background and experience of interviewer and respondent make it easier to maintain an impersonal role? These are some of the questions that could usefully be considered in any examination of the personal–impersonal dimension of interviewer–respondent interaction.

FLEXIBILITY IN FORMULATING QUESTIONS

For nonschedule interviewing, the flexibility with which the interviewer can learn to use a variety of question forms and types may be a useful criterion of competence. In our training of nonschedule interviewers, we noted that, before they underwent training, students varied considerably in the types of questions they employed; during training, they varied in their ability to become aware of the forms they were using and to increase and vary their questioning techniques. The following composite descriptions of the inexperienced and the trained nonschedule interviewer will illustrate this difference, among others.

The inexperienced interviewer working without a schedule and formulating his own questions is generally very anxious about the lack of preformulation; he is fearful that he will be unable to keep the interview going. Sometimes, he will prepare and memorize a set of questions, even though this defeats the purpose of the nonschedule interview. Alternatively, he may, immediately after asking a question, become preoccupied with formulating the next question. In either case, he listens only superficially, at best, to what the respondent says. The successive questions are likely to have interviewer antecedents or no antecedents rather than respondent antecedents, and the interviewer is likely to show a strong preference for closed questions. When he does ask an open question, he frequently restates it almost without pause in the form of a closed question.

Many beginners are very fearful of silences and avoid them by jumping in with a question. The beginner also frequently interrupts a response in his haste to ask the next question. After listening to the respondent tell about some experience, he sometimes will recount some similar experience he has had, and the interview becomes, for a time, a social conversation.

Because the interviewer is not listening carefully to what the respondent is saying, and because he often focuses more on the interpersonal relationship than on the response material, much of what the respondent brings up is not carefully explored through clarifications, extensions, summaries, and confrontations. Often, because the interviewer has not developed a conceptual framework in advance to guide him in selecting content, there will be many abrupt and illogical transitions. Of the wide variety of question techniques described in chapters 6 through 10, the interviewer will use a very limited range, with little variation within this range.

If the foregoing description seems exaggeratedly unfavorable, it is only because it represents a composite of errors. Although not every one of them appears in the efforts of every untrained or unskilled interviewer, each of them is familiar to anyone who has trained interviewers. Although successfully trained and experienced interviewers vary widely among themselves in the techniques they use, it is possible, nevertheless, to identify certain general differences between their styles and those of the inexperienced or unskilled nonschedule interviewer.

The over-all impression gained by observing the experienced interviewer or listening to a tape recording of the interview is that the flow of communication is smooth and that the response material is being given full and careful consideration. Rather than impose his questioning framework on the respondent, the interviewer adapts his pace, idiom, and thought patterns to those of the respondent. In part, he achieves this effect through relating his questions to information the respondent has given in answer to the preceding question or earlier in the interview. Because of this technique, the respondent appears to have considerable control over the topics, even when the interviewer is in fact maintaining considerable control. The skilled interviewer follows up partial statements and cues more carefully and tolerates fewer ambiguities and internal contradictions in the response material. In the initial stage of the interview, when introducing a new topic, the experienced interviewer often uses a number of open questions to get some idea of the kind of information the respondent is best equipped to provide and the manner in which he finds it most congenial to provide it. The skilled interviewer is more likely to drop a line of inquiry that seems ineffective and to return to it at a later time when he deems it more profitable.

Although both unskilled and skilled interviewers use premises and expectations, those of the unskilled interviewers are more often uninformed, whereas those of the skilled interviewers are more likely to be informed and to predict correctly the response the respondent would make.

The variation between interviewers in flexibility to adapt interviewing techniques became apparent in an experiment conducted by Dohrenwend (in press). Four interviewers, all of whom had had considerable experience and training in the use of various question forms, were trained to conduct experimental interviews; in the first half of the interview, they had to maintain tight control (questions had to be closed and had to have prior questions as their antecedents or had to break with the last response), and, in the second half, they had to maintain a low degree of control (questions had to be open and to have prior responses as their antecedents). The interviewers were required, also, to ask either all objective or all subjective questions, in accordance with an experimental design.

Two of the four interviewers had much more difficulty than the other two in controlling their interview techniques. To obtain eight interviews meeting these specifications, the four interviewers required eight, nine, fourteen, and eighteen trials respectively.

One possible explanation of these differences is that the two interviewers who required the least number of interviews in order to meet the experimental criterion had less difficulty in gaining and maintaining respondent participation. But postinterview ratings made by the respondents indicate no differences among the interviewers on this dimension. The degree to which each of the four interviewers was able to dominate his respondents might constitute another explanation, and a review and analysis of the tape recordings of the interviews suggests that the two less successful interviewers showed a tendency to adapt their pattern of interviewing to that of the respondent; this suggests that the explanation of dominance is tenable. Although tape recordings of the four interviewers created the impression that the two who were more successful, and more dominant, sounded very cold, they were rated very favorably by all their respondents.

If the forms and patterns of questions or the general style used by a person is employed as a criterion for the evaluation of interviewers, the evaluation should be made only after the interviewer has obtained some training and experience. Richardson (1954) has found that the initial level of interviewer performance before training is a poor indicator of his performance after training and experience.

Further systematic work is necessary for the development of criteria based on the interviewer's flexibility of style and his ability to exploit the advantages of the entire range of question forms; the economy and availability of tape recorders makes such experimentation readily feasible, and it seems to offer a highly fruitful approach to the assessment of a major element of interviewer competence.

THE ETHICS OF THE INTERVIEWER

Although consideration of his ethical standards and values may constitute a difficult and highly subjective way to characterize an interviewer, the subject of ethics arises repeatedly in discussions among experienced interviewers. The following summary, which encompasses most of the points raised, applies to observers as well as to interviewers.

Interviewers should be able to refrain from violating the values and taboos of the respondent set; must maintain a professional attitude toward the study, both in formal and informal situations; must maintain confidences and the security of written response materials; and must refrain from criticism and gossip. In addition, they should refrain from passing judgment on others' behavior or on social situations, and they should be able to keep their own convictions and be committed to the scientific approach. They should be able to respect other people's customs, values, and mannerisms, no matter how different from their own.

There is no uniform code of ethics agreed on by all investigators, and interviewers may become involved in or be invited to join studies in which procedures are used which conflict with their own ethics.[6] Covert interviewing, asking certain kinds of questions, misleading respondents or withholding certain information from them, or even the study of certain subject matter may produce in the interviewer a conflict between his professional responsibilities and his ethical values. If the interviewer does not recognize the conflict, or if he resolves it inadequately, his performance may deteriorate severely, regardless of his basic competence.

The Problem of Interviewer Selection

Our review of the interviewer's task in the various types of interview and our listing of the several personality and performance characteristics which may be related to competence in certain types of interviewing were intended to delineate areas requiring research rather than to provide clear-cut criteria for the selection of interviewers or interviewer trainees. Until such further research produces results, recruiting competent interviewers must depend on three approaches: the use of experienced interviewers, personal selection, and training.

THE USE OF EXPERIENCED INTERVIEWERS

After reviewing the studies of interviewers employed for schedule interviewing, Hyman (1954, pp. 300–301) concludes:

In summary, the weight of evidence supports the conclusion that we may expect superior performance from the more experienced interviewer. Two qualifications should be made, however:

[6] The American Psychological Association has published *Ethical Standards for Psychologists*. The American Sociological Association has distributed to its membership *Code of Ethics (First Draft)*. See also A. J. King and A. J. Spector, "Ethical and Legal Aspects of Survey Research," *Amer. Psychol.*, 1963, **18** (4), pp. 204–208. The Society for Applied Anthropology has published a statement on ethics in *Hum. Org.*, 1963–64, **22** (4), p. 237.

1. Any apparent superiority of experienced interviewers may be due as much to selective turnover (the better interviewer remains longer on the staff) as to the beneficial effects of experience itself. Whatever the reason, the length of experience still seems valid as a predictor of performance.
2. It seems that the research agency should be cautious about hiring interviewers with particularly long experience with another agency, but this should obviously depend on the degree of similarity of the work of the two agencies.

One common pitfall in hiring experienced interviewers is the assumption that experience in conducting one type of interview under a specific set of circumstances and conditions is a qualification for all kinds of interviewing. For example, a woman who has had several years' experience as a marriage counselor may be totally unqualified to conduct exploratory interviews with parents and children on child-rearing practices. Similarly, an interviewer whose experience is based entirely on market-research schedule interviewing may be quite unsuited to nonstandardized interviewing. If the type of interview, the subject matter, the characteristics of the respondents, or the circumstances and conditions of the study differ considerably from those to which the interviewer is accustomed, his prior experience may well prove more of a hindrance than an advantage, and a person with no previous interviewing experience trained for the specific study may be more effective.

SELECTION AND TRAINING

Although large numbers of persons have been and are currently employed in research interviewing, there are no tests available that are effective instruments for selection. Research agencies employing schedule interviewers may use as a guide certain demographic characteristics—e.g., age, sex, and social class—which, from past experience, they have found to be related to effective performance. Such measures, however, provide only a very coarse screening of applicants and cannot discriminate within the broad characteristics that they specify. The fact that several research directors, such as Hyman (1954) and Riesman (1958), believe that effective and ineffective interviewers exhibit personality differences suggests that personality measures may be developed. But most predictive instruments in social science can select or reject with any certainty only a small proportion at the two extremes of the population. For this reason, a large number of applicants would be needed in relation to the positions available, and such a situation rarely occurs in social research.

Another form of selective test for schedule interviewers consists of evaluation of the applicant in a simulated interview situation after he has been instructed in his task. This form of selection is a more direct measure when it is used in conjunction with a probationary period of training and performance and may prove to be the most effective selection procedure now available. In the selection of nonschedule interviewers, a test of performance before training does not appear to be predictive of performance after training (see p. 344). Some investment in the training of applicants seems necessary before an evaluation of competence would have much predictive value.

As we noted earlier in this chapter, it is not difficult to obtain from experienced research directors a list of the characteristics they consider desirable in a nonschedule interviewer. But the qualities comprising such a list are most unlikely to be embodied in any single human being, much less in one available as an interviewer. At present, the number of people interested in doing nonschedule interviewing is not so much in excess of the demand that procedures can profitably be employed to identify only those candidates who show the highest promise. Instead, initial selection realistically must be restricted to screening out those people who seem likely to find interviewing an unpleasant and rigorous experience and those who seem likely, even after training, to upset the respondents. For the remainder of those interested in becoming interviewers, some diagnosis of potential ability, supplemented by individual training based on an initial appraisal of skills, appears to be the most promising way to obtain optimum performance.

TRAINING

Procedures for training schedule interviewers have been well developed. In general, field supervisors familiarize the interviewers with the schedule of questions, the use of alternative questions, the conditions under which certain questions are to be omitted, and the coding of answers. Trainees are often paired off to role-play an interview which the supervisor either observes and criticizes or tape-records for later review. After role-playing, the interviewers often conduct several practice interviews with people not included in the study and discuss these experiences with the supervisor. Interviewers are also given practice in describing the purpose of the interview and the sponsorship of the study, and, in some projects, supervisors play the role of particularly recalcitrant respondents to provide the interviewers with an opportunity to deal with situations they will probably encounter in the field. The accuracy and completeness of recording are emphasized in training, and work is checked against tape recordings of practice interviews.

It is probable that much of the nonschedule interviewer's training consists of an apprenticeship or assistantship with the principal investigator, since a considerable understanding of the subject matter and the informational needs of the study is essential. But, as we have noted earlier, the principal investigator, regardless of his skills as a social scientist, may be severely deficient in the interpersonal skills required in interviewing. As a consequence, nonschedule interviewers frequently are forced to go into the field virtually untutored in the skills of formulating questions or developing and maintaining satisfactory participation with the people they wish to study.[7]

A number of investigators (e.g., Du Bois, 1937, p. 293) believe that an increase in self-awareness is an essential part of training.

By a thorough awareness of his techniques the individual field worker should develop great range, flexibility and control in handling human material. Even in the arts articulateness and awareness in techniques are not necessarily handicaps. In those social disciplines which profess to be sciences they become obligatory.

Whereas Du Bois suggests self-awareness in terms of professional techniques, Mead (1952) has argued strongly in favor of giving field workers a disciplined awareness of their own cultural position; and Nadel (1951) and Kluckhohn (1955) suggest that field workers should undergo psychoanalysis.

[7] Richardson (1952) describes procedures used for training students at Cornell.

13

SOME CHARACTERISTICS

OF RESPONDENTS

Although every interview study is intended to collect information from a series of individual respondents, the investigator, before considering the selection of individuals, must make some prior decisions about the characteristics of the set of respondents as a whole. A set of respondents may consist, for example, of a random sample of householders in a large city, the inhabitants of a small, isolated agricultural community, the membership of a labor union local, or a group of children who are severely backward in their reading ability. Given a specific research problem, the investigator must determine, insofar as he has freedom to do so, the general nature of the set of respondents that will most effectively suit his purpose. Although his choice is largely dependent, of course, on the purpose of the research, there are enough factors in the selection of the set of respondents to warrant a separate examination of its general characteristics before scrutinizing the characteristics of individual respondents.

The application of such criteria may, at first glance, appear to violate sampling procedures in current use. These procedures, however, generally come into play for selecting individual respondents in order to generalize the results from the sample selected to the total population of respondents. Or, if the total population of respondents is interviewed, the criteria for defining the population must be made explicit. In either case, the results apply only to the single population until further studies are conducted to reproduce the findings using another population. In practice, investigators do not systematically report the procedures used for selecting the set of respondents, whether it be a union local, a hospital, a town, county, or state. There does not seem to be any convincing reason why the particular union, hospital, town, etc. should be a random sample of one from the total population of unions, etc. To use the criteria that we shall suggest can facilitate the conduct of the study and save time, effort, and funds. If the results produced by the study appear promising, a second population and set of respondents may be selected with better knowledge of the variables significant for describing the population and those that should be held constant or varied in the second and, if necessary, successive studies. Although selecting, for a first study, a population that presents serious problems in participation may constitute an interesting challenge, there is no basis for believing that the results obtained from a population that is difficult to deal with will be more generalizable than those from a population that participates readily.

Selecting the Set of Respondents

FREEDOM OF CHOICE

Occasionally, the research question completely specifies the respondent set. For example, if the purpose of the study is to determine the attitudes of school teachers in the city of Toledo toward inservice courses during a given year, or to determine the current leisure activities of the Colgate University class of 1958, or to evaluate the experiences of registrants at a particular international conference on mental health, the respondent set is clearly identified. The only choice left to the investigator is whether to study the total population or to use some sampling procedure.

But if the research question is broadened, the degree of choice is considerably greater. If, for example, the purpose of the study is to determine the attitudes of American teachers toward inservice courses, or to determine the leisure activities of American college graduates, or to evaluate the experience of registrants at mental health conferences held in the United States and Europe during a two-year period, the size of the population of potential respondents is increased enormously and the investigator must develop criteria for deciding *which* teachers, college graduates, or conference participants to select as a respondent set.

When the research question is posed in still more abstract or conceptual terms, the investigator may have even greater latitude. For example, in studies of the social effects of technological change, or of the factors which influence the rate of weight gain in children in the first four years of life, or of the relationship between the expression of aggression in projective tests and its expression in interpersonal behavior, the investigator potentially has a tremendous number of respondent sets from which to select. In the study of weight gain, for example, the investigator might attempt to find a geographic area in which there are extremes of affluence and poverty and select infants from the two extremes for study, or he might use as his set the infants brought to the local well-baby clinic.

IDENTIFICATION OF RESPONDENTS

Some research problems enable the investigator to define and identify respondents quite readily. In a study dealing with the exercise of authority by police sergeants, for example, once a specific police force is selected and permission to conduct the study is obtained, the investigator uses the same definition of "sergeant" as is used by the force, and the sergeants are easily identifiable by their uniform or through the police-force records.

In other studies, definitions and identification of respondents may be a major problem. In a study of community leaders, for example, an operational definition of "leader," for use in selecting respondents, poses many theoretical and practical difficulties. It may require a general descriptive definition for use by a number of key respondents—e.g., newspaper reporters, businessmen, physicians, ministers, and lawyers—for the identification of persons who in their opinion fit the description.

The identification of a respondent set may become a problem because of the scarcity of persons who fit the criteria. In a study by Dembo (1959) on the effects of certain child-rearing practices on two- and three-year-old children with cerebral palsy of a specified degree of severity, finding the number of children necessary for the study became a major investigation because of the low prevalence of cerebral palsy. Any strict sampling procedure for the study was impossible because no complete enumeration of the population of children with cerebral palsy was available.

In studies of illegal and illicit behavior, the investigator will often encounter major difficulties in identifying a set of respondents because of their need for concealment.

INFLUENCE OF THE RESEARCH PURPOSE

The selection of the respondent set is influenced also by the purpose of the study. In the standardized study, the investigator, in reporting results, must make explicit the characteristics of the people to whom the results apply. He must also make certain that the respondents he selects either represent or constitute the population about which he wishes to generalize. In the standardized interview, therefore, the characteristics of the set of respondents must be defined and the set preselected. The investigator must also estimate in advance the nature of the participation he is likely to receive from the respondent set. If a high refusal rate is encountered, the results of the study will be equivocal because those interviewed may no longer be a random sample of the population. The only way to determine the nature of the bias in such results is to persuade a sample of those who refuse to participate to change their minds and then compare the responses of the respondents with those of the original nonrespondents. This is a difficult and expensive procedure. If, in the pretest of a study, a sizable proportion of the respondent set refuses to be interviewed, the investigator should seriously consider selecting another set of respondents, if the research question permits it.

In the nonschedule nonstandardized interview, the enumeration of the set of respondents is rarely possible at the outset of the study, except in general terms. Because exploratory research depends largely on the progressive articulation and revision of a conceptual framework achieved through close interplay with the collection and organization of data, the investigator may, at different stages in the research, seek respondents who can outline and summarize a wide range of data, respondents who can verbalize their own feelings and values, and respondents who can provide, either spontaneously or in interchange with the investigator, ideas, hunches, and insights, or a fresh point of view.

DEGREE OF HOMOGENEITY OF THE RESPONDENT SET

Respondent sets can usefully be considered in terms of the degree of homogeneity of their personal characteristics. When standardization of interviews is essential, the greater the homogeneity of the respondents, the greater the likelihood that a schedule interview can be used effectively. A high degree of homogeneity may also permit the selection of interviewers who have particular experience and skills with the kind of respondents selected.

As the homogeneity of the respondent set decreases, it becomes progressively more difficult to design a schedule of questions that will be meaningful and relevant for all respondents, because of the variety in the modes of thinking, language usage, comprehension, intelligence, and so forth. Respondent heterogeneity also places heavier demands on the skills of the interviewer, whether or not a schedule interview is used.

Criteria for Selecting the Set of Respondents

In addition to the specific characteristics of respondent sets that need to be considered in planning interview studies, there are some general criteria that are useful in making an advance estimate of the adequacy of a set of respondents or in selecting one of several alternate sets. The application of each of these criteria must always be qualified by the phrase "other things being equal," since it is possible to introduce bias through the rigid application of any one criterion. For example, if the criterion of articulateness and communicativeness, which we shall discuss below, leads the investigator to select a set of respondents that can provide information easily and precisely, he must recognize that this set may be very different in other characteristics—educational level, similarity in background to that of the investigator, and so on—and, hence, may be less representative of the population to which he intends to generalize. Despite this limitation, however, the following criteria may be useful as a guide for the interviewer who wishes to compare two respondent sets or to check on the adequacy of a single one.

ACCESSIBILITY

Accessibility is used here in two senses. First, the population must be reachable by the interviewer, available for interviewing, and willing to participate in the study. As we note in Chapter 4, the degree or the quality of the respondent set's participation cannot always be predicted, but at least some information—the experience of prior interviewers, the existence of restrictive ordinances, the existence of a series of gatekeepers, and other characteristics—is usually available in advance. Much depends, of course, on the nature of the study but, given a specific study and two or three possible respondent sets, the investigator can often make a judgment as to which set is likely to be more accessible and then check this estimate in the light of his early experience with the set he selects.

In the second, and simpler, sense, accessibility means nothing more than proximity of the respondent set to the investigator's base of operations. If the investigator can find an appropriate set of respondents within commuting distance of his own institution, he will save the time, expense, and stress involved in travel, and he will have available both colleagues for consultation and personnel to recruit for the study. The novelty of a more distant site can occasionally blind investigators to the disadvantages that result from distance. On the other hand, too close proximity of the study to the investigator's home base can lead to complications. He may find that his social relationships extend into the respondent set and that he is obtaining confidential information about personal friends or persons he knows in roles other than that of respondents. Some investigators who have attempted to study institutions while they are members of these institutions have found that situations of this sort can lead to conflict of interest, role conflict, and confusion.

ARTICULATENESS AND COMMUNICATIVENESS

If possible, the respondent population should be able to communicate information easily and precisely. This means that, if the choice lies, for example, between two marginal social groups, the one that is more fluent in the interviewer's native language and less isolated from intercourse with outsiders would be preferable. This criterion of articulateness, it should be noted, applies to *sets* of respondents and not to individual respondents. Within the respondent set, if it has not been preselected on some sampling basis, it is natural for interviewers to favor the more articulate respondents, who are often the more perceptive as well. The interviewer should bear in mind, however, that articulateness may produce bias and that some seemingly inarticulate respondents can, in time, provide very useful information.

AVAILABILITY AND STABILITY

If the study is a longitudinal one, availability and stability become crucial criteria. A set or respondents may appear to be accessible and yet be (or become) unavailable or (for long-term studies) unstable. Some respondent sets that are initially accessible become unavailable when harvests, peak employment periods, mass vacation periods, and so forth change their regular habits and abodes. Some neighborhoods are notably unstable; some suburbs, for example, show an annual turnover as high as 20 per cent, and certain urban areas (notably rooming-house districts) an even higher rate. Some occupational groups (migrant laborers and construction workers, for example) move from place to place; other groups (waitresses and retail clerks) have high turnover. It still may be important to study such populations over time, but the interviewers must be realistic about the problems of migration and consider whether follow-up procedures are feasible.

PRIOR EXPERIENCE

The respondent's prior experience with interviewers may be an advantage or a disadvantage, depending on the nature of the experience and the nature of the study. In some cases, the population's familiarity with research and interviewing can save the interviewer much time and effort in explaining his role and purpose. On the other hand, if the population has recently had an unpleasant experience with a research study—or with a journalist interviewer or a team of door-to-door salesmen posing as interviewers—it may be wise to consider selecting an alternative set of respondents.

Status Characteristics of the Individual Respondent

A number of investigators have written about their experiences with or impressions of respondents whom they have interviewed, and some of this information may be useful to the investigator in his selection of respondents. He must note, however, that the generalizations we have assembled below are impressionistic rather than systematically developed and that, like all generalizations, they can never be confidently applied to an individual respondent. Thus, they will be most useful if regarded as probability statements rather than taken at face value.

POSITION OF THE RESPONDENT IN THE STRUCTURE OF THE ORGANIZATION OR COMMUNITY

A number of investigators have commented on differences in the type of information they can best obtain from the top and middle levels of an organization. The Webbs (1932, p. 137) found:

It is . . . almost axiomatic with the experienced investigator that the mind of the subordinate in any organization will yield richer veins of fact than the mind of the principal. This is not merely because the subordinate is usually less on his guard and less severely conventional in his outlook. The essential superiority lies in the circumstance that the working foreman, managing clerk or minor official is himself in continuous and intimate contact with the day by day activities of the organization. He is more aware than his employer is of the hetero- geneity and changing character of the facts, and he is less likely to serve up generalizations in which all the living detail becomes a blurred mass or is stereotyped into rigidly confined and perhaps obsolete cate- gories.

Smigel (1958), in a study of lawyers, makes the interesting point that lawyers lower in the hierarchy of a firm became anxious if asked to talk on the level of policy and generalization and pre- ferred discussion of procedures and routines within policies. They accepted more interviewer control, and their responses were more detailed and factual. Campbell (1955), in an experimental study, found a slight trend supporting the Webbs' thesis: Navy yeomen (enlisted personnel performing secretarial duties) were able to make more accurate ratings of morale among submarine crews than officers. Whereas the Webbs refer to the collection of factual data, Dean (1954) comments on the subjective data that can be ob- tained from a subordinate who must adapt to superiors. He points out that the subordinate generally develops insights to cushion the impact of authority and that he may be hostile and therefore will- ing to "blow his top."

The leaders of an organization, aside from serving as respond- ents, can play important roles as informal advisers to the interviewer on the best way to initiate and conduct the study and as gate- keepers who will have an important voice in deciding whether to allow the study to take place. (The role of leadership is discussed in detail in Chapter 4.)

Several investigators have commented on the relationship be- tween the respondent's willingness to participate in the interview and his position in the community structure. Merton (1947, p. 308), in a study of community housing, found that the particularly cooperative respondents occupied the following distinctive posi- tions in the local social structure:

. . . local leaders, active participants in organized and informal group life, persons who identify themselves with the community, etc. There was also some indication that the more fully the informants are incorporated into the local network of personal relations, the higher the proportions giving marked cooperation.

In a study of a small town, Vidich and Shapiro (1955) concluded that the community-minded segment of the middle class was eager to cooperate. The local aristocracy tended to refuse to be interviewed, and the lower income groups were suspicious and fearful of the researchers. Those with double occupations who did not participate in organized community affairs tended to be perfunctory as respondents.

Changes of membership or position in a community or organization may provide people with insights or make them especially willing to provide the interviewer with information. Dean (1954, pp. 235–236) specifies the following types of potentially useful respondent:

The outsider, who observes phenomena from the viewpoint of another culture, social class, community, and so forth

The nouveau, who is in transition from one role or status to another and, hence, is particularly sensitive to the tensions of new experience

The outs, who are out of power but "in the know," critical of the "ins," and eager to reveal discrediting information about them.

The following statements summarize the material we have reviewed about how the respondents' positions in the community or organization may equip them to provide the interviewer with specific types of information. Respondents who have a high degree of freedom of movement within a community or organization have a wide range of opportunity to observe its structure and operations, but the type of information they possess, although it is useful for gaining over-all perspective, may be totally lacking in detail on the stresses and strains felt by someone with a more narrowly defined role. The marginal man, although he may have insights that the full member does not have, may have little detailed factual information about the society, subculture, or group to which he is marginal. Moreover, there is always the danger that marginals, outs, and *nouveaux* will provide the interviewer with a caricature rather than a picture in correct perspective.

LEVEL OF EDUCATION AND
SOCIO-ECONOMIC STATUS

To judge from their published reports, there may be some tendency for interviewers to encounter more better educated and middle-class respondents than less educated and lower-class respondents. Johnson (1955), in a study of intergroup relations, found that he came to know best the better educated segment of the community. Vidich and Shapiro (1955), in a community study, also came to know a disproportionate number of persons of higher prestige and better education. Merton (1947), in his study of a planned community, reported that the more highly educated clerical and semiprofessional respondents were more cooperative than those with low education and in blue-collar occupations. In none of these accounts, however, does the author specify whether his knowing a disproportionate number of such respondents is due to their greater accessibility, their greater congeniality, or their superiority as respondents in relation to the study.

A very much more specific picture of the differences noted between ten upper- and ten lower-class respondents is provided by Strauss and Schatzman (1960, pp. 207–208), who analyzed tape recordings of interviews in an investigation of a disaster.

... [The middle class] respondent usually meets the invitation to tell his story with a fairly lengthy elaborate and well-ordered narrative of events; hence less clarification is necessary. If asked to clarify a point, he does so fairly directly, or at least gives further detail in such a way that the interviewer is not left with numerous other details to clarify. . . . [T]o keep the account unfolding . . . the interviewers used such comments as "Tell me more about . . . ," "and then . . . ," and "You said that. . . ." It is as if the interviewer were occasionally touching and controlling a rolling snowball to keep it going and on the right track. . . .

With the lower-class respondent, it is hard work keeping tight control over the interview lest it fall apart altogether. To a direct query the respondent, of course, may answer to the point. But with great frequency he answers the question and then follows his imagination wherever it may take him.

... [T]he usual interview probes that are not so very different from the ordinary utterances of educated conversation become blunt instruments for eliciting information [from lower-class persons].

Although Strauss and Schatzman do not report it, the interviewers' backgrounds were probably more comparable to that of the middle-class respondents. Also, the interviewers had had little time to become familiar with people in the research area because they entered the area in the wake of a disaster and began interviewing with as little delay as possible. Moreover, the results reported may be due, in part, to lack of time and flexibility on the part of the interviewers and the use of techniques inappropriate for respondents with backgrounds different from their own.[1] The interviewer's adaptation of his language usage in a direction that will make it more understandable and congenial to respondents has been described by Whyte (see p. 231). Whyte had, however, lived and worked for some time in the Italian slum that was the site of his study.

CHARACTERISTICS OF ELITES

A number of investigators have described their experiences in interviewing respondents of high educational level and high social class: a French government and business elite (Lerner, 1956), a legal elite (Smigel, 1958), an industrial elite (Kincaid & Bright, 1957), and an academic elite (Riesman, 1958). In these studies, difficulties were experienced in the use of a schedule interview in which the interviewer confined himself to asking questions and recording answers. Interviewers found themselves forced to modify the more conventional role of the survey interviewer. Their experiences can be summarized in the following points.

---

[1] Riesman (1964, p. 523) has commented as follows on these findings:

We ourselves have listened to a number of these same tapes, and in a few instances were driven to interpretations rather different from those of Schatzman and Strauss. For many respondents what mattered most was the theodicy problem: why had the disaster hit, killing those it killed and sparing others? Directly or indirectly, they wanted the interviewer's opinion, whereas the latter was trained only to want theirs—a technique which, coupled with hailing from Chicago and carrying tape recorders, gave an inevitable impression of godlessness. Once the respondent discovered that the interviewer was not going to debate theodicy, he either resignedly vouchsafed the minimum factual data called for by the embarrassed interviewer or refused to make any effort to put himself in the interviewer's place. To be sure, many respondents did appear to lack the psychic mobility, the "projectivity" necessary for putting themselves in the place of the other; but so, too, did some interviewers.

(*1*) *Respondents actively resent the restrictions placed on them by the interview schedules.*

Riesman (1958, p. 33) reports, for example, that among historians, economists, and political scientists there was frequent resentment against what appeared to them mechanical or stereotyped questions. The academic *avant garde* was tantalized by schedule questions which seemed to raise issues but did not permit respondents to follow them up in their own way.

(*2*) *Respondents demand a more active interplay with the interviewer than the conventional schedule interview permits.*

The academic group studied by Riesman (1958, p. 117) preferred active participation by the interviewer, not the neutrality and task orientation which appeared to take them and their world for granted. Lerner (1956, p. 194) reports in his study of French intellectuals that unless the interviewers acted as foils for conversation and argument, the respondents would refuse to be interviewed. Many of his respondents enjoyed the give and take of skillful debate and dialectic. A more active role on the part of the interviewer has generally been discouraged by writers on interviewing, on the grounds that the expression of ideas and opinions will bias the response. The interviewers of elites, however, did not feel that a more active role had this effect. This may well be due to the status relationship between the interviewer and the respondent and to the self-confidence and security of the respondent.

(*3*) *Respondents are intelligent, quick-thinking, and at home in the realm of ideas, policy, and generalization.*

These qualities place high demands on the ability of the interviewer. In interviewing a business elite, Kincaid and Bright (1957) interviewed as a two-man team, thus doubling the probability of picking up cues and developing ideas. Because elites are busy people who set a high premium on time and because they tend to prefer task orientation (see pp. 282–283), the interviewer must quickly establish his competence, by displaying a thorough knowledge of the topic or, lacking such knowledge, by swift and accurate conceptualization of the problem and shrewd questioning. In general, elites seem comfortable with questions of broad content and with a high proportion of open questions; questions embodying expectations do not appear to influence responses. In the course of the interview, considerable variation will occur in the degree of control, with interviewer and respondent each at times assuming the questioner's role.

The studies of elites demonstrate the special role demands placed on the interviewer. They suggest, also, that, unless the interviewer complies with some of these demands, respondent participation is likely to deteriorate or be withheld altogether. These studies do not indicate, however, the extent to which the interviewer's compliance with the respondents' demands influences the accuracy of the data obtained. It is possible that, in a schedule interview, provided the questions are appropriate and have been well tested and the interviewer thoroughly understands their content and can induce the respondent to complete the schedule, the data may be valid even if the respondent becomes thoroughly exasperated.

SOCIAL MOBILITY

The individual who has been socially mobile—who, in the course of his lifetime, has moved a considerable distance up or down in the social structure—may be a good respondent for several reasons. He may be able to empathize with various social levels, and he may receive communication from more of them than the person who is "to the manor born." The interviewer must bear in mind, of course, that some socially mobile persons reject with considerable violence anything connected with their origins, but this is not universally true, and many socially mobile persons retain an understanding of and sympathy with some of the values and views of other levels.

RESPONDENTS WHOM INTERVIEWERS ARE MOST LIKELY TO ENCOUNTER

The experience of a number of investigators indicates that there are certain types of respondents whom the interviewer is likely to encounter in the early stages of a community study if he is readily identifiable. Marginal men, isolates, and people who readily identify with the interviewer are easily approached and may even go out of their way to talk to him. Some individuals perceive the interviewer as a person through whom they can obtain something—advice, increased power, communication with the outside world, help in undertaking reforms they think are important, or a gain in prestige by virtue of their association with him (see p. 66).

There is wide variation in the amount of time people have to spare, and the interviewer is more likely to find respondents among those who have more time available—older people, housewives who are not busy with a large number of children, and people in jobs in which periods of busyness alternate with periods of idleness, such as storekeeping or hotel clerking. The time of the day, the day of the week, and the season of the year may cause wide variation in the amount of spare time people have, especially those whose employment tends to be seasonal. If the interviewer is aware of these differences, he can use them to advantage. But, although this knowledge makes it easier for the interviewer to gain participation, the implications for bias are clear enough.

Two systematic comparisons have been made of the types of persons an interviewer is likely to come in contact with in the course of studies involving nonstandardized interviewing. In each case, a random sample of the community was compared with the set of respondents actually used.

In a study of intergroup relations, Johnson (1955), himself a bachelor and a Negro, found that he came to know considerably more males than females and that he tended to know the better educated persons in the community. He knew more single, separated, or divorced than married persons. He knew most of the NAACP members, most of the persons who belonged to two or more organizations, a good many of the more regular church attenders, and relatively few of the persons who did not participate in these activities. Finally, he knew a large proportion of those Negroes who had expressed militant or aggressive racial attitudes when interviewed and relatively few of the "lassitudinous" persons, the "insulates," and the "avoiders." This difference, however, was related to educational level because the better educated Negroes tended to be more militant.

Vidich and Shapiro (1955) made a similar comparison in a study of social and psychological correlates of community activity in a rural community with an adult population of about 1,500. They found that the contacts of the investigators were biased in favor of individuals with higher prestige. The researcher, who was male, tended to know more males than females. He knew more better educated than less educated people. Members of the labor force, whether self-employed or not, were less likely to be interviewed than housewives, retired people, and the like.

Despite somewhat different research purposes, these two studies show considerable agreement as to the types of person with whom the researcher is likely to come in contact when using nonstandard-ized interviewing. Advance awareness of the kinds of respondent the interviewer is most likely to meet can forearm him against in-troducing serious bias into the data he collects—bias that may be reinforced by the fact that respondents who agree to participate tend to pass the interviewer on to friends who belong to the same cliques or groups and who may have a similar point of view. Al-though the interviewer cannot expect to obtain full information about the respondent set before he begins interviewing, he can gain some understanding of the composition and structure of the community or organization he plans to study through a variety of documentary sources (see p. 88) and through the use of selected respondents (see p. 114) early in the study.

The respondent characteristics described in the foregoing pages are related to demographic variables such as age; education; and occupational, economic, and social status. Hence, although the interviewer must use these relationships tentatively and cautiously, he can, by advance study of the demographic characteristics of the respondent set, predict with reasonably high probability some of the characteristics of the individual respondent. On the basis of these predictions, he may be able to adapt his interview form and style to take these characteristics into account.

Certain other respondent characteristics are purely idiosyncratic and cannot be predicted on a demographic or other basis. The characteristics described below are likely to be encountered in many respondents but the interviewer cannot predict their presence; he can only detect them after the interview has begun. Once he detects them, however, he can, within the limits set by the form of the interview, adapt his questioning and his behavior so as to take them into account.

Personal Characteristics of Respondents

INTEREST IN HUMAN BEHAVIOR

In many communities and organizations there are a few individuals who are naturally shrewd and reflective observers of behavior and who take special interest in the people, the community, and the society to which they belong. Although there are no cues by which they may be readily identified, such as being in a central position in the communications network, the investigator may be directed to them by the members of the community who recognize these qualities. The characteristics of these students of behavior are very similar to those suggested by the Webbs (see p. 299). Although such individuals can be most valuable respondents, the interviewer must be aware that the social or personality factors that produced this interest and detachment may bias the information that they provide.

PREFERRED STYLES OF INTERPERSONAL RELATIONS

Cumming, Dean, and Newell (1958) have suggested the following classification, derived from Parsons' pattern variables, to describe modes of social interaction that respondents prefer in an "intensive free interview situation."

This schema elaborates the distinction made in our discussion of participation (Chapter 4), where we used Parsons' terms, "universalistic" and "particularistic," to describe respondents who prefer an emphasis on subject matter and ideas and a somewhat businesslike, impersonal relationship restricted to the task at hand or, on the other hand, a broader, more intimate social relationship in which personal relations are stressed more than subject matter.

	SPECIFIC	DIFFUSE
	Approval Seekers	*Esteem Seekers*
NEUTRAL	Businesslike and efficient. Seek approval for job well done.	See the interview through moral or evaluative eyes. Seek esteem for their qualities, achievements, and opinions. View the interview as a way of advancing knowledge.
	Response Seekers	*Total Acceptance Seekers*
AFFECTIVE	Enjoy personal contact but do not try and extend it beyond the interview.	Strain toward total acceptance. Try to turn the interview into a mutual and affective relationship. Wish the relationship to extend beyond the interview and often suggest social visits.

Here we shall point out only that the Cumming, Dean, and Newell classification of respondents, although couched in different terms, is almost identical in meaning with the classifications of interviewers suggested by Hyman (1954 [task involvement versus social orientation]) and Riesman (1958 [blue stocking versus market research]). In our discussion of interviewer–respondent relations (see Chapter 14), we shall examine some of the questions raised by these classifications, which are by definition interactive.

PREFERENCES FOR DIFFERENT STYLES
AND TECHNIQUES OF QUESTIONING

As we have already noted (Chapter 12), interviewers differ greatly in the form and pattern of interviewing they find most congenial and in the extent of their versatility in the use of different forms and techniques. In the present chapter, we note differences in the ways in which respondents prefer to be interviewed —or in the ways in which interviewers believe that they can most effectively elicit information from respondents. Elites and intelligentsia appear to prefer a nonschedule interview and quick, intelligent, and provocative questions which stimulate their thinking and give them considerable freedom to use their knowledge and imagination. Without rather tight control by the interviewer, Strauss and Schatzman (1960) suggest, lower-class respondents may wander off the subject and have difficulty maintaining continuity in the interview process. In our own experience, we have encountered respondents of very similar educational or background characteristics who differ greatly in the type of questioning they prefer. Although some clearly relish taking off from and elaborating on an open, rather general question and can continue to give relevant and full responses with little direction from the interviewer, others become anxious and disturbed unless they are asked very specific and generally closed questions. For such respondents, an interview in which most questions are closed, in which question antecedents are generally prior questions rather than prior responses, and in which little attempt is made to explore unexpected responses would seem preferable.

Because there is some relationship between social class and intelligence and between elite or intelligentsia status and intelligence, it would appear that persons of different intelligence levels prefer different modes of questioning. Although the interview literature has dealt with the problem of interviewing the highly intelligent respondent, little or no systematic attention has been given to the problem of eliciting information from respondents of low intelligence.

The extent to which respondents differ in their preferences for various forms and patterns of questioning has not been studied extensively. Similarly, there is no empirical evidence on whether the use of the respondent's preferred style of questioning most effectively produces the response qualities sought by the interviewer. In some circumstances, catering to the preferences of the respondent may prove distinctly deleterious to response quality, as we shall note below in connection with garrulous and reticent respondents.

GARRULITY AND RETICENCE

Because so much of his training and effort is devoted to the development of respondent participation—"getting the respondent to open up"—the interviewer is sometimes surprised to encounter a respondent who is delighted to talk freely and openly with little or no persuasion, who is so eager to talk that the interviewer's problem becomes one of curbing and stopping the spate of responses.

Garrulity may be due to any of a number of factors. If the respondent feels lonely or isolated, he may seize on the interview as an opportunity for talk. If he is expert or enthusiastic about the subject matter of the interview, his garrulity may be a spontaneous expression of his enthusiasm, an earnest desire to inform the interviewer, or an attempt to impress the interviewer with his expertise. In other circumstances, garrulity can be used as a verbal smoke screen in an attempt to hide significant facts from the interviewer or to mislead him without appearing uncooperative. The following techniques, we have found in our experience with nonschedule interviewing, may be effective in reducing the length and increasing the relevance of garrulous responses.

Silences are unlikely to restrict output. Discreet use of the guggle by the interviewer puts the respondent on notice that the interviewer wishes to say something. If used a few times, the guggle may stop the respondent but, if it is unsuccessful, the interviewer can seize a moment when the respondent pauses for breath to break in with a summary of what has been said. This has the effect of stopping the immediate momentum of the respondent's train of thought. At the end of the summary, provided it is accurate, the respondent is almost bound to affirm it. Immediately after this affirmation, the interviewer interjects a question which breaks with the preceding content and introduces a shift in topic. Being "quick on the draw" with this question is essential if the respondent is not to regain control of the interview. Although frequent abrupt changes of topic and breaks with prior content are not generally recommended, they can prevent the garrulous respondent from gathering too much momentum on any one topic.

Increasing the proportion of closed to open and narrowing the scope of questions gives the interviewer greater control of both subject matter and length of response. Because the garrulous respondent will probably provide more information than is called for by a closed question, this form is unlikely to produce the degree of brevity of response that it would in a less garrulous respondent.

If all of the foregoing techniques fail, outright interruptions are likely to be necessary, and the interviewer will have to judge the frequency with which he can interrupt without losing the participation of his respondent.

Reticence, like garrulity, may be due to several factors. The respondent may be generally taciturn in all his relationships. He may be participating minimally because there are pressures on him to participate even though he is resentful of the interviewer or some aspect of the study. Or he may have a vested interest which the study appears to threaten. Regardless of the specific reasons for respondent reticence, the following techniques—which are generally the opposite of those used with the garrulous respondent—have proved effective.

If open questions followed by interviewer silences do not elicit responses, the interviewer may increase his use of closed questions which narrow the breadth of the content. If the respondent answers each question minimally, the interviewer may, through a series of closed questions, delineate the various topics and territory he wishes to cover in the interview. Although the reticent respondent may not open up on the basis of individual questions, the pattern that the series of questions maps out may provide sufficient incentive to talk, or a specific question may trigger off a fuller response. Once fuller responses begin, the interviewer can relax his control of the interview by moving to less directive techniques —open questions and questions with respondent antecedents, for example. Asking extension questions about prior, brief responses may provide the key to opening up the respondent. In some cases, the use of deliberately distorted premises and assumptions may be useful—as is discussed in chapters 7 and 9.

In the schedule interview, although the interviewer has no freedom in the wording of questions, he may be forced to break away from the requirement of presenting uniform stimuli with garrulous or reticent respondents if he is to get through the schedule with the former or prevent a large number of "no answers" or "don't knows" from the latter.

As the foregoing discussion indicates, there is often a conflict between the mode of questioning the respondent finds congenial and the mode that the interviewer must employ to obtain responses that are useful for the research purpose. Yielding to the respondent's preferences may produce responses of poor quality; on the other hand, the use of a mode of questioning that is uncongenial to the respondent may result in the loss or the deterioration of his full and willing participation.

As the reader may have noted, a number of personal dimensions applied to the respondent in this chapter and to the interviewer in the preceding one are equally applicable to both. And some of them—e.g., status relationships and preferred modes of personal interaction—can be understood only in the context of interviewer–respondent interaction. It is for this reason that we devote the next chapter to some aspects of the interaction between interviewer and respondent.

14

FURTHER ELEMENTS OF THE INTERVIEWER–RESPONDENT RELATIONSHIP

In the two preceding chapters, we focused attention on the interviewer and the respondent separately. The interview, however, is an interpersonal relationship between two people, and the suitability of each of them for his task as interviewer or respondent depends not only on his individual characteristics but also on his interaction with the other person. In this chapter, we shall focus on interpersonal factors.

Social Relationships and Interview Relationships

Although a skillfully conducted interview may appear to be highly similar to a social conversation, in certain respects they differ sharply. Because we have all had extensive experience with social conversations, a consideration of these differences may broaden our understanding of the relationships involved in an interview.

INITIATION OF THE RELATIONSHIP

A casual two-person social relationship may be initiated by either party and may begin on any of a number of grounds—witnessing an event, a common experience, desire for the companionship of someone who appears interesting or attractive, or simply desire for self-expression. The interview, by contrast, is initiated almost always by the interviewer, usually because the respondent possesses information that the interviewer seeks, and always for the sole purpose of eliciting this information.

The initiation of a casual social relationship is usually governed by certain norms of the society in which it takes place. Generally speaking, it is more acceptable for a man to initiate a relationship with a woman than vice versa, for the older person to approach the younger, for the person of higher status to initiate and control the relationship than the person of lower status. Moreover, a casual relationship is generally not initiated unless each party to it perceives that the other is willing or, at least, not preoccupied with some other activity.

The interview relationship, by contrast, is almost always initiated by the interviewer, regardless of whether the personal characteristics of the interviewer and respondent make it appropriate for the interviewer to take the initiative. For example, a young woman interviewer may initiate an interview relationship and maintain the initiative through being the questioner even though the respondent is a man for whom this pattern of behavior in a social relationship would seem peculiar. A high-status, middle-aged executive, accustomed to initiating and controlling interpersonal relations in his work environment, may have difficulty in adapting to a young interviewer whom the executive regards as having far lower status than himself and who asks the executive to take the role of respondent.

People vary widely in the frequency and ease with which they engage in new social relationships. The person who has grown up in a small family or in an urban environment, who has changed his place of residence frequently, or whose work involves dealing with many people is likely to have a great deal of experience in forming new interpersonal relationships with strangers. On the other hand, the person who has spent most of his life in the same small community, who has known most of his associates for as long as he can remember, or whose work brings him into contact with very few people may experience some difficulty in establishing a relationship with a person of unknown status who is a newcomer to his social environment.

This is not to imply that people who are experienced in meeting strangers invariably enjoy the process, or that people who are inexperienced invariably find strangers threatening. It does mean, however, that the interviewer, no matter how eager he may be to "get down to business," must be sensitive to the difficulties of respondents who are unaccustomed to strangers. He must recognize that such people are likely to assimilate him into "stranger" roles with which they have some familiarity—tourists, salesmen, and the like—and he, therefore, must take time to work out a relationship that suits his own purposes but also has some degree of resemblance to what the respondents are accustomed to.

CONGENIALITY

Most social relationships involve participants who are considerably similar in background, interests, values, norms, and intelligence level. These shared elements help to ensure that the rules and norms governing social relationships will be implicitly understood and observed by both parties. Lacking this basic congeniality, a social relationship can nevertheless be maintained on the basis of some strong common interest—political, recreational, occupational, and so forth.

In the interview relationship, however, there is often neither basic congeniality nor commonality of interests. And, although it is always possible for two strangers to find some common ground, the interviewer's primary task is to use all the available time for eliciting information. Often, it is necessary to use some time for teaching the respondent how best to play his role in the interview, but the use of interview time for the development of a social relationship is, in terms of the primary task of gathering information, strictly speaking, wasteful.

This ideal definition of the interviewer's task, however, can rarely be achieved in practice. As we point out in chapters 3 and 4, the participation of the respondent may be difficult or impossible to gain unless the interview situation offers him at least some elements of a social relationship. Moreover, as we note in our discussion of the characteristics of the interviewer (Chapter 12), certain types of interviewer are incapable of maintaining complete task orientation, and they themselves require some social elements in the interview. Hence, most interviews are, in fact, compromises between the strict requirements of gathering information and the "wasteful," but often necessary, elements of a social relationship.

The congeniality that is characteristic of a social relationship and that may be necessary, to some degree, in the interview relationship implies at least a modicum of spontaneity between the participants. Spontaneity, however, carries with it certain dangers. Since the interviewer cannot feel the same toward all the respondents that he must deal with, too high a degree of spontaneity entails the danger that he will communicate his feelings of liking or antipathy to the respondent. Such differences in affective tone between one interview and another decrease the degree of standardization, may lose participation if the interviewer expresses negative feelings toward the respondent, and, if there is communication among respondents, may produce conflicting accounts of the interview experience. Yet a complete absence of spontaneity, either real or apparent, may make the interview so wooden, stilted, and uninteresting that participation may be jeopardized. Hence, once again, compromise is necessary to avoid the difficulties of excessive or insufficient spontaneity and congeniality.

Whereas the duration of a social relationship is indeterminate, the interview relationship has served its purpose as soon as the interviewer has obtained all the information he needs. If the interview is relatively brief and impersonal, its termination will probably present no difficulty. If, however, the interview has required a number of sessions, in which, from the viewpoint of the respondent, a congenial social relationship has developed, the interviewer must plan the termination carefully. If he thinks only in terms of the interview task, he may terminate the relationship too abruptly and offend the respondent, who, from his own point of view, may interpret abrupt termination as discourteous and unfriendly. If the respondent communicates his umbrage to other potential respondents and if he is influential, he can severely damage the participation of the other respondents.

MUTUALITY

In a social relationship, it is customary for both parties to develop a mutually satisfactory balance between giving and receiving information. Generally, such a relationship involves the matching or swapping of stories, anecdotes, gossip, self-revelation, or ideas. Although one of the parties may emerge as more influential in determining the choice of subject matter and the direction and duration of the conversation, such leadership may shift back and forth so that, in the long run, both parties have a sense of mutuality.

In interviewing, on the other hand, the task of gathering information calls for a largely unilateral relationship, the interviewer taking the leading role in questioning the respondent or in guiding him in the shaping of his answers. If the interviewer, either because of his personal needs or because of needs he perceives in the respondent, drops his role of questioner and launches into personal anecdotes, an exchange of views, or other personal matters, or if he permits the respondent to assume the role of questioner, he will inevitably prolong the interview beyond the point of maximal usefulness; moreover, he will risk biasing the responses through the disclosure of his own views and values.

On the other hand, if the interviewer maintains his role of questioner too rigidly, restricting the respondent to answering questions, the balance of give and take to which the respondent may be accustomed may become so distorted as to strain the relationship. The danger of such imbalance was clearly apparent in a study that Richardson, Hastorf, and Dornbusch (1964) conducted on the nature of the verbal categories people use when they give free descriptions of others. The initial question was, "Tell me about [the name of the person]." When the respondent stopped talking, further interviewer attempts would be made to elicit a description as complete as possible. These attempts could not, however, take the form of questions suggesting categories of perception to the respondent. The interviewers could say, for example, "Please tell us some more," but not, "Do you like him?" In pretesting interviews, they found that even highly cooperative respondents found such an extreme one-way flow of information uncomfortable because it differed so from normal conversation. To prevent tension, the interviewer was permitted to introduce comments about information that had been provided by the respondent in earlier response material. For example, if a respondent had said that a child was two-and-a-half years old, the interviewer might say, "He has had his second birthday, then?" These questions were almost nonsensical, and the answers were of no relevance to the interview purpose, but they did succeed in reducing the mounting tension and correcting the extreme imbalance.

In attempting to maintain a balance in the give and take of information that is acceptable to a respondent, the interviewer must construe "information" in its widest sense, involving much more than the spoken word. With this in mind, the interviewer can maintain a balance satisfactory to the respondent by means other than the ratio of the number of words he speaks to the number that the respondent speaks. For example, the interviewer can improve the balance by temporarily permitting the respondent to ask questions instead of answering them, by providing information about himself, by moving away from the subject matter of the interview for a brief interlude, by being an attentive listener, and by providing clues, both verbal and nonverbal, that he is receiving and thoughtfully synthesizing the respondent's information. The opportunity to talk to an attentive listener may be an enormously rewarding and rare event for a respondent, and the gratification the respondent receives from being listened to in return for giving information may be sufficient to give him a satisfactory sense of balance. Often, however, the maintenance of a balance requires that the interviewer provide the respondent with some information in return for the respondent's information. The next section describes the various ways in which this can be done.

Kinds of Information the Interviewer May Provide

As we have noted, the interview can rarely be restricted to the minimal requirements of information gathering but, in addition, must generally modify or incorporate some of the elements of the respondent's customary form of social relationship. The inter-

viewer cannot assume that the respondent should do all the adapting to the interview relationship; he must, to some degree, meet
the respondent's needs and expectations, working out, within the
interview, a mutually acceptable role and providing the respondent
with some information, which may or may not be related to the
subject matter of the interview.

INFORMATION ABOUT THE SUBJECT MATTER

In nonstandardized interviewing, particularly in the early stages,
the interviewer is likely to have very little specific information
about the subject matter of the study, despite his having gained
what he can from documentary sources. His respondents, if he
has selected them judiciously, know much more than he does, and
he is unlikely to be able to give them information that they do not
already have. The relationship between interviewer and respondent in such a situation is similar to that between student and
teacher, and the interviewer can make the experience interesting
and rewarding to the respondent by demonstrating attentiveness,
the ability to assimilate new information swiftly and intelligently,
and the ability to ask perceptive questions. During this stage, the
interviewer may develop conceptualizations that provide the respondent with new insights.

Occasionally, in the early stages of exploratory interviewing, a
respondent will attribute to the interviewer considerably more
knowledge of the subject matter than he in fact possesses. This can
create something of a dilemma for the interviewer. If he does not
correct the respondent's exaggerated estimate, he may get response
material that is completely beyond his understanding and, hence,
is of little use to him. On the other hand, he may feel that a con-
fession of ignorance is inappropriate and that, if he is able to "pick
it up as he goes along," he is likely to save a great deal of time and
learn more than he would if his respondent felt that a more rudi-
mentary level of response would be acceptable or that distortions
would not be detected. If the interviewer chooses to admit his
relative ignorance, it is possible that the respondent will be willing
to respond at the appropriate level, but it is also possible that he
will be less interested in providing information or will respond
superficially or with distortion. Often, the dilemma is resolved by

the respondent's becoming so involved in the subject matter, partly as a result of skilled listening and encouragement by the interviewer, that some of these gaps in the interviewer's information are filled in rather quickly.

In later stages of a study, when the interviewer has acquired considerable knowledge of the subject matter, the amount of information he discloses to the respondent will depend on a number of factors. If a respondent appears interested and cooperative from the outset, there is little need for the interviewer to delineate the subject area before beginning with the questioning. But some respondents who have many demands on their time may be unwilling to devote time to an interviewer unless he can very quickly demonstrate through his questions that he is competent to deal with the subject matter of the study. Such respondents may, at the outset, temporarily assume an interviewer's role in order to assess by direct questioning the interviewer's knowledge and competence. Moreover, a respondent who is very well informed on the subject matter of the interview may not know the level of sophistication in which to frame his responses until he has obtained some estimate of the interviewer's current understanding of the subject matter.

If the subject of the interview is threatening to the respondent, the interviewer's disclosure of his knowledge requires careful thought and judgment. In some situations—for example, in the study of an organization or community that is generally closed to outsiders—any knowledge that the interviewer discloses to the respondents is likely to heighten their suspicion of him. And, if he reveals information that he could have obtained only from one of the respondents, such a revelation may be seen as evidence that he does not respect confidences. On the other hand, skillful disclosure of his knowledge may have two possible advantages with respect to eliciting or heightening respondent participation: First, disclosing what he knows, regardless of whether his information is flattering or injurious to the respondent, may be provocative enough to arouse interest and response in a respondent who might otherwise be reticent or apathetic. Secondly, disclosing what he knows, and occasionally whom he knows—especially if the subject matter is a sensitive or difficult one—may encourage the respondent to participate fully because of his realization (*a*) that the interviewer knows too much to be satisfied with a superficial or evasive answer or (*b*) that the interviewer is thoroughly accustomed to dealing comfortably with the kind of information about which the respondent is embarrassed or uncomfortable.

The foregoing comments apply primarily to the nonstandardized and the nonschedule standardized interview, because the schedule interviewer is permitted little discretion in playing his part. It is not so easy for the schedule interviewer to provide the respondent with information about the subject matter, but there are two approaches that can be used. By building into the schedule hypothetical situations to which the respondent is asked to react or by providing a range of alternatives for the respondent's selection, the schedule can communicate to the respondent some of the investigator's, if not the interviewer's, information about the subject matter. If, in the course of the interview, it becomes apparent that the respondent is becoming disturbed by the imbalance of the flow of information, the interviewer may have to depart from the schedule in order to restore the balance, even at the cost of reducing standardization between interviews.

When he discloses information about the subject matter, the interviewer must be certain that he is doing it to satisfy the respondent's needs rather than his own. It is not uncommon for inexperienced interviewers to disclose more information than the situation calls for, either because *they* rather than the respondent are made uncomfortable by the imbalance or because they believe that showing considerable knowledge of the subject matter will enhance their status in the eyes of the respondent. At best, such unnecessary disclosure of information simply wastes time that could be devoted to eliciting response material. At worst, it may irritate the respondent by preventing him from providing as much information as he would like and by confusing him as to his own and the interviewer's role.

INFORMATION NOT RELATED TO SUBJECT MATTER

Although some respondents will not be troubled by the imbalance of the flow of information and although others, more sensitive to the imbalance, are content to have it redressed in terms of the subject matter of the interview, still others—those who are more socially oriented and less task oriented—are likely to demand information of a more personal nature. How, then, can the interviewer select from his background and conversational repertory elements that will help and not hinder his interview purpose? We can make only a few tentative suggestions.

There are a number of conversational gambits which make it difficult to return to an interview relationship—for example, the matching of a respondent's story or anecdote with another which typically begins, "Oh, that reminds me," or "You know, I have an uncle who had an experience just like that." In giving information about himself, it is generally wise for the interviewer to restrict himself to factual information and not to discuss his values, opinions, and feelings. Provided the factual information does not reveal the interviewer's position with respect to subjects dealt with in the interview, such information is less likely to influence the respondent than knowledge of values and attitudes. Perhaps the greater danger is that, in discussing his feelings and values, the interviewer may become so personally absorbed in self-revelation that he neglects his primary purpose. Moreover, this satisfaction of his personal needs may turn the interview into a social relationship, which makes further interviewing more difficult. (In chapters 3 and 4, we discuss the kinds of information that can be helpful in gaining the participation of respondents.)

If the respondent lacks confidence, has difficulty in expressing himself, or feels anxious, verbal encouragement, support, and thanks may be helpful. If the interview takes place in the respondent's home, there may be a photograph, picture, magazine, book, some artifact, some piece of furniture, or some architectural feature that appeals to the interviewer and that he can refer to appreciatively.

Another basis for this kind of interchange is provided by experiences or interests common to interviewer and respondent. These may be anything from baseball to children, war experience to "women's talk," places both have visited, or an interest in jazz. The respondent is likely to be helpful in finding some common interests, for these constitute one almost universal foundation for conversation.

If the interviewer and respondent come from similar backgrounds, the interviewer will have some idea of the topics that are commonly used in small talk: the weather, crops, sports, or some recent news event. This small talk can, if it is used skillfully by the interviewer, provide an interlude during or after the interview in which the respondent can gain some respite from what may be for him a novel and difficult relationship.

It is preferable to delay such an interchange until the respondent has obtained enough experience in the interview relationship and has learned enough about his role as a respondent so that the addition of this more social element does not confuse the primary role relationship. The interchange of information not directly relevant to the primary role relationship is certainly not unique to interviewing. It occurs between lawyer and client, doctor and patient, teacher and student. Its basic purpose is to facilitate the primary role relationship.

INFORMATION REVEALED BY THE COMPONENTS OF QUESTIONS

Even if the interviewer sees no need to provide information about the subject matter in order to correct the imbalance of information flow, he will inevitably communicate to the respondent something of his knowledge of the subject matter by the questions he asks and the ways in which he formulates them. Different forms of questions convey different amounts of information.

In the early stages of the study, when the interviewer knows very little about the subject matter, he will be likely to use echoes, extensions, clarifications, and summaries. In addition, his questions at this stage are more likely to have broad than narrow scope and he is likely to use more open questions than he will when he has learned more about the subject matter. In terms of their antecedents, his questions are more likely to refer to prior responses than to his own prior questions.

As his knowledge of subject matter increases, he may use expectations and assumptions with greater probability that they will correctly reflect information and predict the intended response. Similarly, he will use closed selection questions, and the range of the alternatives they include will reflect the range of his knowledge. The antecedents of his questions may increasingly be his own prior questions or the respondent's earlier responses; thus, they will increasingly reveal his frame of reference, as well as the direction of his thinking and the scope of his knowledge. To the extent that the interviewer has knowledge and awareness of the question forms he is employing, he may use this knowledge as one way of varying the amount of information he provides in his questions.

INFORMATION REVEALED BY THE INTERVIEWER'S USE OF DOCUMENTS

Documents can be used in a variety of ways to communicate a variety of information to the respondent effectively and economically. Letters of introduction, for example, give the respondent detailed and convincing information about the interviewer. But documents can also be used as stimulus materials to replace or supplement questions. In projective psychological tests, the purpose is to elicit information inaccessible to direct questioning; hence, the stimulus is an ambiguous picture or ink blot which the respondent structures on the basis of his prior experience rather than on the basis of interviewer questions.

Documents may be used as visual aids to facilitate responses dealing with factual information. For example, in a study by Collier, photographs taken of every house in a community were used in a group interview in order to obtain information about the households. Collier also used photographs of social events to identify the participants who were known to the respondent. In a third aspect of the study, Collier took photographs of a factory which he used to stimulate discussion with the respondent about his recollection of events, the photographs providing an opportunity for the respondent to discuss his attitudes and values in relation to the objects photographed. In addition to photographs, scrapbooks, maps, and other documents and objects in the possession of re-

spondents have been utilized by the interviewer.[1] W. F. Whyte
(1954) has used a series of drawings of products manufactured by
craftsmen as a way of stimulating discussion on the reasons why
the craftsmen preferred making some objects rather than others.

Preferred Styles of Interpersonal Relations
of Interviewer and Respondent

In the two preceding chapters, we note the various classifications
that have been used to describe the preferred styles of interpersonal
relations of the interviewer (see p. 281) and the respondent
(see p. 308). Although the terminology varied, the types of behavior described are rather similar, as the following table indicates.

Interviewer	Respondent
Task involvement	Approval seekers
(Hyman, 1954)	(Cumming et al., 1958)
Blue stocking	Esteem seekers
(Riesman, 1958)	(Cumming et al., 1958)
Market research	Response seekers
(Riesman, 1958)	(Cumming et al., 1958)
Social orientation	Total acceptance seekers
(Hyman, 1954)	(Cumming et al., 1958)
The intrusive interviewer	Total acceptance seekers
(Hyman, 1954)	(Cumming et al., 1958)

A number of interesting questions are raised by these parallel
classifications of interviewers and respondents. If we assume that
the interviewer has sufficient skill to play each of these interpersonal

[1] Collier (1957) has reported that when the interviewer and respondent look
at a stimulus photograph together, the relationship becomes more impersonal and
less affect laden. When one of the authors reported this to an experienced interviewer, she commented that in schedule interviewing she found it was very
effective to sit beside the respondent so that both could read the schedule of
questions rather than sitting opposite the respondent reading the questions from
a schedule hidden by a clip board. Further experience is needed to determine the
conditions under which the impersonal focus of attention provided for interviewer and respondent by this technique facilitates the interview.

roles—blue stocking or market research, task or social orientation—
to what extent should he try to meet the preferences of the respondent? Should the extent of this accommodation vary with the
type of interview? Hyman (1954, p. 79) argues that, in the schedule
interview, socially oriented or intrusive interviewers increase the
sensitivity of the respondent to the social aspects of the situation
and may thereby bias responses in the direction of the interviewer's values. He expresses a general preference for the task-oriented,
nonintrusive interviewer, but he does not qualify this preference in
terms of the preferences of the respondents, and his emphasis is on
the avoidance of bias rather than some of the other criteria of
evaluating responses that we suggest in Chapter 5.

Our own impressions are that the interviewer must attempt to
accommodate to the preferred style of the respondent to the extent
necessary for gaining and maintaining his participation, but that
within the range of respondent requirements the more effective
interviewer–respondent relationship is in the direction of more
task orientation and less social orientation.

The foregoing discussion assumes that the interviewer can vary
at will the type of interpersonal role he plays in order to adopt the
role congenial to the respondent. Unfortunately, there has been
little examination of this question in the interview literature. The
evidence cited of the differential ability of four experienced interviewers to make their style of interviewing conform to rather rigid
prescriptions (see p. 286) suggests that there is considerable variation in the flexibility of interviewers. Goldman-Eisler (1952, 1954)
measured the time that three psychiatrists spent in talking and gesturing while interviewing five reserved and five talkative patients.
She found that each psychiatrist used silences consistently, regardless of whether the patient was reserved or talkative. Although
some variability in talking and gesturing occurred for each psychiatrist from one interview to another, there was still consistency
in the relative differences among the psychiatrists. These studies
suggest that there are limitations on the degree to which interviewers can adapt their behavior to that of different respondents.

APPENDIX

A STUDY OF SELECTED
PERSONALITY CHARACTERISTICS
OF SOCIAL SCIENCE FIELD WORKERS

Stephen A. Richardson

In Chapter 12 we note that, although scattered impressions were available about the relationship between personality characteristics and skill in nonstandardized interviewing, few empirical studies had been done. Because we concluded that the nonstandardized interview offered more freedom of behavior to the interviewer than other forms of interviewing and demanded the widest range of skills, we carried out an empirical study to test whether personality characteristics are related to competence in nonstandardized interviewing.

To achieve this primary purpose it was necessary to test the following additional hypotheses:

1. Personality characteristics will not change as the result of training in nonstandardized interviewing.

2. Performance skill in nonstandardized interviewing will change as the result of training but in differing amounts for different individuals.

These two additional hypotheses are based on the following reasoning. An essential element in the definition of personality is the *stability* of a disposition to act in a certain manner. Thus any selected measures of personality must be tested to determine whether they do in fact remain unchanged for each subject over

---

A more detailed account of this study is available in S. A. Richardson (1954).

the time period under investigation and in the face of the training given in interviewing.

If performance skills in nonstandardized interviewing are so stable that training does not change the level of skill, the initial level of skill shown by a neophyte interviewer is then sufficient basis for selecting "good" interviewers, and no training is necessary. If this is the case, there is no need for personality measures to predict performance. If, however, training does change the skills of the students and there is no correlation between the levels of skills before and after training, the initial level of skill in interviewing cannot be used to predict the outcome of training. If these two secondary hypotheses are confirmed, personality measures obtained before training may predict the outcome of interviewer training.

In addition to the skills required for obtaining information during the interview, nonstandardized interviewing requires the ability to gain and maintain the cooperation and participation of the people studied (field relations). Nonstandardized interviewing is also frequently done in conjunction with observation. The three bodies of skill—interviewing, field relations, and observation—are frequently embraced under the title "field methods," and it is customary to combine these methods in a single course. Because of the interdependence of the three skills, we decided to examine personality characteristics in relation to field relations and observation as well as to interviewing.

Methods

Two sets of subjects were used in the study. The first set consisted of experienced field workers (ten men and four women) who had had broad training and experience in interviewing and observation in studies of organizations and communities. All were working at Cornell, but most had had prior research experience at other universities. Although these fourteen do not constitute a systematic sample from a known population of field workers, they can be considered as fairly representative. This set will hereafter be called *experienced*.

The second set consisted of twenty (fifteen women and five men) Cornell upperclassmen and graduate students who had applied for admission to a one-semester seminar in field methods, prerequisites for which were two courses in the social sciences but no training or experience in field methods. Again, although no sampling procedure was used in selecting the students, it is reasonable to believe that they were representative of students who apply for training in field methods.

For the experienced interviewers, ratings of competence were obtained from supervisors and measures of personality derived from a test which will be described in the following section. Measures of both performance and personality were made after the subjects had obtained training and experience.

The second set of subjects, the twenty students, were given initial tests to assess their level of skill in interviewing, field relations, and observation and were given the same personality test as the experienced set of subjects. The students were then randomly divided into a training group of eleven, who were given a semester of intensive training by an experienced teaching staff in field methods; this training consisted of reading and discussion, simulated situations devised in a classroom setting, and actual experience in a small research project. The remaining nine students were used as a control group and were given no training or experience in field methods during the semester. Hereafter the student experimental and control groups will be called *trained* and *controls*.

At the end of the semester, the trained and control sets were again measured for the same personality characteristics and for performance skills in field methods. By using the "before and after" design, we could determine the effect of the training in field methods both on ability in interviewing and observation and on selected personality characteristics. The use of experienced and student field workers in the two parts of the design provides independent measures of the relationship between personality characteristics and field-method skills. The summary of the design of the study is contained in Table 13.

TABLE 13. *Summary of Experimental Design*

	I	II	
		EXPERIMENTAL OR TRAINED SET	
		TRAINED SET	CONTROL SET
	EXPERIENCED	OF STUDENTS	OF STUDENTS
TIME	$(n = 14)$	$(n = 11)$	$(n = 9)$
Before training		Battery of personality and performance tests	Battery of personality and performance tests
During semester		Classroom and field experience given in field methods	No field-methods experience obtained
After training		Battery of personality and performance tests	Battery of personality and performance tests
		Supervisors' ratings made of field-methods skills	
After training and professional experience	Supervisors' over-all rating of field-methods skills Personality test		

DESCRIPTION OF PERSONAL CHARACTERISTICS

The selection of specific personality variables believed to be associated with skill in interviewing stemmed from careful descriptions of the personal qualities demanded by the task. Because of the paucity of published descriptions of the personal characteristics of interviewers who use nonstandardized methods fifteen experienced research directors were asked: What skills and personality characteristics would you look for in selecting a field worker for nonstandardized interviewing and observation? We included observation because the literature on field work stresses the close relationship between interviewing and observation. There was high consensus in the fifteen responses as well as an implicit assumption that every characteristic suggested would be helpful in both interviewing and observation. The following composite list of their recommendations retains insofar as possible the original language and terminology of our respondents.

The skills necessary in field methods were stated to be:

1. A memory for details and names.
2. An ability to write clearly.
3. Conscientiousness in recording data and in writing reports.
4. Ability to analyze feelings.
5. Ability to take the role of a watchful onlooker.
6. Ability to relate to all social classes and to function in an unstructured situation.
7. Ability to approach total strangers and to participate in a wide variety of small talk.
8. Ability to think ahead of the informant.
9. Ability to identify and win the support of people in the organization or community.
10. Ability to make the informant feel at ease.
11. Ability to structure one's role in a realistic nonthreatening way.
12. Ability to avoid partisan identification.
13. Ability to track down and evaluate rumors and antagonisms connected with the research operations.
14. Ability to keep the ultimate objectives of the research project in mind while interviewing.
15. Ability to pick up quickly the technology common to the organization or community in which one is working.
16. Ability to create for oneself a role of field worker that is understandable to the people whom one is studying.
17. Ability to fit data to a theoretical structure and yet not distort data by imposing an unsuitable conceptual framework.
18. Ability to observe a situation while involved in that situation.

19. Awareness of alternative techniques of field work with no emotional investment in any one method.

20. Flexibility in recording data; i.e., ability to operate either completely from memory or by taking full notes.

21. A sense of timing; i.e., how fast to move in when working from superficial to highly affective subjects and also how fast to move in on a group or situation.

22. Ability to keep from probing into problems he or the respondent can't handle.

23. Ability to be warm enough so that people will want to talk, but not so hot or pressing that he becomes a threat.

24. Ability to analyze data and to work with some degree of independence; i.e., to think about the situation effectively while actually in the field.

Certain characteristics can better be classified as personal qualities:

25. Humility, modesty, integrity, respect, sympathy, curiosity about people and the subject.

26. Insight, patience, fortitude, wonder, sincerity, sincere appreciation of people.

27. Ability to find satisfaction in being with, listening to, and trying to understand people and society.

28. Ability to take a passive role.

29. Probably the willingness to strive to please and win approval. This would involve watching and weighing situations in order to adapt oneself as perfectly as possible.

30. A controlled but creative imagination, either as a natural attribute or as the effect of having a reflective life forced on oneself, with the consequent tendency toward a rich fantasy life.

31. Ability to make a good first impression. Neither too much the "native" nor too much the "outsider." The ability to look "different" from the native in a way one is expected to look.

32. Ability to hide one's feelings and not to become aggressive. Ease in adopting local grammar and colloquialisms quickly but not in a manner that seems forced or unnatural.

33. Ability to keep wondering what is going on.

34. Ability to allow something that has been said to be misinterpreted and let it pass; i.e., to accept being misunderstood.

35. Ability to listen to prejudiced, false, or malicious statements and continue to give support to the speaker.

36. Humor, especially to be able to see oneself as others see one.

37. Ability to empathize with others but not to the point of losing oneself. Emotional stability.

38. Ability to include data that contradict hypotheses in order to modify, revise, or reject initial hypotheses.

39. Ability to keep personal projections at a minimum and yet retain insight.

40. Open friendliness rather than withdrawn curiosity.

41. Ability not to be resentful at unfavorable field situations.

42. Ability to tolerate love and hostility in others and in oneself.

43. Ability to take rebuffs.

44. Flexibility and the ability to shift role readily.

45. Sensitivity to feel what the other person feels but the ability to resist either being immobilized by it or being forced to act in a particular way.

46. Ability not to become anxious if not immediately accepted.

47. Ties and satisfactions outside the research activities.

48. Does not have to use people and exert power over them.

49. Ability to respond to feelings as well as to words.

50. Not aggressively socially mobile.

51. Does not take a markedly moralistic view of the world.

52. A person whose thinking tends to run off in a great many directions and who seeks out widespread implications, rather than a person who has a clearly, highly organized mind.

Finally, some ethical requirements were included in the descriptions:

The field worker should not violate subcultural values and taboos. He should be able to interpret research projects in line with established policy, both in formal talks and informal conversation, to maintain confidences and security of notes, and to refrain from criticism and gossip. He should be able to keep himself from passing judgment on others' behavior or on social situations. He should be able to respect other people's customs, values, and mannerisms.

PERSONALITY MEASURES

Some of these personal characteristics are similar in style and content to some of the variables used in the Thematic Apperception Test (hereafter called TAT). In this test the subject is shown a set of standard pictures and asked to make up a story about each. The stories are then analyzed to determine the degree to which defined personality variables are present or absent (H. A. Murray, 1943; S. S. Tompkins, 1947).

The TAT has been widely used for testing people with backgrounds similar to those of subjects used in this study, and its authors believe that even a person sophisticated in the social sciences would find it difficult to formulate responses so as to give a distorted measure of his personality. For these reasons selected TAT variables were used as the personality measures for this study.

For each of the personality characteristics measured in this study a prediction was made as to whether its relationship with over-all field-methods competence would be positive or negative (Table 14).[1]

TABLE 14. *TAT Variables*

		PREDICTION
1. Receptivity:	To enjoy contemplation, or the reception of sensuous impressions.	+
2. Dominance:	To try to influence or manipulate the behavior, sentiments, or ideas of others. To lead, manage, govern. To coerce, restrain, imprison.	−
3. Affiliation:	To seek or form friendly relations with a person or persons. To enjoy persons of either sex.	+

[1] A rationale for the predictions made and how the definitions derive from descriptions of field workers is contained in Richardson (1954).

4. Dependence: The tendency of the hero of the story to strongly need, seek out, or rely on some other person or persons for emotional support, advice, direction, or motivation.   −

5. Counteraction: To strive in the face of defeat or disappointment. To be energetic in recouping after failure. To meet damaging press with renewed vigor.   +

6. Achievement: To work at something important with energy and persistence. To strive to accomplish something creditable. Ambition manifested in action.   +

7. Symbolic aggression: Emotional and verbal—to hate, be angry, engage in a verbal quarrel. To curse, criticize or ridicule.   +

8. Intraggression: To blame, criticize, reprove, or belittle oneself for wrongdoing, stupidity, or failure. To suffer feelings of inferiority, guilt, remorse. To punish oneself physically, to commit suicide.   −

9. Value judgment: A strong tendency of the characters in the stories, or the writer, to make value judgments in terms of good and bad, about the thoughts, decisions, and activities of other persons or groups.   −

10. Humor: An abundance of good-natured joking or satirical insights.   +

11. Introspection: A deep and intimate understanding of how many kinds of characters depicted feel and think about themselves, but not in relation to other people.   +

12. Human relations: Insights into the complex of feeling relationships between the people depicted in the stories.   +

| 13. Diversity: | The portrayal of a variety of people with their differing roles, feelings, and relations to one another. | + |

The TAT test, as we indicated in Table 13, was administered to the experienced group once and to the student group twice. The test was administered to groups of subjects varying in size from four to twelve. Instructions to subjects followed the form recommended by Murray (1943, p. 3), except that subjects wrote the stories instead of narrating them and were given a time limit of seven minutes per story and told the time limit in advance. Seven TAT pictures were used in the following sequence: 1, 2, 4, 5, 13 MF, 8 GF, 6 GF. When the TAT was administered the second time to the student group, four months later, the pictures and procedures were identical except for the added instruction: "Please write different stories from those you wrote when you took the test the first time."

The only information given the scorers of the TAT protocols was the sex of the subject and the picture about which each story was told. The "before" and "after" test protocols of the students in the trained and control groups, and the one test of the experienced group were mixed in random order so that the scorers had no way of knowing which two protocols were written by the same subject, which set a subject belonged to, or whether any single protocol was a "before" or "after."

The scoring procedure consisted of the following steps:[2]

[2] The following further procedures were used in the scoring of tests of reliability.

Four judges scored the protocols of all the subjects independently. After the independent scoring, the four judges were formed into two teams of two, and each team worked independently. The two members of a team compared their scores, discussed the basis of their judgments, and reached a final agreement on a score which would represent their team. The method of scoring in teams was developed by Malcolm C. Preston and was used in a project described by M. C. Preston et al. (1950). To prevent the norms of the two judges in each team from diverging from other teams as might occur in the course of scoring a large number of protocols, the members of the judging teams were systematically rotated after every fifth protocol. This scoring procedure provided for each subject four individual judgments and two subsequent team judgments for each variable used in the study.

The reliability of the two team judgments for each variable ranged from .83

1. The judge first read the seven stories comprising each protocol and for each story identified the character with whom the subject had identified himself (the hero of the story). The rules for making this selection were those suggested by Murray.

2. The judge then reread the protocol considering the intensity, duration, frequency, and importance in the plot of the variables to be scored in relation to the hero of each story.

3. On the basis of the amount of evidence found for the variable, the judge then assigned a score for the variable based on the seven pictures. Complete absence of the variable was scored 0; the slightest suggestion of the variable in an intense form or the continued presence of the variable of a milder form was assigned a

----

for human relations to .54 for dominance, with a median of .75 (product moment correlation with Spearman-Brown correction).

When several sources of random error can be distinguished, the sources cannot be separated by means of the customary correlational approach. For this reason, an analysis of variance test was also used to measure the variance attributable to judges, to errors in subjects' responses, and to differences between subjects. It provides measures of the reliability of the judges' ratings and of the variation in subject responses. The test applied to the ratings made independently by four judges indicates that satisfactory judge reliability was achieved in only 23 per cent of the sets of judgments. The ratings, however, discriminate between subjects for every one of the variables. *This suggests that, although there was considerable variation among judges, there was substantial agreement in the rank ordering they assigned to the subjects.*

The procedure of team judgments was used to determine whether reliability could be improved. Eighty-two per cent of the sets of team judgments achieved satisfactory reliability. *These results are highly suggestive of improved reliability when team judgments are used.* (Because of the different and small number of degrees of freedom in the two kinds of judging, no exact measure of the difference between the two forms of judging is possible.) There is danger that in order to reach agreement the two judges forming a team will compromise in the direction of the mean score. This might increase the reliability of the two team ratings and at the same time reduce the variation in the ratings made. That this was not a serious danger is suggested by the fact that 79 per cent of the sets of team ratings discriminate among subjects. Reliability of team measures may be impaired by learning taking place during the scoring which would enable one team member to better predict how the other team member would score. If this occurred, a higher agreement between team scores would be expected in the second half of the scoring than in the first half. This was checked by means of a split half test, which demonstrated no significant increase in agreement in the second half over the first half.

Although team ratings do discriminate less well between subjects than individual ratings, this loss of discrimination is outweighed by the increase in agreement in judges which teams obtain.

maximum score of 5. Scores of 2, 3, and 4 were assigned for intermediate intensities of expression.

This procedure was used for all the variables except value judgment, humor, introspection, human relations, and diversity. Here the judges did not score in relation to the hero of the stories but based the score on general evidence in the stories, wherever this evidence may have been contained.

The study design requires that, in addition to personality measures, measures of skill in interviewing, observation, and field methods be obtained for each subject. Because the measure of field methods obtained for the *experienced* and *student* groups of subjects were not identical, it is necessary to describe each in some detail. These descriptions are necessary not only for reporting the methods but also for interpreting the results obtained.

PERFORMANCE MEASURES OF EXPERIENCED FIELD WORKERS

All field directors who had first-hand knowledge of the skills of the fourteen experienced field workers were asked independently for an over-all rating on a four-point scale of each field worker's level of competence. Initially more than fourteen experienced field workers were included but individual workers were dropped if fewer than two ratings were obtainable or if there was more than a one-point difference in the ratings obtained. Because we shall be comparing these ratings of competence with those of the trained students it is useful to briefly examine the basis of judgment from which the ratings are made for the experienced group.

The criterion of over-all field-methods performance obtained for the experienced group was essentially the type of evaluation which field directors customarily make of the workers whom they supervise. In actual research operations, field directors have the additional advantage of being with the field worker where the task is his major responsibility, under conditions far removed from university life. Thus the directors can see how the field worker withstands the stresses of full-time field work. In some respects, however, field directors are in an unfavorable position to make an evaluation of the workers whom they supervise. Evaluations are made primarily not from the worker's interviewing but from his field notes, which are judged in the light of the director's general knowledge of the field situation and on such criteria as copiousness, literary quality, the types of data covered, and internal consistency. Because the field director is rarely present at the situations observed or at the interviews, it is very difficult for him to judge the validity of the notes. The over-all evaluation is likely to be fairly heavily weighted by considerations of the worker's competence in interpersonal relations, the congeniality of his ethics and values with those of the director, and his intellectual ability.

The evaluation of the experienced field workers in the study was based on performance in more than one field situation and was made by a number of supervisors. The existence of several independent supervisors' ratings for each experienced field worker provides some check on the consistency of supervisors' judgments.

PERFORMANCE MEASURES
STUDENT INTERVIEWERS

In order to obtain separate measures of the interdependent skills of interviewing, observation, and gaining and maintaining the participation of the people under study as well as an over-all measure of field-methods skills, and in order to overcome some of the limitations of field supervisors' ratings, we devised independent tests for each of these main skills. These tests were also necessary to compare the trained and control groups of students because the control group was not trained and thus its skills could not be assessed during training.

The subjects were asked to conduct a half-hour interview with a person who had participated in a meeting a week earlier. The purpose of this nonstandardized interview was to determine both what had happened and how the participants had felt at that meeting. The interviewer had not been acquainted with the respondent prior to the interview and had little knowledge of the nature of the meeting or the identity of the participants. The interviewers took no notes during the interview, but immediately afterward they wrote from memory a report covering the data elicited during the interview. The over-all measure of interviewer competence was based on how well the interviewer gained the respondent's participation, the form and types of questions the interviewer employed, and the quality and quantity of the information the interviewer recorded. The student reports were compared with typed transcriptions of tape recordings of the interviews.

Two tests of field observation were administered, one involving a dramatic audition, the other a motion picture. In the audition test, four drama students were given twenty minutes in which to invent and prepare a five-minute skit or play, which they were then to act. The explanation to the drama students, the rehearsal, and the play were observed by the trained and control groups, who formed the audience. The audition was tape-recorded and photographed[3] to provide a record against which the students' reports were compared.

The trained and control groups were told that they were to observe both what happened and how the participants felt during the audition. No notes were to be taken at the audition by the students. After the audition the subjects wrote a report to reconstruct as fully as possible what had happened. The measure of observation competence was based on the amount and type of correct information obtained, the distortions made in reporting, and the form in which the report was written.

The motion picture was a color-sound film especially produced to provide a measure of ability to make a selective report of an event and to make interpretations from the behavior observed. The situation filmed was part of a school-board meeting. The criteria used to judge observation competence were the same as those used in the audition test.

Two tests—one involving a letter, the other a telephone call— were used to determine the degree of skill with which field workers deal with certain problems in gaining the participation of the people who are to be studied.

In the letter test, a proposed research project in an organization

3 A camera was used that took one photograph every five seconds.

was described to the students. They were instructed to assume the roles of field workers who were to carry out the research and to write letters to a person in charge of the organization asking for an appointment to discuss the proposed research. The purpose of the appointment was to win the cooperation of the person in charge.

In the telephone test, a research project to be carried out in a number of communities was described to the students. Each student was instructed to take the role of a field worker and to make a telephone call to an influential person in the community and ask for an appointment to discuss the research. The role of the influential person was played by a member of the research staff. Each telephone call was tape-recorded to provide a basis for systematic evaluation of performance.

The measure of field relations competence for both these tests was based on the student's conception of the relationship between himself and those he was studying and on how he planned to use the meetings being arranged.

The scores on the interview, observation, and field relations tests were each converted into rank orders for the trained and control groups of students. For each student the rank orders on each test were summed and one over-all rank was obtained and designated as a measure of field-methods skills.

Three members of the training seminar staff supervised the trained group both in the field project and in the classroom. Each of these supervisors, together with three or four students, formed a team, and each team undertook a field study of the organization and functions of a church in a small town. Because field observation was carried out for the most part by the whole team observing the same situations, the supervisors had an unusually good opportunity to evaluate the observation reports written by their team members. In addition to having seen the situation, the supervisors were able to compare the field notes written by each member of the team about the same situation. The supervisors were present in social situations when the students carried out informal interviewing of the persons present and, whenever possible, listened to these interviews without breaking into the conversation. Supervisors were able to observe the way in which the students developed and maintained interpersonal relations with the people whom they were studying and, from these observations, were able to evaluate the students' field-relations skills. These could also be gauged by the comments that people in the field made about the students when the students were not present.

The supervisors' evaluations were in part also based on the work done by the trained group in simulated tasks in a classroom setting where students observed socio-dramas, interviewed people, discussed the tape recordings of the interviews with their supervisors, and discussed case studies in field relations.

On the basis of these kinds of evidence, at the end of the training period each of the three supervisors made independent ratings for each trained student on interviewing, observation, and field-relations skills. Although the supervisor was best able to rate the students on his own team, all three supervisors knew all the students well, had supervised some of their work or had listened to tape-recorded practice interviews, and had read all the students' field notes.

The independent ratings were then compared, and a final agreement was reached on each rating for each trained student. An over-all evaluation of each student's field-methods skills was obtained by combining the rankings for each skill into an over-all ranking. The tests had the advantage of providing uniform scoring procedures and uniform conditions in which student performance could be compared. Furthermore, recording the interviews and the situations observed permitted a detailed analysis of the accuracy of student reporting in both interviewing and observation and of the techniques used by the students in the interview and telephone field-relations test.

The tests had obvious disadvantages in that they could not simulate many of the conditions that occur in actual field work, such as the stresses that develop when the worker is for long periods of time among people with backgrounds very dissimilar from his own, the hostility sometimes encountered, and the complexities involved in dealing with respondents many of whom know and communicate with one another.

Results

CHANGES IN PERSONALITY AND PERFORMANCE MEASURES OVER A FOUR-MONTH PERIOD

The four-month interval and intensive training in field methods had negligible effects on the thirteen TAT measures. No significant changes in TAT measures occurred in the trained or control group during the time interval. Only one variable (diversity) increased $(P < .01)$ for the trained group, owing to the joint effect of the time interval and the training.[4]

Changes in interviewing skills did occur as a result of training—for the most part in the predicted direction—but there was wide variation in the degree to which individual students changed as the result of training. The relationship between the before and after tests was low and insignificant. Hence, initial level of interviewing performance before training is a poor predictor of the outcome of training.

This confirmation of the two hypotheses stated on page 328 permits the TAT measures before training to be used to predict the outcome of training if the characteristics measured by the TAT are related to the skills exhibited after training. Furthermore, because initial level of performance cannot be used to predict outcome, it is important to determine whether TAT measures can predict.

THE RELATION BETWEEN THE TAT VARIABLES AND THE OVER-ALL MEASURES OF FIELD-METHODS PERFORMANCE

The correlations between TAT variables and over-all measures of competence in field methods are given in Table 15, which includes only variables with significant or near-significant relationships. Taking into account whether predictions were confirmed by one

---

[4] t tests were used to determine whether changes in measures occurred.

TABLE 15. *Correlations between TAT Variables Measured before Training and Over-all Measures of Field Competence after Training*[5]

TAT VARIABLE	PREDICTION	EXPERIENCED FIELD WORKERS ($n = 14$)	STUDENTS TESTS AFTER TRAINING ($n = 11$)	SUPER-VISORS' RATINGS	RESULTS CONFIRM OR CONTRADICT	PREDICTION ($P < .10$)
Human relations	+	.59*	.53*	.11	Confirmed	Experienced and student
Introspection	+	.67†	.44‡	.24	Confirmed	Experienced and student
Receptivity	+	.45‡	.00	.48‡	Confirmed	Experienced and student
Diversity	+	.51*	.25	.04	Confirmed	Experienced only
Symbolic aggression	+	.51*	.21	-.16	Confirmed	Experienced only
Affiliation	+	.20	.47‡	.49‡	Confirmed	Student only
Intraggression	–	.45‡	.59*	.01	Contradict	Experienced and student
Value judgment	–	.75†	.02	-.32	Contradict	Experienced only
Counteraction	+	-.11	-.27	-.60*	Contradict	Student only
Dependence	–	.13	.67*	.29	Contradict	Student only
Achievement	+	-.14	-.48‡	-.45‡	Contradict	Student only

5

	*	†	‡
	5%	1%	10%
$n = 11$	.53	.73	.43
$n = 14$	.46	.64	.39

or both of the sets of subjects and whether the correlations are significant ($P < .05$) or near significant ($P < .10$), the TAT variables which best predict over-all skill in field methods are listed in rank order, beginning with strongest confirmation of prediction.

The person who shows over-all competence in field-methods scores, as predicted, high in the following TAT variables:[6] human relations, introspection, receptivity, diversity, symbolic aggression, affiliation.

For five additional TAT variables, relationships or near relationships with over-all measures of field methods were found, but they were opposite to those predicted. These TAT variables and the direction of their correlations with over-all field-methods measures are as follows: intraggression: $+$; value judgment: $+$; counteraction: $-$; dependence: $+$; achievement: $-$.

No direct contradictions occur between results for the two groups, although there is some discrepancy with regard to value judgment.

The results raise a number of questions which require further analysis of the data. For example, why were the predictions of the relations between TAT variables and performance that were based on the thinking of experienced field supervisors no better than chance? Why did more confirmation of predictions appear in the experienced group of field workers and more relations contrary to prediction in the student group? The following analysis will be aimed at these questions and others. Any findings uncovered must serve as a basis for hypotheses which require testing and confirmation in further studies.

The predictions tested were based on the thinking of experienced field-work supervisors. Because these individuals implicitly assumed that field-methods skills are highly positively correlated with one another, no separate predictions were made for interviewing and observation. This assumption is not borne out by the measures of performance after training. *The correlation between interviewing skills and observation skills is low and insignificant.* We shall now examine further this unexpected finding by relating the TAT variables to the more specific performance skills of interviewing and observation.

---

[6] For definitions of these personality variables see pp. 335–336.

RELATIONS BETWEEN TAT VARIABLES AND
INTERVIEWING AND OBSERVATION

Correlations for the trained group between TAT variables before training and measures of interviewing and observation after training are shown in Table 16. Competence in interviewing is positively related to the following TAT variables: human relations ($P < .05$); symbolic aggression ($P < .05$); affiliation ($P < .05$); intraggression ($P < .05$); diversity ($P < .10$); dominance ($P < .10$).

Competence in observation is positively related to the TAT variables: introspection ($P < .05$), receptivity ($P < .05$), intraggression ($P < .05$), dependence ($P < .10$); it is negatively related to counteraction ($P < .05$), achievement ($P < .10$), humor ($P < .10$).

The only TAT variable that is significantly correlated with both interviewing and observation tests is intraggression.

By contrast, when TAT variables before training are correlated with measures of interviewing and observation before training only two significant relationships were found.[7] This contrast suggests that TAT variables can predict the outcome of training in interviewing and observation, but cannot predict the level of interviewing and observation skills before training.

The incomplete agreement between the results for the experienced group and those of the teaching group shown in Table 15 can now be examined in the light of Table 16. Because the reliability of the TAT measures is satisfactory, any lack of agreement must be due to differences in the over-all measures used of field-methods performance.

The following evidence suggests that the ratings of over-all field-work competence made for the experienced group were more weighted for interviewing and less weighted for observation than the ratings and test scores of the teaching group. Two TAT variables—diversity and symbolic aggression—were related to over-all performance for the experienced set only.

In the trained set, the same two TAT variables were related to interviewing but not to observation. On the other hand, four variables—affiliation, counteraction, dependence, and achievement—

[7] A negative correlation between humor and interviewing ($P > .10$) and a positive correlation between affiliation and observation ($P > .05$).

TABLE 16. *Correlation between TAT Variables Measured before Training and Measures of Skills in Interviewing, Observation, and Over-all Field Methods after Training*[8]

TAT VARIABLES AND PREDICTIONS		TRAINED STUDENTS						EXPERIENCED FIELD WORKERS
		INTERVIEW		OBSERVATION		OVER-ALL FIELD METHODS		OVER-ALL FIELD METHODS
		Supervisor Rating	Test score	Supervisor rating	Test score	Supervisor rating	Test score	Rating
Human relations	+		.63*				.53*	.59*
Introspection	+				.57* .49†		.44†	.67*
Receptivity	+			.60*	.48†		.48†	.45†
Diversity	+		.44†					.51*
Symbolic aggression	+		.59*					.51*
Affiliation	+	.73‡	.59*			.49†		
Intraggression	−		.55*		.58* .61*		.47† .59*	.45†
Counteraction	+			−.74‡	−.52†	−.60*		
Dependence	−				.51†		.67*	
Achievement	+			−.42†		−.45†	−.48	
Humor	+				−.51†			
Dominance	−		.46†					

8 * = p > .05
† = p < .10
‡ = p < .01
Where two correlations are given for observation tests this indicates results from both tests.

were related to over-all performance for the trained set only. In this case, three out of four of the same variables—counteraction, dependence, and achievement—were related to observation but not to interviewing for the same group. If the results of tables 15 and 16 are compared with the predictions, we find that in the two cases —diversity and symbolic aggression—where the predictions are confirmed for the experienced set only, Table 16 shows that the variables were related to interviewing for the trained set. On the other hand, three predictions—counteraction, dependence, and achievement—are contradicted by the results from the trained set. Table 16 shows that each of these variables was related to observation.

INTERVENING VARIABLES

Before proceeding with the analysis, let us examine the possible influence of intervening variables. Two such variables suggested in the literature on the TAT are length of story, or protocol (H. A. Murray, 1943, p. 8), and sex of the subject tested (G. Lindzey & M. Goldberg, 1953). First, then, to examine the effect of length of story, two tests were made.

1. Correlation between the number of words written and the field-methods performance measure.

2. Correlation between the number of words written and each of the TAT measures which have been found to be related to field-methods performance.

Results of these two tests for the experienced group show a significant positive relationship between the number of words written and the over-all rating on field-methods skills ($P < .01$). Moreover, of the seven variables that are positively related to the over-all measures of field-methods skills, six are also positively related to the number of words written in the TAT protocol. For the experienced group, then, both tests suggest that the number of words written was an intervening variable that influenced the relation between TAT scores and performance measures. For the trained group, however, neither of the tests shows any significant correlations.

These results suggest that the experienced worker is evaluated to a large extent on the basis of his field notes. Because the supervisor is rarely present at the event described, he is not in a position to evaluate the accuracy of the notes and hence must restrict his evaluation to the richness of the data reported, the amount of coverage, and the clarity of communication of the feelings and interpersonal relations of the people interviewed or observed. On the other hand, the supervisors of the trained group were in an unusually advantageous position to assess the accuracy of the students' notes written under field conditions. The supervisors were in the field with the students, the students subsequently wrote their notes, and the fact that three or four students were generally observing the same event produced several reports for comparison. All these conditions provided the supervisors with external checks on the accuracy of the students' reports. The writer of the TAT stories, unhampered by reality, is maximally free to describe persons and social situations. The results obtained on the relation between the number of words written and performance suggests, then, that supervisors of field workers may be overinfluenced by the literary quality and fluency of the notes they obtain from field workers. Here we have another clue to the lack of agreement in the construction of the over-all measure of field methods used for the experienced group and the students.

Secondly, a test of sex difference in TAT variables showed no significant differences. The sex composition of the trained and experienced groups is not, then, an intervening variable.

VALUE JUDGMENT

The largest discrepancy between prediction and results occurred for the variable value judgment. The predicted negative relation between value judgment and field-methods skills was based on wide agreement among field supervisors that a field worker who has a markedly moralistic view of the world is likely to distort the research data he collects and to antagonize respondents through his inability to refrain from passing judgments.

The results show that for the trained group value judgment does not show any significant correlations, but there is a shift from negative correlations before training to positive correlations after training. For the experienced group the results show a positive relationship ($P < .01$), which is in the opposite direction to that predicted.

Several pieces of evidence may be used to interpret these results:

1. In order to determine the relation between fantasy behavior exhibited in a TAT story and overt behavior in everyday life, ratings of overt behavior were obtained. The three field supervisors were asked to read the definition of each TAT variable and then to rate each student in the experimental group on the basis of his behavior on each variable as this behavior manifested itself during training. This was done after the supervisors had known the students for four months. The relationship between value judgment exhibited in the TAT and value judgment displayed in overt behavior was positive and significant ($P < .05$). This indicates that persons who exhibit high value judgment in TAT stories do so also in life situations.

2. Correlations between value judgment and the skill of observation and interviewing show a consistent trend toward positive increase with training.

3. If persons can be made aware of their tendency to make value judgments, they may learn to control it. The degree to which this control may be developed can in part be tested. Observation reports made by the trained group in the tests before and after training were analyzed to determine the extent to which they contained explicit and implicit value judgments.[9] During training, supervisors stressed the need for making value judgments explicit in their field notes and pointed out to students the implicit value judgments that appeared there. The measures of implicit, explicit, and total value judgments in the observation tests were correlated with TAT measures of value judgment. The results are contained in Table 17.

[9] An explicit value judgment is one which makes clear that the judgment is based on personal opinions and values. Students were taught to identify their value judgments by placing them in parentheses and adding their initials. In an implicit value judgment the maker gives no sign of recognition that he has made a value judgment.

TABLE 17. *Relation between TAT Variable Value Judgment and Value Judgments Made in Writing a Report on a Situation Observed*
[*Experimental Group Only* $(n = 11)$]

VALUE JUDGMENTS MADE ON OBSERVER'S REPORT	TAT VARIABLE VALUE JUDGMENT
Before	
Explicit value judgment	x[10]
Implicit value judgment	.42
Total value judgment	.45[11]
After	
Explicit value judgment	.09
Implicit value judgment	−.42
Total value judgment	−.37

The results show that before training the correlation between value judgments made in observers' reports and value judgment in the TAT is positive and near significance, whereas after training these trends reverse, and there is a negative correlation. This evidence suggests that with training field workers can learn to control their value judgments in writing field notes. This suggests why the predicted negative relationship between value judgment and field-work competence was not obtained.

To interpret why a positive relationship was found for experienced field workers, it is necessary to go beyond the data presented. Autobiographical material of experienced field workers contains frequent references to strong interest in humanitarian values and social reform. These field workers felt that social research is a more desirable approach to achieving change than direct and possibly hasty action—sentiments well expressed by W. F. Whyte (1955, pp. 280–283). Such motivational values will be an important self-selective factor for field workers, especially for extended periods of field work where conditions frequently cause considerable emotional stress and sometimes physical discomfort. A strong humanitarian value system may be an important aid to sensitive per-

[10] No rank correlation run because of large number of ties in ranks.
[11] $P < .10$

ception of social behavior through providing an intuitive set of conceptual categories with which the person makes observations.

In summary, then, a person with high value judgment will at first find this a hindrance in field work, but with training this may be overcome. High value judgment for certain values may provide a set of implicit conceptual categories that sensitize the field worker to social behavior and provide an important motivational factor for doing field work.

DISCREPANCIES BETWEEN PREDICTIONS AND RESULTS

There are two major underlying ideas in the field supervisors' personality descriptions which were used to formulate the TAT variables and the predictions:

1. Individuals who possess sensitivity of perception, understanding, and liking for people will be competent at the actual process of data gathering by observation and interviewing. This can be called "sensitivity."

2. The field worker's role is inherently stressful. Some people possess personality characteristics that make them particularly vulnerable to these stresses. This can be called "vulnerability." The TAT variables chosen for the study relate to one or the other of these two categories as shown in Table 18.

Table 18 shows that all variables based on the premise of sensitivity gave results which confirmed the predictions. On the other hand, four out of five variables based on the premise of vulnerability gave results opposite to that predicted. What does this rather striking finding mean? The answer appears to lie in the measures of field-work performance that were used. The variables based on sensitivity were aimed at predicting the performance skills related primarily to data collecting. These variables were tested against measures of data-collecting skills and the predictions were confirmed. The variables based on vulnerability were intended to predict how well a person could do field work effectively for long stretches of time during which the stresses inherent in the role would become increasingly felt. For the trained group, performance measures of observation, interviewing, and over-all field-

TABLE 18. *Extent to Which Results Confirm or Reject Predictions Made and Assumptions Underlying Definition and Prediction*

OUTCOME OF PREDICTION	VARIABLE	PREDICTION	TRAINED GROUP TEST RESULTS	TRAINED GROUP SUPERVISOR RATING	EXPERIENCED GROUP	THINKING UNDERLYING VARIABLE
Prediction Confirmed	Affiliation	+	+	+		Sensitivity
	Receptivity	+	+		+	Sensitivity
	Human relations	+	+	+	+	Sensitivity
	Introspection	+	+		+	Sensitivity
	Diversity	+	+	+	+	Sensitivity
	Symbolic aggression	+	+		+	Vulnerability
Prediction Contradicted	Counteraction	+	−	−		Vulnerability
	Dependence	−	+			Vulnerability
	Intraggression	−	+		+	Vulnerability
	Achievement	+	−	−		Vulnerability
	Humor	+	−			Vulnerability

methods competence were used. The training experience during the seminar was carefully planned to avoid stressful situations. Thus the TAT variables based on vulnerability were not related to the trained group's ability to withstand stress. This explains why TAT variables based on sensitivity confirmed predictions. It does not account for why four out of five of the TAT variables based on vulnerability were related to performance but gave results opposite to those predicted.

Table 19 shows whether the variables categorized as sensitivity and vulnerability relate to competence in interviewing, observation, or both and whether the prediction is confirmed or contradicted.

TABLE 19. *TAT Variables Related to Interviewing and Observation Which Can Be Categorized by Sensitivity or Vulnerability*[12]

INTERVIEWING	OBSERVATION	INTERVIEWING AND OBSERVATION
Affiliation*‡	Counteraction†§	Intraggression†§
Human relations*‡	Dependence†§	
Diversity*‡	Humor†	
Symbolic aggression†‡	Achievement†§	
	Receptivity*‡	
	Introspection*‡	

Five out of six variables classified under vulnerability are related to observation. Every one of these variables contradicts the predictions. This result suggests, then, that the personality characteristics which field supervisors assume make a field worker most vulnerable to the stresses inherent in the role are the same characteristics which predict competence in observation. In other words, the person who is a highly competent observer is the one who is most sensitive to the stresses of field work and possibly least able to withstand them.

[12] *Sensitivity
†Vulnerability
‡Prediction confirmed ($P < .10$)
§Prediction contradicted ($P < .10$)

Summary and Conclusions

The purpose of the study was to explore the personality character-istics of social science field workers. In practice the role and func-tion of the nonstandardized interviewer frequently require him also to be an observer. This close relation in functioning between non-standardized interviewing and observation has led to the widespread belief that the skills of interviewing and observation are usually combined in the same person and that a good interviewer is also a good observer. The author initially subscribed to this view and made a set of predictions about the relationship between person-ality characteristics and over-all skill in field methods, assuming the skills required for interviewing, observation, and field relations to be highly positively correlated. Although relationships were found[13] between personality and over-all measures of the field-methods skills, the prediction of the direction of the relationship was no better than chance.

Contrary to the general belief, we found the skills of nonstand-ardized interviewing and observation to be unrelated. Although the correlation is low and statistically insignificant, these skills are not mutually exclusive and a few people will be skillful in both.

When the relationship is examined between personality and the separate skills of interviewing and observation, the results suggest that the effective interviewer enjoys people, seeks friendly relations with them, and has insight into the complex of feeling relationships among widely varying types of people. He is a persistent evaluator and judge of himself and others, and he possesses considerable latent hostility.

The competent observer has understanding of how people think and feel about themselves. He is a contemplative, passive, and receptive person who needs some other person or persons for emo-tional support, advice, direction, or motivation. He is self-critical and easily discouraged, and he lacks humor and the persistence and energy to get things done.

A characteristic stressed by experienced field workers in non-

[13] Using a form of the TAT.

standardized data collection in communities and organizations is the ability to withstand stress. Our findings suggest that the competent observer is the person who is most sensitive to the stresses of field work and possibly least able to withstand them.

The most competent experienced field workers were found to have strong value judgments as reflected in the TAT. This was contrary to a prediction based on the views of experienced field supervisors, who believed that a person with strong value judgments is likely to introduce bias and distortion into the research data he collects and to antagonize the people with whom he deals. In analyzing the relations between high value judgment and competence in field work, we found that, with training, students can learn to recognize and control their value judgments in writing field notes. Strong value judgment may be linked to the "reformist" orientation of many social scientists; it may generate heightened awareness and sensitivity and provide considerable motivation.

High value judgment requires careful self-control if the interviewer is to fulfill his role successfully. This may require a compensatory expression of these feelings when the interviewer is away from the field situation. This compensatory mechanism may explain the tendency of some field workers to indulge in derogatory remarks about the people they are studying and a tendency toward invidious gossip. Field supervisors should recognize that under certain conditions there may be an important need for the expression of value judgments by field workers. A recognition of this need may be of help to experienced workers who feel considerable guilt after the expression of such feelings, if such expression offends their ethical beliefs. The expression of value judgments is related also to the expression of hostility. In both the experienced and trained groups there is a positive relation ($P < .05$) between value judgment and intraggression. The person who needs to judge himself also needs to judge others. This combination suggests that such people may be highly conscientious in their work.

The evidence shows that field supervisors use as criteria of field-worker competence—in addition to low value judgment—the copiousness, lucidity, and literary quality of field notes, the probable ability of the field workers to withstand stress, and interviewing skill as judged from ability in interpersonal relations. The use of these criteria may prevent the identification of sensitive, accurate observers who may not have competence in interpersonal relations and are likely to be vulnerable to the stresses of field work.

Although the skills of interviewing and observation before training were found not to predict the level of skill after training, TAT measures before training can be used to predict the outcome of training in interviewing and observation.

It was not intended that this study should develop an instrument for selecting field workers. Such an aim would require somewhat different procedures and would be academic in terms of the present supply and demand for field workers. The TAT can be employed to advantage in making an early assessment of the potential abilities of students for interviewing and observation. This would be an aid in planning individual training. For example, if competent observers are needed, a person predicted to be a potentially competent observer and possessing few of the personality characteristics suitable for interviewing could be given specialized training in observation combined with training in field relations to minimize the stresses that might develop from lack of prior knowledge and the mistakes that can ensue from such ignorance (Richardson, 1952). On the other hand, if some skill in observation and interviewing are necessary, special emphasis on interviewing might be given in training.

The results suggest the need for developing further procedures for diagnosing a field worker's strengths and weaknesses. This knowledge can result in the best utilization of available personnel for the specific research purpose.

BIBLIOGRAPHY

Adorno, T. W., Frenkel-Brunswik, Else, Levinson, D. J., & Sanford, R. N. *The authoritarian personality.* New York: Harper, 1950.

Albig, W. Two decades of opinion study: 1936–1956. *Publ. Opin. Quart.*, 1957, **21**, 14–22.

Argyris, C. *Understanding organization behavior.* Homewood, Ill.: Dorsey Press, 1960.

Bain, R. K. The researcher's role: a case study. In R. N. Adams & J. J. Preiss (Eds.), *Human organization research: field relations and techniques.* Homewood, Ill.: Dorsey Press, 1960. Pp. 140–152.

Baldamus, W. Incentives and work analysis. *Univer. Birmingham Stud. Eco. & Soc.*, 1951, No. A1.

Bartlett, F. C. *Remembering.* Cambridge: Cambridge Univer. Press, 1932.

Becker, H. S. The professional dance musician and his audience. *Amer. J. Sociol.*, 1951, **57**, 136–144.

Becker, H. S. A note on interviewing tactics. *Hum. Org.*, 1954, **13** (4), 31–32.

Beezer, R. H. Research on methods of interviewing foreign informants. *George Washington Univer. Hum. Tech. Rep.*, 1956, No. 30.

Benedict, Ruth. *The chrysanthemum and the sword.* Boston: Houghton Mifflin, 1946.

Benney, M., Riesman, D., & Star, Shirley A. Age and sex in the interview. *Amer. J. Sociol.*, 1956, **62**, 143–152.

Berelson, B. R., Lazarsfeld, P. F., & McPhee, W. N. *Voting.* Chicago: Univer. Chicago Press, 1954.

Bingham, W. V. D., Moore, B. V., & Gustad, J. W. *How to interview.* (4th rev. ed.) New York: Harper, 1959.

Birdwhistell, R. Body motion. *Hum. Org.*, 1952, **11** (1), 37.

Bronfenbrenner, U. Personal communication. 1951.

Burling, Temple, Lentz, Edith M., & Wilson, R. N. *The give and take in hospitals: a study of human organization.* New York: G. P. Putnam, 1956.

CAMPBELL, A., CONVERSE, P. E., MILLER, W. E., & STOKES, D. E. *The American voter*. New York: John Wiley & Sons, 1960.

CAMPBELL, D. T. The informant in quantitative research. *Amer. J. Sociol.*, 1955, **60** (No. 4), 339–353.

CANNELL, C. F., & AXELROD, M. The respondent reports on the interview. *Amer. J. Sociol.*, 1956, **62**, 177–181.

CANNELL, C. F., & KAHN, R. L. The collection of data by interviewing. In L. Festinger & D. Katz (Eds.), *Research methods in the behavioral sciences*. New York: Dryden Press, 1953. Pp. 327–380.

CANTRIL, H. *Gauging public opinion*. Princeton, N.J.: Princeton Univer. Press, 1947.

CANTRIL, H. & STRUNK, MILDRED (Eds.). *Public opinion 1935–1946*. Princeton, N.J.: Princeton Univer. Press, 1951.

CAUDILL, WILLIAM. *The psychiatric hospital as a small society*. Cambridge, Harvard Univer. Press, 1958.

COCHRAN, W. G., MOSTELLER, F., & TUKEY, J. W. *Statistical problems of the Kinsey report*. Washington, D.C.: Amer. Statist. Assn., 1954.

COLLIER, J., JR. Photography for social science. Stirling County studies report No. 430. Unpublished manuscript. Cornell Univer. Dept. Anthrop.

COLLIER, J., JR. Photography in anthropology: a report on two experiments. *Amer. Anthrop.* 1957, **59**, 843–859.

COUCH, A., & KENISTON, K. Yeasayers and naysayers: agreeing response set as a personality variable. *J. abnor. soc. Psychol.*, 1960, **60**, 151–174.

CUMMING, ELAINE, DEAN, LOIS R., & NEWELL, D. S. What is morale? A case history of a validity problem. *Hum. Org.*, 1958, **17**(2), 3–8.

DAVIS, A., GARDNER, B. B., & GARDNER, MARY R. *Deep south*. Chicago: Univer. Chicago Press, 1941.

DEAN, J. Participant observation and interviewing. In J. T. Doby (Ed.), *An introduction to social research*. Harrisburg, Pa.: Stackpole, 1954. Pp. 229–252.

DEMBO, TAMARA. Personal communication. 1959.

DEMBO, TAMARA, LEVITON, GLORIA L., & WRIGHT, BEATRICE A. Adjustment to misfortune: a problem of social-psychological rehabilitation. *Artif. Limbs*, 1956, **3** (2), 4–62.

DEXTER, L. A., Role relationships and conceptions of neutrality in interviewing. *Amer. J. Sociol.*, 1956, **62**, 153–157.

DOHRENWEND, BARBARA SNELL. The effects of open and closed questions on respondents' answers. *Hum. Org.*, in press.

DOHRENWEND, BARBARA SNELL, & RICHARDSON, S. A. Directiveness and non-directiveness in research interviewing: a reformulation of the problem. *Psychol. Bull.*, 1963, **60**, 475–485.

DOHRENWEND, BARBARA SNELL, & RICHARDSON, S.A. A use for leading questions in research interviewing. *Hum. Org.*, 1964, **23**, 76–77.

DU BOIS, CORA. Some psychological objectives and techniques in ethnography. *J. soc. Psychol.*, 1937, **8**, 285–300.

FEAR, R. A. *The evaluation interview*. New York: McGraw-Hill, 1958.

FESTINGER, L., RIECKEN, H., & SCHACTER, S. *When prophecy fails*. Minneapolis: Univer. Minnesota Press, 1956.

GOLDMAN-EISLER, FRIEDA. Individual differences between interviewers and their effect on interviewees' conversational behavior. *J. ment. Sci.*, 1952, **98**, 660–670.

GOLDMAN-EISLER, FRIEDA. A study of individual differences and of interaction in the behavior of some aspects of language in interviews. *J. ment. Sci.*, 1954, **100**, 177–197.

GORDEN, R. L. An interaction analysis of the depth-interview. Unpublished doctoral dissertation, Univer. Chicago, 1954.

GORDEN, R.L. Dimensions of the depth interview. *Amer. J. Sociol.*, 1956, **62**, 158–164.

GOTTSCHALK, L., KLUCKHOHN, C., & ANGELL, R. (Eds.) *The use of personal documents in history, anthropology, and sociology*. New York: Soc. Sci. Res. Counc., 1945.

GROSS, N., & MASON, W. Some methodological problems of 8-hour interviews. *Amer. J. Sociol.*, 1953, **59**, 197–204.

GRUENBERG, E. M. A population study of disability from mental disorders. *Ann. N. Y. Acad. Sci.*, 1963, **107**, 587–595.

GUEST, L., & NUCKOLS, R. A laboratory experiment in recording in public opinion interviewing. *Int. J. opin. attit. Res.*, 1950, **4**, 336–352.

GURIN, G., VEROFF, J., & FELD, SHEILA. *Americans view their mental health*. New York: Basic Books, 1960.

HASTORF, A. H., & CANTRIL, H. They saw a game: a case study. *J. abnorm. soc. Psychol.*, 1954, **49**, 129–134.

HEBB, D. O. Emotion in man and animal: an analysis of the intuitive processes of recognition. *Psychol. Rev.*, 1946, **53**, 88–106.

HILDUM, D., & BROWN, R. W. Verbal reinforcement and interviewer bias. *J. abnorm. soc. Psychol.*, 1956, **53**, 108–111.

HOVLAND, C. I., & JANIS, I. L. (Eds.) *Personality and persuasibility*. New Haven: Yale Univer. Press, 1959.

HUGHES, C. C., TREMBLAY, M.-A., RAPOPORT, R. N., & LEIGHTON, A. H. *People of cove and woodlot: communities from the viewpoint of social psychiatry*. New York: Basic Books, 1960.

HUNT, M. The case of flight 320. In W. Haddon, Jr., E. A. Suchman, & D. Klein, *Accident research: methods and approaches.* New York: Harper & Row, 1964. Pp. 721–742.

HYMAN, H. H. *Interviewing in social research.* Chicago: Univer. Chicago Press, 1954.

HYMAN, H. H., & SHEATSLEY, P. B. The Kinsey report and survey methodology. *Int. J. opin. attit. Res.,* 1948, **2,** 183–195.

JAQUES, E. *The changing culture of a factory.* New York: Dryden Press, 1952.

JOHNSON, R. B. Personal communication. 1951.

JOHNSON, R. B. The nature of the minority community: internal structure, reactions, leadership, and action. Unpublished doctoral dissertation, Cornell Univer., 1955.

KINCAID, H. V., & BRIGHT, MARGARET. The tandem interview: a trial of the two-interviewer team. *Publ. Opin. Quart.,* 1957, **21,** 304–312.

KINSEY, A. C., POMEROY, W. B., & MARTIN, C. E. *Sexual behavior in the human male.* Philadelphia: W. B. Saunders, 1948.

KLUCKHOHN, C. The personal document in anthropological science. In L. Gottschalk, C. Kluckhohn, & R. Angell, *The use of personal documents in history, anthropology, and sociology.* New York: Soc. Sci. Res. Counc., 1945.

KLUCKHOHN, C. Personal communication. 1955.

KOLLER, E. Personal communication. 1960.

KORNHAUSER, A., & SHEATSLEY, P. B. Questionnaire construction and interview procedure. In Claire Selltiz, Marie Jahoda, M. Deutsch, & S. W. Cook, *Research methods in social relations.* New York: Henry Holt, 1959. Pp. 546–587.

KRASNER, L. Studies of the conditioning of verbal behavior. *Psychol. Bull.,* 1958, **55,** 148–170.

LAMB, R. K. Suggestions for a study of your hometown. In R. N. Adams & J. J. Preiss (Eds.), *Human organization research: field relations and techniques.* Homewood, Ill.: Dorsey Press, 1960. Pp. 422–430.

LAZARSFELD, P. F., & THIELENS, J. W. *The academic mind.* Glencoe, Ill.: Free Press, 1958.

LEIGHTON, A. H. Personal communication. 1950.

LEIGHTON, DOROTHEA C., HARDING, J. S., MACKLIN, D. B., MACMILLAN, A. M., & LEIGHTON, A. H. *The character of danger.* New York: Basic Books, 1963.

LENSKI, G. E., & LEGGETT, J. C. Caste, class, and deference in the research interview. *Amer. J. Sociol.,* 1960, **65,** 463–467.

LENTZ, EDITH M. Personal communication. 1953.

LERNER, D. Interviewing Frenchmen. *Amer. J. Sociol.*, 1956, **62**, 187–194.

LINDZEY, G., & GOLDBERG, M. Motivational differences between male and female as measured by the Thematic Apperception Test. *J. Pers.*, 1953, **22** (1), 101–117.

LINK, H. C. An experiment in depth interviewing. *Publ. Opin. Quart.*, 1943, **7**, 267–279.

LITWAK, E. A classification of biased questions. *Amer. J. Sociol.*, 1956, **62**, 182–186.

MACCOBY, ELEANOR, & MACCOBY, N. The interview: a tool of social science. In G. Lindzey (Ed.), *Handbook of social psychology*. Cambridge, Mass.: Addison-Wesley, 1954. Pp. 449–487.

MACMILLAN, A. M. Lecture on field methods. Cornell Univer., 1952.

MACMILLAN, A. M., & LEIGHTON, A. H. People of the hinterland. In E. H. Spicer (Ed.), *Human problems in technological change*. New York: Russell Sage Foundation, 1952. Pp. 225–243.

MANDLER, G., & KAPLAN, W. K. Subjective evaluation and reinforcing effect of a verbal stimulus. *Sci.*, 1956, **124**, 582–583.

MARCUS, I. M., WILSON, WILMA, KRAFT, I., SWANDER, D., SUTHERLAND, F., & SCHULHOFER, EDITH. An interdisciplinary approach to accident patterns in children. *Monogr. Soc. Res. Child. Develpm.*, 1960, **25** (2).

MEAD, MARGARET. The training of the cultural anthropologist. *Amer. Anthrop.*, 1952, **54**, 343–346.

MERTON, R. K. Selected problems of field work in the planned community. *Amer. sociol. Rev.*, 1947, **12**, 304–312.

MERTON, R. K., FISKE, MARJORIE, & KENDALL, PATRICIA L. *The focused interview*. Glencoe, Ill.: Free Press, 1956.

MOSCOVICI, S. Attitudes and opinions. *Annu. Rev. Psychol.*, 1963, **14**, 231–260.

MURRAY, H. A. *Thematic Apperception Test manual*. Cambridge: Harvard Univer. Printing Office, 1943.

NADEL, S. F. *Foundations of social anthropology*. London: Cohen and West, 1951.

NAHOUM, C. *L'entretien psychologique*. Paris: Presses Univer. France, 1958.

NUNNALLY, J. C. The nation's mental pulse. *Contemp. Psychol.*, 1961, **6**, 263–264.

OSGOOD, C. *Ingalik material culture*. New Haven: Yale Univer. Press, 1940.

PAUL, B. D. Interviewer techniques and field relationships. In A. L. Kroeber (Ed.), *Anthropology today*. Chicago: Univer. Chicago Press, 1953. Pp. 430–439.

PETTIGREW, T. F. Regional differences in anti-Negro prejudice. *J. abnorm. soc. Psychol.*, 1959, **59**, 28–36.

PRESTON, M. C., MUDD, EMILY HARTSHORNE, PELTZ, W. L., & FROSCHER, HAZEL B. An experimental study of a method for abstracting the content of social case records. *J. abnorm. soc. Psychol.*, 1950, **45**, 628–646.

QUAY, H. The effect of verbal reinforcement on the recall of early memories. *J. abnorm. soc. Psychol.*, 1959, **59**, 254–257.

RICHARDSON, F. L. W., JR. Personal communication. 1950.

RICHARDSON, S. A. Training in field relations skills. *J. soc. Issues*, 1952, **8** (3), 43–50.

RICHARDSON, S. A. A study of selected personality characteristics of social science field workers. Doctoral dissertation, Cornell Univer., 1954. (Publication 9922 Univ. Microfilms, Ann Arbor, Michigan.)

RICHARDSON, S. A. Organizational contrasts on British and American ships. In James D. Thompson et al. (Eds.), *Comparative studies in administration.* Pittsburgh: Univer. of Pittsburgh Press, 1959.

RICHARDSON, S. A. The use of leading questions in non-schedule interviews. *Hum. Org.*, 1960, **19** (2), 86–89.

RICHARDSON, S. A., HASTORF, A. H., & DORNBUSCH, S. M. Effects of physical disability on a child's description of himself. *Child Develpm.*, 1964, **35** (3), 893–907.

RIECKEN, H. W. The unidentified interviewer. *Amer. J. Sociol.*, 1956, **62**, 210–212.

RIESMAN, D. Some observations on the interviewing in the teacher apprehension study. In P. F. Lazarsfeld & W. Thielens, Jr., *The academic mind.* Glencoe, Ill.: Free Press, 1958. Pp. 266–370.

RIESMAN, D. *Abundance for what? and other essays.* Garden City, N.Y.: Doubleday & Co., 1964.

ROETHLISBERGER, F. J., & DICKSON, W. J. *Management and the worker.* Cambridge: Harvard Univer. Press, 1946.

ROGERS, C. R. *Counseling and psychotherapy.* Boston: Houghton-Mifflin, 1942.

ROGERS, C. R. The non-directive method as a technique for social research. *Amer. J. Sociol.*, 1945, **50**, 279–283.

ROTH, J. A. *Timetables.* New York: Bobbs-Merrill, 1963.

ROY, D. F. Participant observation as a technique for sociological investigation of factory situations. Unpublished manuscript, 1953.

ROY, D. F. Work satisfaction and social reward in quota achievement: an analysis of piecework incentive, *Amer. sociol. Rev.*, 1953, **18** (5), 507–514.

SALZINGER, K., & PISONI, STEPHANIE. Reinforcement of verbal affect responses of normal subjects during an interview. *J. abnorm. soc. Psychol.*, 1960, **60**, 127–130.

SALZINGER, SUZANNE. Rate of affect response in schizophrenics as a function of three types of interviewer verbal behavior. Paper read at Eastern Psychol. Assn., Atlantic City, March 1956.

SASLOW, G., MATARAZZO, J. D., PHILLIPS, JEANNE S., & MATARAZZO, RUTH G. Test–retest stability of interaction patterns during interviews conducted one week apart. *J. abnorm. soc. Psychol.*, 1957, **54**, 295–302.

SKINNER, CORNELIA OTIS. Trial by Kinsey. *New Yorker*, 1950, **26** (May 27), 29–31.

SLOCUM, W. L., EMPEY, L. T., & SWANSON, H. S. Increasing response to questionnaires and structured interviews. *Amer. sociol. Rev.*, 1956, **21**, 221–225.

SMIGEL, E. O. Interviewing a legal elite: the Wall Street lawyer. *Amer. J. Sociol.*, 1958, **64**, 159–164.

SMITH, M. B., BRUNER, J. S., & WHITE, R. W. *Opinions and personality.* New York: John Wiley, 1956.

STEINER, G. A. *The public looks at television.* Chicago: Univer. Chicago Press, 1963.

STEPHAN, F. F. Public relations and research interviewing. *Publ. Opin. Quart.*, 1964, **28**, 118.

STERN, W. (Ed.) *Beitrage zür Psychologie der Aussäge* (Contributions to the psychology of testimony). Leipzig: J. A. Barth, 1903–1906.

STERN, W. *General psychology: from the personalistic standpoint.* New York: Macmillan, 1938.

STRAUSS, A., & SCHATZMAN, L. Cross-class interviewing: an analysis of inter-action and communicative styles. In R. N. Adams & J. J. Preiss (Eds.), *Human organization research: field relations and techniques.* Homewood, Ill.: Dorsey Press, 1960. Pp. 205–213.

STUKAT, K.-G. *Suggestibility.* Stockholm, Sweden: Almqvist & Wilsell, 1958.

SULLIVAN, H. S. *The psychiatric interview.* New York: W. W. Norton, 1954.

TOMPKINS, S. S. *The Thematic Apperception Test.* New York: Grune and Stratton, 1947.

TURHAN, M. Yüz ifadelerinin tefsiri hakkinda tecrübi bir tetkik (an experi-mental investigation concerning the interpretation of facial expressions). *Istanbul Univer. Yayinlar.*, 1941, No. 149.

VIDICH, A. J., & SHAPIRO, G. A comparison of participant observation and survey data. *Amer. sociol. Rev.*, 1955, **20**, 28–33.

WALLIN, P. An appraisal of some methodological aspects of the Kinsey report. *Amer. sociol. Rev.*, 1949, **14**, 197–210.

WARNER, W. L., & LUNT, P. S. *Social life of a modern community.* New Haven: Yale Univer. Press, 1941.

WEBB, S., & WEBB, BEATRICE. *Methods of social study.* New York: Longmans, Green, 1932.

WEST, J. *Plainville, U.S.A.* New York: Columbia Univer. Press, 1945.

WHIPPLE, G. M. The observer as reporter: a survey of the psychology of testimony. *Psychol. Bull.*, 1909, **6**, 153–170.

WHYTE, W. F. Interviewing for organizational research. *Hum. Org.*, 1953, **12** (2), 15–22.

WHYTE, W. F. Personal communication. 1954.

WHYTE, W. F. *Street corner society.* (Enlarged ed.) Chicago: Univer. Chicago Press, 1955.

WIGMORE, J. H. *A treatise on the Anglo-American system of evidence in trials at common law.* Vol. 3. (3rd ed.) Boston: Little, Brown & Co., 1940.

WILLIAMS, R. *Strangers next door.* Englewood Cliffs, N.J.: Prentice-Hall, 1964.

WINDLE, C., McFANN, H., & WARD, J. The effect of various interview techniques in evoking fear responses. *J. clin. Psychol.*, 1955, **11**, 171–173.

WOLFENSTEIN, MARTHA. The emergence of fun morality. *J. soc. Issues*, 1951, **7** (4), 15–25.

YOUNG, PAULINE. *Scientific social surveys and research.* New York: Prentice-Hall, 1949.

INDEX